Recycling derelict land

Recycling derelict land

Edited by
GEORGE FLEMING
BSc, PhD, FEng, FICE, FRSA

Professor and Head of Division of Water Engineering
and Environmental Management, Department of Civil
Engineering, University of Strathclyde, Glasgow

T̄I Thomas Telford, London

Published for the Institution of Civil Engineers by Thomas Telford Ltd,
Thomas Telford House, 1 Heron Quay, London E14 9XF

First published 1991

British Library Cataloguing in Publication Data
Recycling derelict land.
 1. Derelict land. Reclamation. Technical aspects
 I. Fleming, George   II. Institution of Civil Engineers
 627′.5

ISBN: 0 7277 1318 3

Typeset in Great Britain by the Alden Press, Oxford, London and Northampton
Printed and bound in Great Britain by Redwood Press Ltd, Melksham, Wiltshire

Contents

1 The marginal and derelict land problem

GEORGE FLEMING, BSc, PhD, FEng, FICE, FRSA
Professor and Head of Division of Water Engineering and
Environmental Management, Department of Civil
Engineering, University of Strathclyde

Since the industrial revolution the UK has witnessed a widespread
increase in the use of land for the processes associated with manufacture.
Such processes have included the mining and quarrying of natural resources, the importation of manufacturing materials, and the conversion of
natural resources to a value product.

Associated with manufacturing has been the increase in the generation
of waste products. These include solid, liquid and gas by-products which
have resulted in the contamination of land, water and air.

Little incentive has been given to industry to reduce or recycle waste or
to make the manufacturing process more environmentally friendly. As a
result, the technological age has inherited a legacy of contaminated land
from the industrial age. The impact on the new age takes a number of
forms: a basic financial burden to rehabilitate sites proposed for new
developments; the problem of assessing the effect of the contaminants on
the water and food resources; the effect of the contaminated land on the
building fabric; the risk to health; and the effect on the ability of the UK
to compete in the international market. For example, the financial burden
of UK Ltd to provide land suitable for development, while at the same
time ensuring that modern standards of health are improved, is part of a
competitive industry.

In an industrialised community such as Europe, much of the land used
for development has a history of previous uses. The reuse or recycling of
land is dependent on the previous use and the state of the land at the time
of the proposed development. That state can be classed in physical,
chemical, or biological terms, and is often so poor that it renders the land
unsuitable for continued use or reuse without major land engineering
works. The state of urban land in Europe has declined as a result of
economic and industrial trends which have rendered an increasing area of
land classified as poor quality.

This book deals with land which is marginal, derelict or contaminated
and which requires engineering input to recycle it to a usable state. It
provides professional engineers with a basis on which to classify types of
derelict or contaminated land and alerts them to the range of environmental and legal considerations to be addressed.

The book is a follow-up to the ICE conference on building on marginal
and derelict land (ref. 1.1) which considered examples of construction or

building works on such land. The present text examines the hazards involved in land recycling and includes specialisms such as hydrogeology, geotechnics, chemistry and biology. The need for an integrated approach to site investigation, covering the physical, chemical and biological state of the land, is emphasised. Data are presented to illustrate analysis and interpretation procedures, which take account of published guidelines on contamination.

The basic problem in land engineering is that no set of guidelines or standards exists which covers the range of conditions found in practice. Every site is unique and requires a unique solution in order to make it suitable for reuse. In the European Community, guidelines differ between member states and no land register exists which allows the previous use of the land to be identified.

The past approach to the problem has by circumstance been piecemeal and the problem has grown through neglect. The present approach is stimulated by a greater awareness of the environment and its impact on economic development and community health.

Whatever the approach to recycling marginal, derelict or contaminated land, it has to be stressed that our understanding of the problem is limited by a number of factors.

The first is the difficulty in identification. No routine procedures have been set down for investigating land prior to development or during a current occupancy.

The second is the reality that whatever solution is proposed for remedying the land problem it cannot be assumed to be permanent. It is important to aim for a permanent solution but the controls on management of the land by future users under the present legislation allow no guarantee. The construction industry has throughout time produced buildings, roads, dams, and all manner of structures which form the infrastructure of our society. They all have a limited design life measured in tens or hundreds of years. Their permanency is dependent on maintenance or refurbishment. It is therefore fundamental that all land engineering of derelict, marginal, or contaminated land should be seen in this context, that the solution to the problem must be based on a design with a finite life, and that monitoring of the solution must be undertaken in order that our understanding of the effectiveness of the land treatment can be assessed. It is also important that future users of the land should be made aware of previous problems in order that monitoring can be effective over an adequate time period. New legislation is required to enable this approach to be effected.

The third factor reflects the inadequacy of our present experience in dealing with the derelict or contaminated land problem. There is insufficient information in existence on past remedial work with which to build confidence on the long term reliability of a range of solutions to a range of problems. This situation will continue for some time to come and will not dissipate until the experience gap has been bridged through the publication of an adequate number of case studies. This book is part of that process.

Definitions and classifications

This text deals with 'derelict land', a term which has been defined (ref. 1.2) as

Land so damaged by industrial and other development that it is incapable of beneficial use without treatment.

The damage to the land can be physical, chemical or biological, and can lead to the land being 'contaminated land', defined (ref. 1.3) as

Land that contains substances that when present in sufficient quantities or concentrations are likely to cause harm, directly or indirectly to Man, to the environment, or on occasions to other targets.

The degree of the dereliction or contamination varies and terms have evolved (ref. 1.4) to describe the extent. For example, partial dereliction, active dereliction, disused derelict land or potential derelict land.

The term 'marginal land' can refer to the agricultural use, or the way in which the land is related to derelict land. Marginal land can be defined as land which lies between two well defined states, the derelict state and the beneficial state. The derelict state has been induced by damage through development. Land in the beneficial state may be either natural or developed but it is not damaged, physically, chemically or biologically. Marginal land falls between the two states. It represents land where the benefits are limited by the natural or developed state, but that state has not been induced by the use of the land. For example, natural poor drained marsh land may be marginal; or soft, loose natural soils may be marginal in relation to their beneficial use for building. The term marginal can also refer to the cost of developing land in relation to the anticipated benefits once development has taken place. This text does not consider the marginal land problem separately but includes both marginal and contaminated land within the derelict land problem.

The definition of derelict land provides one general classification of the problem. A more detailed classification is also required in order to identify the factors contributing to dereliction. Such a detailed classification enables a register to be set up and from that register a set of maps of different scales to be developed. The preparation of maps and drawings is an important step toward an understanding of the problem at both local and national levels.

A number of classification systems are available, which allow land to be mapped according to range of categories. The reader is referred to a summary of the methods published elsewhere (ref. 1.4).

Causes of dereliction and contamination

Dereliction and contamination are caused by industrial or other land uses inflicting physical, chemical or biological damage on the land. The main land uses are classified (ref. 1.5) as shown in Table 1.1.

The problems of dereliction and contamination are traditionally considered as site-specific, and principally due to spillage, storage, or seepage of damaging materials, or due to working practice on the site, neglect, or the disposal of waste in either the solid or liquid form. Examples of sites

Table 1.1 Industrial land classifications

0. Agriculture, forestry, and fishing
1. Energy and water supply industries
2. Extraction of metals, manufacture of metals, mineral products, and chemicals
3. Metal goods, engineering and vehicle industries
4. Other manufacturing industries
5. Demolition and construction
6. Distribution, hotels and catering, repairs
7. Transport and communications
8. Banking, finance, insurance, and business services
9. Other services

susceptible to dereliction or contamination have been identified by the Interdepartmental Committee on the Redevelopment of Contaminated Land (ICRCL) (ref. 1.6) and are shown in Table 1.2.

The contamination and subsequent dereliction of land can also take place due to atmospheric deposition. Such deposition includes acid-forming constituents, heavy metals, and radionuclides. Recent research in the Civil Engineering Department at Strathclyde University (ref. 1.7) has indicated that heavy metal concentrations in soils are often higher in rural areas used for agriculture than in city centre sites. This conclusion is based on results obtained from a detailed survey of two areas in central Scotland. Typical results are shown in Fig. 1.1.

In other research, by the Scottish Universities Reactor Research Centre (ref. 1.8), it has been observed that the radionuclide contamination of soils in the UK due to fall-out from the Chernobyl disaster has been significant. The study (ref. 1.9) is based on a new aerial monitoring method. Such radionuclide contamination over large areas can affect water and food resources and represents a new dimension in the concept of derelict and contaminated land.

Table 1.2. Examples of sites on which contaminants may be found

Landfills and other waste disposal sites
Gasworks
Sewage works and farms
Scrap yards
Railway land
Oil refineries, petroleum storage sites
Metal mines, smelters, foundries
Chemical works
Munitions production and testing sites
Asbestos works
Tanneries
Paper and printing works
Industries making or using wood preservatives

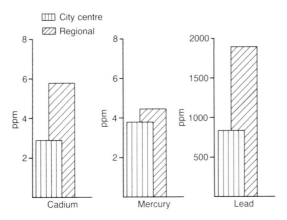

Fig. 1.1. Metal levels found in soils in Glasgow city centre and the surrounding area, parts per million (ref. 1.7)

Both the above examples emphasise the need to be more than site-specific when studying the derelict and contaminated land problem. The causes can be locally dominated or regionally dominated. For example, the emissions from a chimney stack may not affect the specific site of the industry causing the emission, but can affect the downwind land which has a completely different use. The causes of dereliction or contamination of land require division into

o   *direct dereliction*: site-specific dereliction due to the user of the land
o   *indirect dereliction*: regional or adjacent dereliction due to a land user or industry located elsewhere.

This distinction is essential if the remedial work to correct the problem is to truly take account of the cause of the dereliction and contamination. For example, in a recent review by the Scottish Development Department (ref. 1.10) of 528 landfill sites in Scotland containing gas-producing waste, 118 were identified as of prime concern and 252 of intermediate concern. Those of prime concern are methane-producing sites located within 250 metres of land containing buildings, underground services or other developments. The migration of landfill gas and the resulting risk of gas explosion can render dereliction in an indirect way, just as radionuclide fall-out or acid rain can render land derelict at much greater distances than 250 metres.

Quantifying risk
The term risk is often defined as the degree or probability of loss or danger of injury. It is often confused with hazard. Risk is a factor which must be assessed by the civil engineer when designing a dam or flood-mitigation system. It is an important factor in the design of a scheme to recycle marginal, derelict or contaminated land. Hazard is the danger from a given process (e.g. a flood). Risk of a hazard is often difficult to

Table 1.3. The main hazards associated with derelict and contaminated land

---

Uptake of contaminants by food plants grown in contaminated soil
Ingestion and inhalation
Skin contact
Phytotoxicity
Contamination of water resources
Fire and explosion
Chemical attack on building materials and building services

---

quantify and the civil engineer is often required to base the assessment on judgement founded on experience. In land recycling, the experience is limited, hence great care must be adopted when using engineering judgement in this field.

The hazards in recycling land are presented in Chapter 3 of this book based on the experience of David Barry, and the analysis and interpretation of data in relation to risk is presented in Chapter 5 of the book based on the experience of Michael Smith.

An important contribution to the subject of quantifying risk is contained in the publication by the Interdepartmental Committee on the Redevelopment of Contaminated Land (ref. 1.6) and is strongly recommended as additional reading on the subject.

The main hazards associated with derelict and contaminated land are listed in Table 1.3 as general headings, not necessarily in order of priority. The ICRCL report presents an important concept in relating the hazard to some measure of the contaminant. That measure is known as the 'trigger concentration'. The concept of trigger concentration and hazard is illustrated in the ICRCL report and is reproduced in Fig. 1.2.

There are three states for a particular hazard, the no-risk state, the significant-risk state, and the unacceptable-risk state. Each state is related to the associated hazard when the land is proposed for a particular use. The threshold between the no-risk state and the significant-risk state is defined by the trigger concentration of the constituent causing the risk. The transition between the significant-risk state and the unacceptable-risk state is defined by an action value of the concentration of the constituent.

At present the ICRCL report publishes 'Guidelines' to determine only the trigger concentrations which indicate the transition between no risk and significant risk. No national or international guidelines or standards exist to define the full range of risk thresholds for derelict or contaminated land. However, the ICRCL guidelines are a valuable first step in quantifying risk.

The hazards (Table 1.3) associated with a particular constituent or group of constituents must be assessed when a particular remedial action is proposed. The remedial actions currently favoured for the treatment of contaminated soil are shown in Table 1.4. To illustrate the problem of determining risk, consider the example of heavy-metal contamination in soil, and the use of the soil for either domestic house building, or for parks

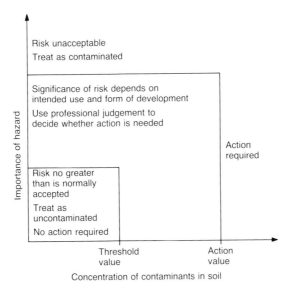

Fig. 1.2. Interpretation of trigger concentrations (ref. 1.6)

and recreational areas. When land is used for housing consideration must be given to the fact that the house owner may use the soil for growing food (e.g. vegetables). The standard or guideline for this use will differ from the recreational use, where the hazard is less likely to be food contamination but rather skin contact and phytotoxicity.

Figure 1.3 shows the ICRCL guidelines for the concentrations of four heavy metals in soil for the two uses. Hence, if a site is being investigated for potential development or recycling for housing, the level of heavy metal should be determined and related to the trigger concentration for that use. Where the concentration lies above the trigger for housing, then site engineering and cost–benefit analysis must be undertaken to engineer the site for the proposed use. Alternatively, the site may be rejected for housing and proposed for recreational development.

However, from the other viewpoint, if we take routine random samples of land in city centre and regional locations, research has shown (ref. 1.7) that heavy-metal concentrations can vary considerably and often do not

Table 1.4. Remedial action currently favoured for the treatment of contaminated soil

Excavation of the contaminated soil
Isolation of the contaminated soil
Chemical, biological or physical treatment
Mixing the contaminated material with clean soil

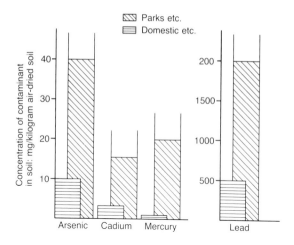

Fig. 1.3. ICRCL guidelines for the concentrations of heavy metals in soil

reflect on the current or past land uses. Figure 1.1 shows results from a recent study (ref. 1.7) where both the city centre and regional heavy-metal concentrations were in excess of the guidelines for use in growing food but within the guidelines for park or recreational use. This is primarily due to the migratory nature of pollutants within the water or air movement systems. It is therefore possible to determine guidelines on current risk for specific sites, but it is much more difficult to establish regional guidelines or to ensure that site-specific guidelines are maintained. The present situation of air-borne or water-borne pollutants being deposited on land is not quantified nor for that matter under control. It is therefore stressed that the land dereliction and contamination problem is dynamic and must have a dynamic solution, involving monitoring in extreme cases.

To illustrate the dynamic nature of contamination, consider the quality of the River Clyde sediments between 1972 and 1988. The Clyde is dredged to maintain a navigable channel and tests undertaken by Strathclyde University (ref. 1.7) and the Clyde River Purification Board (ref. 1.11) show a marked decline in the pollution by heavy metals, as illustrated in Fig. 1.4. Such a decline is due to a combination of factors, including the introduction of the Control of Pollution Act 1974 and the Rivers (Prevention of Pollution (Scotland)) Act 1951, the change in the industrial activity in the area and the recession in the use of the port by shipping during the period. If, however, the European directive on the control of dumping waste at sea is fully implemented, then the disposal of dredged material must be transferred to land. The importance of the quality of the sediments will become the major consideration in the design of a land disposal plan and in turn will affect the contamination status of the land used for disposal.

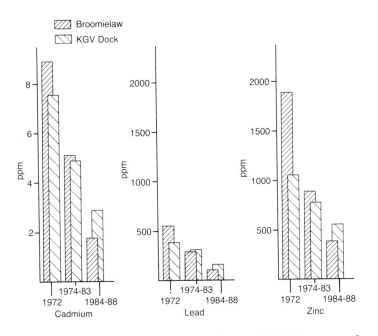

Fig. 1.4. Trace metal levels in Clyde estuary sediment, 1972–88 (courtesy of Clyde River Purification Board)

Subsequent chapters of this book deal with the difficulty of identifying the problem, assessing the hazard, proposing a solution and verifying that the solution works in the long term.

The scale of the problem

The size of the derelict and contaminated land problem is considerable in the UK, but varies regionally depending on historical land use. For example, in a survey (ref. 1.4) for England and Wales between 1974 and 1982, the inherited dereliction increased from 43 272 to 45 683 hectares (a hectare being 10 000 square metres). This increase was during a period when a considerable land area was rehabilitated. The increase must also be seen against a background of increased awareness of environmental issues.

The current statistics concerning land made derelict through contamination are based on surveys which only represent specific classes of land, such as spoil heaps, excavations, pits, railway land, Ministry of Defence land and other limited sources of dereliction. The surveys do not include hydraulic fills or colliery-discard lagoons, marshland, or soft soil sites. Hence, it is not possible to fully quantify the scale of the problem, particularly the scale of contamination induced by atmospheric fall-out or other pollutant migration paths.

Considerable research is required in the field of contaminated and derelict land in order to quantify the scale of the problem and its dynamic nature.

The role of the civil engineer

The indentification of dereliction and contamination of land before a change is made to a proposed new use has traditionally been undertaken by the civil engineer as part of the routine site investigation. Such site investigation is essential to determine the physical parameters for designing the building, structure, or other development proposed for the site. Other developments include waste repositories for a range of wastes, industrial facilities, hospitals, water and sewage treatment systems, roads and reservoirs.

Dereliction and contamination on site can affect the building or use of the land and is a fundamental aspect considered by the civil engineer at the design stage. Examples include sulphur attack on mortar, methane gas explosion, water pollution and risk from toxics.

The civil engineer is therefore directly concerned with the derelict and contaminated land problem through the professional responsibility for site investigation, design, supervision of construction and maintenance of completed works. The civil engineer is also responsible for the public health and safety aspects of recycling land to an improved use.

The civil engineering profession is uniquely placed to deal with the derelict and contaminated land problem, since the formation of the civil engineer throughout his or her education and training provides a range of skills necessary to deal with what is a multidisciplinary problem. Such skills include municipal engineering, public health engineering, soil science and geotechnics, geology, water and environmental management, structural and building design engineering, construction management, surveying and waste treatment.

References

1.1. Institution of Civil Engineers. *Building on marginal and derelict land.* Thomas Telford, London, 1987.
1.2. Ministry of Housing and Local Government. MHLG, London, 1966, circular 59/66.
1.3. Smith M.A. (ed.). *Contaminated land: treatment and reclamation.* Plenum Press, New York/London, 1985.
1.4. Bridges E.M. *Surveying derelict land.* Oxford Science Publications, Clarendon Press, Oxford, 1987.
1.5. Central Statistical Office. *Standard industrial classification.* HMSO, London, 1980.
1.6. Interdepartmental Committee on the Redevelopment of Contaminated Land. *Guidance on the assessment and redevelopment of contaminated land.* Department of the Environment, London, 1983, ICRCL 59/83.
1.7. Fleming G. *et al. Feasibility study on the use of dredged material from the Clyde estuary for land renewal.* University of Strathclyde, Glasgow, 1988.
1.8. Baxter M.S. *et al. A feasibility study of airborne radiometric study for UK fall-out.* Scottish Universities Research and Reactor Centre, Glasgow, 1988.

1.9. Sanderson D.C.W. and Scott E.M. *Aerial radiometric survey in West Cumbria, 1988.* Scottish Universities Research and Reactor Centre, East Kilbride, 1989, report to MAFF.

1.10. Scottish Development Department. *Review of landfill sites in Scotland.* SDD, Edinburgh, 1989.

1.11. Clyde River Purification Board. Personal communication, 1989.

2 | Controls on the reuse of derelict land

MIKE JACKSON, BA, PhD, CBiol, MIBiol, FRSH, MREAIS
Head of Division of Environmental Health,
Department of Civil Engineering, University of Strathclyde

TOM CAIRNEY, BSc, PhD, CEng, MICE, MIWEM
Dean of Faculty of Construction, Liverpool Polytechnic

During the 1980s, central government has consistently encouraged the reuse of derelict sites within the urban areas. Under the sponsorship of the Department of the Environment (DoE), this has tended to take the form of very large reclamations (e.g. the Thamesmead (London) and Beaumont Leys (Leicester) sites, and the Liverpool, Stoke and Gateshead garden festival reclamations), with the major development initiative resting with the local authorities. In Scotland similar sponsorship by the Scottish Development Agency has enabled the siting of the Glasgow Garden Festival on derelict dockland. With the recent interest in inner city dereliction (which is actually no more than an extension of the same reuse of urban land policy), the Department of Trade and Industry will assume a more dominant role (ref. 2.1) and this is likely to lead to many and smaller reclamations, in which private sector firms will be encouraged to have a major role.

To accelerate the beneficial reuse of disused land, government has made available a wide range of financial incentives (e.g. the Derelict Land Grant, the Urban Development Grants, the Urban Regeneration Grant, the Urban Programme and access to the EEC's Regional Development Fund), and is encouraging the streamlining of the development control processes by setting up urban development corporations (based on the successful Merseyside and London docklands models) in the areas where urban dereliction is, and has been, a major long term problem.

The advantages of urban reclamation are, of course, obvious. The local economy receives a direct and immediate boost, even in the initial construction phase; in the longer term, the rates revenue of the local authority rises as a site is brought back into economic use; employment prospects are improved; and the simple removal of visible dereliction can so improve an area that private sector businesses are eager to bring in their own investments. Thus local authorities (irrespective of their political complexion) tend to be eager to co-operate with the government's policy.

However, local authorities do have statutory responsibilities to control developments so that the public is not exposed to hazards, risk or nuisance, and these statutory obligations can place an authority in the position where it cannot fully support the national policy. For example, the local authority may favour the reclamation of a derelict site for reuse as a public amenity (say, a public park), whereas the central government bias is to promote reclamation for uses which encourage job opportunities and thus give an economic return. Also, the local authority might well want a considerable time to evaluate a developer's proposals, whereas the emphasis of central government is to speed up reclamation works wherever possible. Furthermore, local authority staff may lack the experience to deal with the more unusual problems that urban reclamation can expose and so be unwilling to advise that planning permission be granted in the form that the developer requires.

In the UK there is no official record of derelict land. In particular, the extent to which land is contaminated is a matter for conjecture or local, and hence limited, knowledge. Even land used by local authorities themselves for such purposes as waste disposal can only be identified with any degree of certainty if it is still in use or if use has only recently been completed.

A pilot study was carried out in Wales in 1984 (refs 2.2, 2.3) which identified 703 potentially contaminated sites. Only one other survey of this type (ref. 1.10) has been carried out in the UK, even though the Government has demanded that all refuse disposal authorities should monitor the evolution of methane gas on disposal sites. Throughout the UK, contaminated land is not usually dealt with unless it causes a nuisance or is required for redevelopment. This situation tends to be different in many other countries. The USA, Canada, the Netherlands, West Germany and France have all allocated resources to monitor and treat land which is regarded as contaminated.

Because neither the scale of the problem nor the extent of any contamination are known, it is not possible to generalise. However, two uses of land which have been widespread and which are known to produce potential hazards are landfill operations for the disposal of waste, and use as a site for gas works.

Generally landfill sites are operated in such a way that they can be used after completion and invariably nowadays the specific use is identified at the planning stage. Thus parks, playing fields, or grazing land are available within a relatively short period after completion of the site, provided that it has been adequately covered with suitable topsoil. Other forms of development may be restricted for some time because of the physical effects of settlement as the refuse decomposes.

Gas works sites, however, were never intended for future development, and on vacation are unlikely to have been covered in any but the most rudimentary manner. Many former gas works sites are near the centres of towns so they are extremely valuable for redevelopment. As each town had at least one such site, and they are now almost without exception redundant, the problem from this source is considerable.

Options for reuse

A number of categories of reuse can be identified, each having its own particular requirements as to the type and extent of contamination that can be tolerated. The siting of the area in question will, to a large extent, influence the reuse option. The distinction is particularly clear between urban and rural sites, but more specifically the type of previous use, such as residential, commercial, light industrial or heavy industrial, might have an influence on the type of reuse required or permitted.

The Government has been keen to see derelict sites in urban areas, particularly inner cities, redeveloped. The Housing Minister, John Patten, is quoted as saying in 1986

> I want to promote building on land which has already been used. Last year we built 45% of the new houses in Britain on land that has been built on before and I want to carry this well past 50% (ref. 2.4).

Unfortunately even with all the good intentions and all the grants and inducements available, the areas where sites are available may not coincide with the areas where sites are required.

Specific options available for reclaimed derelict sites are considered below.

Housing

The wholesale demolition of properties in clearance areas is largely a thing of the past in the UK. However, previously cleared sites will still lie derelict in many urban areas and there is a growing move to utilise these sites to reverse the trend of previous decades of moving populations out of towns.

Most of of these sites, having previously been used for housing, present few engineering problems, although unfilled sewers and manholes or insufficiently infilled subfloor areas could cause occasional problems. The use of these sites by fly tippers may have produced problems, however, if toxic material has been deposited. Such tipping by unlicensed operators has caused problems in some areas and would necessitate treatment or removal of the waste before the land could be developed for housing.

Of more importance, because it would be on a larger scale, is the possibility of reusing waste disposal sites or contaminated industrial sites. The generation of methane or carbon dioxide gas on a site and the possibility of toxic chemicals or heavy metals being in the upper layers of the soil are at odds with housing development. A number of explosions have occurred in homes built over or near sites generating explosive gases as a result of decomposition of tipped material. It must be remembered also that such gases can migrate laterally through the ground and explosions have occurred at distances of up to 500 metres from the site of generation of the gases. Such gases can continue to be generated for a number of years, and even after that may be trapped beneath impervious strata where any disturbance may liberate them to migrate upwards.

A number of heavy metals have given cause for concern in gardens. Although these have not always resulted from previous activity by man on that land, they do indicate the need for caution in building housing over land where much material may be present. Some highly toxic materials such as cadmium have been found to accumulate in some garden vegetables, to the potential hazard of the consumers.

Horticulture, agriculture and forestry

Where land is to be used for horticulture, agriculture or forestry, the possibility of settlement is of less significance except where buildings, particularly glasshouses, may be erected. The extent to which toxic materials in the soil are important varies according to the crops grown. Edible crops in horticultural premises could be particularly at risk; however, as fertile soil is needed for horticulture, early use of a site for this purpose, after contamination from previous use, is unlikely.

Grass and cereal crops in agriculture may also be at risk, although perhaps to a lesser extent than some horticultural crops. One cannot discount the possibility of physical harm being caused to grazing animals from materials such as glass shards, metals or plastics, which can work their way to the surface. Adequate covering with topsoil should prevent this but must be carried out competently and conscientiously in order to do so.

In the case of forestry, the requirement is to provide a site on which the young trees can become established and on which the toxic materials will not produce harmful effects on the trees. A suitable depth of fertile soil is obviously necessary for the root growth, together with a sufficiently compacted soil to enable the trees to maintain a secure position.

Industry

Where land is to be used for industry, probably the physical factors are initially most important, in order to provide an acceptable site in engineering terms. However, the generation of gases is likely be undesirable, if not unacceptable. The presence of a moderate amount of contamination below ground level is unlikely to cause problems after construction of the site, because little ground disturbance, other than possible landscaping, is likely to be required. However, if any part of the site is required for other purposes, such as a waste disposal area, the presence of reactive material already in the ground could be of major importance.

Recreation

If the aim is to provide open parkland, then the same requirements apply as for agricultural use. Caravanning and camping sites may also require similar provisions. There is not the necessity for level or minimally sloping surfaces for recreational areas, as little, if any, building work will be necessary and an undulating site will create more interest and give greater scope for separating various uses. This might be an important cost-saving where spoil or waste tips are used, as levelling these could be costly.

The provision of nature reserves requires little in the way of preparation of the site beyond the necessity to ensure that all contamination is well covered. In some cases, such as quarries or gravel pits, filling the extraction area with water creates a cheap and easy method of providing a reserve for birds and other water flora and fauna.

An area of water may be wanted within a park, for sporting activities. Excavation into contaminated land will obviously disturb contaminated material. In addition such material may dissolve in the overlying water, or, if insufficient care is taken in the construction, such water may leach the contamination into a watercourse.

Problems and decisions

The first essential when developing land is to know whether or not the site in question is contaminated. That is, a definition of contamination is required. The British Standards Institution has brought out a draft code of practice for the identification and investigation of contaminated land (ref. 2.5). The Royal Commission on Environmental Pollution, in their eleventh report (ref. 2.6), recommended such a proposal as a 'worthwhile objective'.

Secondly, it is necessary to know the extent of the contamination. This means the actual area of ground contaminated and the degree to which such contamination is present. The recommendation by the Interdepartmental Committee on Redevelopment of Contaminated Land (ICRCL) (ref. 2.7) that there should be two 'trigger concentrations' (Fig. 1.2) gives some help as to the definition of degree of contamination. Basically if the lower levels are not exceeded the site may be suitable for most forms of redevelopment. If the higher levels are exceeded, 'action of some kind, ranging from minor remedial treatment to changing the proposed use of the site entirely, is then unavoidable'. For any concentrations between the two levels must be judged according to the toxicity, reactivity and persistence of the substance concerned.

The decisions to be taken by the developer and the enforcing authority, with regard to the site, are the following.

- ○ *Is the land suitable in engineering terms?* For this aspect, possible earth movement and slope stability, drainage, settlement and gas generation must be taken into consideration.
- ○ *Is the land suitable in health terms?* This may require a survey to determine the extent of the contamination, but knowledge of previous use of the land will be invaluable.

Physical hazards include glass shards, asbestos, metals and plastics, and gas generation. As low-level radioactive waste may be disposed of by burial, this must also be considered as a potential hazard when developing old waste-disposal sites. The hazard from such material may well be very slight (depending on the length of time of burial), but will inevitably cause a furore if the material is uncovered.

Chemical hazards include a wide range of toxic substances, including heavy metals, pesticides, solvents, and mixtures whose identification is unknown and extremely difficult to determine. It is important to remember that many toxic substances, such as polychlorinated biphenyls (PCBs) and some pesticides, have been developed specifically to have a high persistence in the environment and are thus not degraded significantly even after a relatively long burial period.

Having decided on the extent of the problem it is necessary to decide whether suitable treatment can make the site usable.

Treatment in situ might be possible in some cases. Excavation and removal might be necessary in others. The cost of these operations will obviously influence the decision as to whether or not to go ahead with any particular proposal.

One of the decisions to be made is whether problems are likely to be caused by the redevelopment of a site which is currently problem-free. If a site used for disposal of hazardous waste is properly maintained during use, and properly capped and covered on completion to ensure no escape of material, it would probably be unwise to introduce any development which would cause disturbance. A simplistic but nevertheless sound 'rule' is that the development should suit the site rather than the site being made to suit the development.

Given the need to avoid conflicts and delays, it is thus worthwhile examining the pivotal role of local authority officers in the reclamation of derelict urban land, and establishing the information that developers should supply to them, and the discussions and procedures that should be followed if a particular reclamation is to be brought to completion as quickly and as cheaply as possible.

England and Wales

Given the differences in legal and administrative processes and procedures, England and Wales are considered together and Scotland is considered as a separate case.

Local authorities and derelict land reclamation

The general term 'local authority' is here used to encompass both the widespread urban district councils (in whose areas most urban reclamations will occur) and the smaller number of newer urban development corporations. Although the latter have rather wider financial powers, and areas of control that more logically cover areas of a similar type of dereliction, both types of body are staffed by town planners, environmental health officers, and building control and environmental pollution specialists who face the same difficulties when asked to control urban reclamation work.

All development work in England and Wales is subject to the provisions of the Town and Country Planning Act 1971. Other Acts (e.g. the Housing and Planning Act 1986, the Building Act 1984) enhance and widen the basic powers of the local authority to control developments for the benefit of the community. Thus before any development can proceed, the local authority's officers have to be convinced that the proposal is both beneficial and safe.

The more obvious problems of urban reclamation are serious, but are within the normal experience of local authority staff. Thus they tend not to create serious conflicts between the local authority and the developers. Such problems are the physical difficulties of working on a congested site; of having vehicle access impeded by a town's normal traffic; of having the hours of allowable working restricted by noise and environmental constraints; of encountering massive foundations or running into areas of poorly compacted tipped material; or intercepting service pipes that appear on none of the plans of the areas's utility services.

Chemically contaminated land, however, is quite another matter.

Contaminated land was first recognised as potentially hazardous in the late 1970s; therefore, few local authority staff will have had any formal education in the subject. It is a subject area that calls for a grasp of organic and inorganic chemistry, hydrology and hydrogeology, sampling strategy, materials science, geotechnics, and gas and fire hazards. As these topics are outside the normal education of town planners, environmental health officers and building control personnel (the three groups of a local authority's staff with whom a developer is most likely to come into contact), it is unsurprising that few local authority staff feel confident to question the technical details of a developer's proposals.

To make matters worse (from the viewpoint of these officers), various ICRCL guidance notes (refs 2.7–2.13) will have emphasised the contaminant hazards that particular past industrial uses of a site can pose, other publications (e.g. ref. 2.14) have stressed that contaminated land is likely to be especially common in the old industrial areas of a town (where dereliction is now commonest), and the latest joint circular from the DoE and Welsh Office (ref. 2.15) details that past industrial use can so contaminate a site that it now may be actively or potentially hazardous to

- o people working on a reclamation scheme
- o the ultimate occupiers or users of buildings erected on the site
- o the materials used in the buildings
- o any food crops that might be grown in gardens or allotments
- o water supplies
- o the environment in general.

This same circular acknowledges that these hazards 'may be a direct threat to the health and safety' and that 'if remedial action is needed in an emergency, there may be additional costs and difficulties', and concludes with the statement (remarkably unhelpful from the viewpoint of a local authority officer who is charged with the statutory duty of protecting the public against unsafe developments) that 'a balance has to be struck between the risks and liabilities and the need to bring the land into beneficial use'.

While the above comments might be seen as over-critical of central government, the DoE and the Welsh Office, they do have to be read in the context of England and Wales having no single body of law describing the standards that should be attained when contaminated land is reused, no code of professional practice on the subject, and no British Standard guidance. This situation conflicts dramatically with that for almost every other type of construction, where developers' proposals can be compared with the guidelines in codes of practice, and is atypical of the situation elsewhere in Europe (e.g. in Holland and West Germany), where both legal statutes and official guidance exist to guide the local authority personnel.

Local authority procedures in dealing with contaminated derelict land

Instead of applying any unified body of law to control the developments on a site which is known or suspected to be contaminated, local authority staff have to follow the guidance of the DoE and Welsh Office (ref. 2.15) and make use of a range of existing laws to ensure that the proposed redevelopment is both acceptable and safe.

Local authority officers are advised by the government circular to treat contamination, or the potential for it, as a material consideration that has to be taken into account in the various stages of the planning process. Thus — ideally — chemically contaminated sites should be identified well before any applications from developers are made to reuse that land. Although this advice is somewhat unreal (since it assumes that a local authority wil be able to find the staff and financial resources to sample the near surface layers of its stock of derelict land, and then the extra funds to pay for the chemical analyses that are required to prove whether or not a contamination risk exists), it has at least encouraged local authority staff to identify the past industrial uses of particular parcels of land and judge (on the basis of the ICRCL guidance notes) whether contamination is likely to exist.

From this desk study, some local authorities then feel able to indicate the type of reuse of the land which could be acceptable. This type of judgement tends to be on the 'scale of sensitivity' basis outlined in the draft code of practice (ref. 2.16) produced by the British Standards Institution in 1983

housing with gardens	most sensitive
allotments	
housing without gardens	
light industrial or office use	
amenity use (e.g. parks)	
car parking	least sensitive

On this basis, only land that is very slightly contaminated would be suggested for a sensitive end-use, as the local circumstances allowed. It would, of course, be assumed that a full site investigation would be carried out (by the developer) to prove the conclusions of the desk study.

A few local authorities with more experienced staff have felt able to go beyond this level of desk study, and have identified the contaminants likely to have been left behind by a particular prior industrial use and the targets which this contamination might attack. On this basis, an old paint factory site, whose surface soils might be highly contaminated by lead compounds, would not be an ideal location for any use that included gardens or allotments, but would not be unsuitable for the building of blocks of flats or a light industrial estate, where, the concrete and tarmac sealing of the site surface would preclude the lead contamination coming into contact with human targets.

While the above types of desk study are sensible and proper, the actual responsibility (under the legal controls that exist) of assessing whether or not a site is suitable for a particular end-use rest *not* with the local authority, but primarily with the developer (ref. 2.15). This gives rise to a considerable potential for conflict, since private sector developers tend not to be interested in the least sensitive reuses of land (since these cannot easily generate profitable incomes) and usually propose the most sensitive reuse (i.e. housing with gardens) since this is the most likely to give rise to the highest profit level, at least in the southern areas of England and Wales.

In such cases, the developer will make an application under the 1971 Town and Country Planning Act for his chosen reuse of the land, and the scene can be set for a long-running battle, which may include the following stages

o   an initial planning application from the developer
o   a rejection of planning permission, often on the grounds of risks to the public, and of inadequacy of information provided by the developer
o   an initial site exploration by the developer to obtain some data on the site contamination
o   a second planning application from the developer
o   a second rejection of planning permission
o   an appeal from the developer to the Secretary of State for the Environment
o   a decision from the Secretary of State for the developer's case
o   a continued conflict situation during the development work, with the local authority using its powers to require the abatement of nuisances under the 1936 Public Health Act, the 1986 Housing and Planning Act, the Control of Pollution Act 1974, the Control of Pollution (Special Waste) Regulations 1980, the regional water authority's by-laws (to prevent pollution of surface or groundwater), and the Building Regulations 1985
o   a completed development which has taken far longer to build than it should and which has so soured relationships that the developer and that local authority are unlikely to be able to co-operate in future.

Preferred procedure for co-operating with a local authority

The scenario outlined above is neither efficient nor (sadly) unusual, and should be avoided.

A far better procedure is where the local authority and the private developer recognise each other's proper interests and co-operate in a development.

An example of such a case could be the proposed redevelopment of a derelict coal stockyard on the edge of a growing town. Over a century or more of use, the surface of the site (to a depth of up to 2 metres) has become heavily contaminated by coaly waste, to the point at which almost every soil sample has a calorific value in excess of 15 000 kJ/kg (a figure well above that indicated as potentially hazardous in the ICRCL guidance note 61/84 (ref. 2.12). Irregular heaps of coal and coaly waste rise up to 5 metres above the surrounding land surface, and surface fires have broken out several times in the past. The site is an eyesore and covers an area of 10 hectares.

Obviously the local authority wishes to have this dereliction removed, and the large area of land brought back into productive use.

A local developer notes that the town's population is still increasing and that the demand for houses (with gardens) is buoyant. Thus he acquires the coal stockyard and decides to develop it as a housing estate, conveniently adjacent to the existing services and the town's shopping area.

However, he realises that the local development plan has zoned the site for industrial use (since the local authority officers never considered that it could be reclaimed for domestic dwellings) and that he will require the co-operation of the local authority's planning officers to have this zoning altered.

Thus he opens discussions with the planning officers on an informal basis. These discussions reveal that the authority could accept the housing development proposal, *if* they could be convinced that the site is not a fire hazard and that no other serious contaminant risk exists on it.

The developer then commissions, at his own expense, a limited site exploration programme to provide basic information on the materials that underlie the site. Samples taken from the trial boreholes are examined to determine their calorific values, their combustion indices, and their general chemical nature (sulphate, phenol, tar and similar coal carbonisation by-product levels).

These data are then examined by the developer's consultants, and the consultant's report is made available to the local authority's planning department. The planning officers, faced with the level of technical detail in the report, bring in their environmental health and civil engineering colleagues, and — possibly — their own specialist consultant, and propose a second informal meeting.

This meeting agrees that the site, in its present state, is potentially combustible, and that site fires could be caused by (say) buried power lines, the surplus heat from basement central heating plants, or the actions of vandals. Thus house-building in the site's existing state would present an unacceptable risk to the future inhabitants. However, the meeting also accepts that the combustion risk is entirely due to the abundance of coal fragments mixed throughout the top 2 metres of the site's soil, that this coal could be recovered economically by an excavation and washing process, and that this could conveniently be carried out as part of the necessary recontouring of the land for the housing estate.

As this agreement was reached with the support of the local authority's specialist staff, the developer feels confident to seek outline planning approval for reusing the site as a housing estate, and to accept the conditions that no houses will be built until the calorific values of the site's soils are reduced to a level acceptable to the local authority.

The local authority's planning committee is presented with this application, together with a recommendation from its own officers that outline planning permission be given for the site's reclamation, that permission also be allowed for the vehicular movements needed to move the recovered coal off the site, and that the full planning permission be considered at a later date once fuller architectural and planning details come to hand. The authority then decides that the development is in line with local needs and that it it can be controlled to ensure an acceptable result, and grants the outline planning permission.

As the reclamation continues, the developer ensures that the local authority's staff are kept aware of all salient facts and brought into the decisions that are taken.

The end result is a successful reclamation that has taken as short a time as the complexities of the site allowed. The ongoing co-operation between the developer and the local authority throughout the reclamation prevented any situations arising that compelled the local authority to serve abatement notices under its various legal powers.

The above scenario is somewhat idealised (although based on an actual redevelopment) but does include all the elements that the authors have found essential.

Scotland

With its separate and distinct legal system, Scotland has its own legislation dealing with planning and the redevelopment of derelict land. However, in some cases it has legislation in common with the rest of the UK, such as most of the legislation dealing with the control of pollution. Even where there is common legislation, the parts that are in force within any particular Act may not be the same in Scotland as in the rest of the UK. Much of the Control of Pollution Act 1974 that has been enacted has been brought into force by commencement dates which have varied considerably between Scotland and the rest of the UK. It is therefore important for developers to bear in mind that, although the same general principles apply throughout the UK with respect to the redevelopment of land, the enforcement and administration may differ.

To complicate matters still further, Scotland has two clearly distinct problems: in the industrial belt and in rural areas. The central belt, including Glasgow in the west and Edinburgh in the east, contains the most heavily populated areas, and naturally the bulk of the industrial activity, which relies heavily in this part of Scotland on traditional industries. In this central belt there has been a decline in the mining, steelmaking, car manufacuring and shipbuilding industries amongst others; this has left large sites which are often of considerable value but which may have associated problems of siting, pollution from the previous activities and so on which must be tackled before they can be reclaimed. The situation is similar in other areas of the UK, such as the north-east of England, where there has been a reliance on the traditional 'heavy' industries.

Outside this industrialised central belt, Scotland is predominantly rural. Here the problems are fewer, but individually they may be greater because of the competing demands for local employment and preservation of the environment. That major problems of land contamination during redevelopment are not confined to highly industrialised areas is evidenced by the discovery of considerable quantities of hazardous asbestos waste uncovered during work at the Faslane submarine base.

One of the main concerns of many countries is the possible contamination of underground water resources. The British Geological Survey (ref. 2.3) suggested that greater priority should be given to this in the UK, but as Scotland is less reliant than the rest of the UK on underground sources for drinking water, there is less pressure to seek out contaminated sites.

Sponsored redevelopment

The redevelopment of derelict dockland in Glasgow as a site for the Glasgow Garden Festival posed an interesting problem. The redundant docks have been infilled over a period and have provided actual or potential sites for industrial and commercial development. The Scottish Development Agency (SDA) has been able to offer some of these sites for redevelopment with attractive grants available for suitable schemes. The garden festival site is one such in which the SDA has assisted and it is expected that employment and income from visitors will be generated. In addition to the normal problems associated with redevelopment, there was an additional feature that Clyde river sediments were used as topsoil for the site. This was seen as solving the problem of disposal of dredging waste and also the problem of importing expensive topsoil from elsewhere. However, the potential problem of heavy metals, pesticides and high salt content in the dredged material had to be considered. It was necessary for a team to carry out extensive monitoring and investigation into the levels of these pollutants and their effects on vegetation. Although this is essentially a once-only operation for a garden festival site, it illustrates the possible unforeseen problems which may occur. The incorporation of sewage sludge into the land poses similar problems of possibly introducing contamination as part of the process of redevelopment. Both chemical and microbiological hazards may be introduced in this manner.

Controls — the theory

In Scotland, the Scottish Vacant Land Survey (SVLS), organised by the Scottish Development Department and the Scottish Development Agency in conjunction with the local authorities, compiles a list of derelict and contaminated land.

The development of contaminated land is controlled by the planning authorities, under the powers contained in the Town and Country Planning (Scotland) Act 1972. Planning is carried out by both regional and district councils. The regional councils are required to produce a structure plan for their area, for approval by the Secretary of State for Scotland. Such structure plans are concerned with policies on land use and development in broad terms, rather than with individual sites. At the district level (or, in the case of some rural areas such as the Highland Region, the regional level), local plans are formulated which require, among other things o   a written statement setting out and justifying policies and proposals for land development

o   a plan defining sites which are suitable for development.

'Development' is defined in the Act as 'the carrying out of building, engineering, mining or other operations in, on, over or under land, or the making of any material change in the use of any building or other land'.

The opening of the land to 'inspect, repair or renew any sewers, mains, pipes, cables or other apparatus by the local authority or statutory undertaking is not a development'. Therefore such works would not require permission and could constitute a risk.

Planning permission is required before development can take place and must be requested initially from the district council. Most applications will be dealt with at this level, but those considered to be major proposals can be 'called up' by the regional authority or by the Secretary of State. Full planning permission, when granted, normally lapses after five years if work has not commenced. Outline planning permission lapses after three years if full permission is not sought in that time.

In its eleventh report, the Royal Commission on Environmental Pollution (ref. 2.6) recommended that the various Ministry bodies should issue planning advice for local authorities, statutory bodies and developers on the redevelopment of contaminated land or land suspected to be contaminated. The Scottish Development Department (SDD) has recently issued such a document as planning advice note 33 (ref. 2.17).

This planning advice note defines contaminated land as 'Land which is incapable of beneficial use unless treated to overcome contamination hazards which pose a potential threat to health and safety for the intended land use.' It advises that the possibility of contamination be considered whenever land which is proposed for development has been previously used for industrial or waste disposal purposes. Where it is 'known, or strongly suspected' that the site is contaminated, the developer will normally be required to carry out an investigation before planning permission is granted. In other cases, planning permission may be granted subject to a satisfactory report. Generally the cost of investigating the possibility is borne by the developer.

Planning advice note 33 recommends that the planning department, in assessing the significance of contamination, should consult the local authority's departments of environmental health, waste disposal, land reclamation, building control, water supply, surveying and engineering, and the Regional Analyst and the Health and Safety Executive.

The environmental health departments of the local authorities have powers under Part 2 of the Public Health (Scotland) Act 1897 to deal with land which may be 'injurious or dangerous to health'. Under the Health and Safety at Work Act 1974, employers have a duty to safeguard the health and safety of themselves and the public when carrying out any work. This would apply to work involving contaminated land.

Where waste is to be removed from a site, whether contaminated or not, it is classified as 'statutory controlled waste', which may only be disposed of by a licensed operator. It may also be classified as 'special waste' and its disposal may thus be subject to the provisions of the Control of Pollution (Special Waste) Regulations 1980.

The Occupiers Liability (Scotland) Act 1960 imposes a duty upon occupiers of premises to ensure that all visitors may enter in safety, even where such persons are trespassing. This Act may have relevance on contaminated sites.

The SDA has powers under the Scottish Development Agency Act 1975 to acquire land that is derelict, neglected or unsightly and to bring it up to improved standards. The Agency has been active in stimulating the development of a number of areas in Scotland. The redevelopment of part of the old docklands to house the Glasgow Garden Festival is described above.

In addition to the grants from such as the Urban Programme and the European Regional Development Fund, which are also available in England and Wales, there are some which are specifically applicable to Scotland. The Land Engineering Fund is available to help develop land which requires treatment before it can be reused. This is administered by the SDA. The Local Enterprise Grants for Urban Projects (LEG-UP) are also administered by the SDA and enable it to give assistance of up to £250 000, or more with Ministerial approval.

Similar sponsorship by the SDA itself enabled the siting of the Glasgow Garden Festival on derelict dockland.

Controls — the practice

Although the procedures outlined above appear fairly straightforward and well regulated, in practice there seems to be considerable scope for improvement, just as in England and Wales. An unpublished survey of planning procedures, carried out by the Environmental Health Division at Strathclyde University during 1985–86, found a wide range of approaches in use by the local authorities. In no circumstances would the planning authorities be prepared to investigate potentially contaminated sites either on public health grounds or to aid their own future planning proposals. However, investigations were often undertaken where the local authority themselves were developing the site. Other developers might, or might not, be required by the planning authority to carry out an investigation.

Although it is a requirement of the planning legislation that local authorities produce a local plan, the survey revealed, for instance, that only one authority had a register of gasworks sites as part of a derelict land survey. This means that the other authorities could have had at least only a vague idea of where these potentially highly contaminated sites were situated.

Thus, in practice, the requirements imposed by the local planning authorities on developers may vary. Some authorities appear not to consider the potential problems of developing a contaminated site, rather concentrating on the traditional planning criteria.

Although the local planning authorities, when considering an application, are not obliged to ensure that the condition of the site is suitable for the proposed development, it is surprising, in view of the legacy they might inherit if something were to go wrong, that they do not give more consideration to this aspect. Of course, if the planning authority grants permission to develop land which is later found to be contaminated, it is not liable. However, it would have problems enforcing any remedial action upon the developers at that stage. In practice the authority might be left with no alternative but to revoke or modify the planning permission and compensate the developer. Because of this a number of developments have been allowed to proceed where otherwise they might not have been. Another example of the problem is that the local authority might be left with a moral obligation to remove contamination even though it had no legal obligation. Such a case occurred recently in the West of Scotland where a developer uncovered a large quantity of asbestos during development work. Because of the high cost of dealing with this material (among other reasons) the developers went into liquidation, leaving the local authority to deal with the problem at a huge cost.

Summary

The law governing the redevelopment of derelict land has been criticised by almost every author on the subject (refs 2.18–2.21) as being inadequate to guide either developers or the local authorities whose duty it is to ensure that development is appropriate and safe. Certainly the vast majority of local authority staff share this viewpoint and find the current vagueness over appropriate development standards a professional limitation.

However, it has to be accepted that derelict sites can pose a remarkably wide range of contamination problems, and that the range of acceptable solutions is likely to be nearly as great.

Thus it seems unlikely that any unified body of new law will appear to control such reclamations, and it seems that co-operation between developers and local authority staff will continue to be the best possible compromise.

Given this situation, a sensible developer will recognise the statutory duties of local authority staff and will endeavour to provide them with the fullest information possible, before they are asked to decide on a planning application. Included in this information should be

o a clear definition of the extent of contamination
o accurate strata and chemical data from each borehole or pit
o an evaluation of the contamination against the ICRCL guidelines (ref. 2.7)
o a clear statement of how the proposed reclamation will overcome the contamination and other site problems.

The developer should be prepared to discuss all these points with the local authority staff and to incur additional expenditure where it proves necessary to obtain a higher level of site information.

References
2.1. Clarke made cities supremo. *The Times*, 1987, 19 Dec.
2.2. Environmental Data Services. *Contaminated land survey in Wales*. ENDS, London, 1984, report 119.

2.3. Environmental Data Services. *High-tech approaches gaining favour for contaminated land clean-up*. ENDS, London, 1987, report 150.

2.4. Environmental Data Services. *The rising issue of contaminated industrial land*. ENDS, London, 1986, report 140.

2.5. British Standards Institution. *Draft for development: code of practice for the identification of potentially contaminated land and its investigation*. BSI, London, 1988, DD 175.

2.6   Royal Commission on Environmental Pollution. *Eleventh report — Managing waste : the duty of care*. HMSO, London, 1985.

2.7. Interdepartmental Committee on the Redevelopment of Contaminated Land. *Guidance on the assessment and redevelopment of contaminated land*. Department of the Environment, London, 1983, ICRCL 59/83.

2.8. Interdepartmental Committee on the Redevelopment of Contaminated Land. *Notes on the redevelopment of landfill sites*. Department of the Environment, London, 1978, ICRCL 17/78.

2.9. Interdepartmental Committeee on the Redevelopment of Contaminated Land. *Notes on the redevelopment of gasworks sites*. Department of the Environment, London, 1979, ICRCL 18/79.

2.10. Interdepartmental Committee on the Redevelopment of Contaminated Land. *Notes on the redevelopment of sewage works and farms*. Department of the Environment, London, 1979, ICRCL 23/79.

2.11. Interdepartmental Committee on the Redevelopment of Contaminated Land. *Notes on the redevelopment of scrapyards and similar sites*. Department of the Environment, London, 1983, 2nd edn, ICRCL 42/80.

2.12. Interdepartmental Committee on the Redevelopment of Contaminated Land. *Notes on the fire hazards of contaminated land*. Department of the Environment, London, 1984, ICRCL 61/84.

2.13. Interdepartmental Committee on the Redevelopment of Contaminated Land. *Asbestos on contaminated sites*. Department of the Environment, London, 1985, ICRCL 64/85.

2.14. Harris M.R. Recognition of the problem. *Reclaiming contaminated land* (ed. Cairney T.C.). Blackie, Glasgow, 1987.

2.15. Department of the Environment and Welsh Office. *Development of contaminated land*. DoE, London, 1987, circular DOE 21/87.

2.16. British Standards Institution. *Draft code of practice for the identification and investigation of contaminated land*. BSI, London, 1983, BSI 83/55992.

2.17. Scottish Development Department. *Planning advice note 33 — Development of contaminated land*. SDD, Edinburgh, 1988.

2.18. McCarthy M.J. Reclamation of a refuse tip for open space and housing development. *Proc. Conf. Reclamation of Contaminated Land, Eastbourne, 1980*. Society of Chemical Industry, London, 1981.

2.19. Gordon J. Planning and site licensing aspects of landfill disposal of waste. *Proc. Landfill Gas Symposium, Harwell, 1981*.

2.20. Smith M.A. *Legal powers and responsibilities in relation to the development of contaminated land*. Building Research Establishment, Garston, 1983, note N16/83.

2.21. Joint Unit for Research on the Urban Environment. *Identification and assessment of contaminated land*. Ecotec Research and Consultancy, Birmingham, 1984.

3 Hazards in land recycling

DAVID BARRY, BE, CEng, MICE, MIHT
Principal Environmental Consultant,
W.S. Atkins Planning and Management Consultants Ltd

Introduction

Hazard, risk and consequence

It is important to establish clearly the difference between 'hazard' and 'risk'. For example, a concentration of methane in air of between about 5% and 15% represents a latent explosion hazard, but only a potential explosion risk: the hazard can only be realised if an ignition source is present. This apparently semantic argument is very important since the most difficult decisions normally facing engineers and their advisors concern the assessment of the risk (i.e. probability) of a hazard arising in a critical location. Thus, for example, if a coal tar deposit (i.e. a hazardous substance) is covered by a concrete slab, the issue to be addressed is that of the risk of either the coal tar migrating to the surface (i.e. within easy reach of contact by humans), or the slab being removed or damaged (resulting in a similar possibility of human contact). In essence, therefore, the potential difficulties presented by chemical and other hazardous substances can only be defined properly when their contexts are understood.

Consequence is a third and critical element in the appraisal of hazardous conditions; indeed it is central to the question of whether or not specific abatement or control measures are taken. For example, the consequences of some development features becoming corroded through potentially aggressive conditions (high risk) might be acceptable when compared with the costs of protecting to a high degree. On the other hand, a low risk of a gas explosion hazard arising in a particular circumstance might be unacceptable due to the potential consequences. Thus, assessments of hazard, risk and consequence are separate but related steps in the design process.

Perception of hazards

The perception by professionals of hazards, and related risks, must not be considered as being synonymous with public perception. It is implicit in all designs that, as far as practicable, the feature under consideration is perceived by all relevant parties as having an acceptable risk, *vis-à-vis* stability or durability, for example. With most conventional engineering designs, there are relatively few difficulties in this regard, but environmental hazards can present more profound problems. This is not aided by the difficulty in many instances of quantifying accurately conditions that are

Table 3.1. Hazard types and target groups

Types of hazard
Toxic; carcinogenic; corrosive; combustible; explosive; asphyxiant; physical

Affected groups/features
Investigation workers; demolition and clearance workers; after-users of site,
especially children; maintenance workers; neighbourhood; building materials;
plant life; water supplies

---

likely to exist. Inevitably, therefore, there is a need, on the one hand, for
greater 'factors of safety' in hazard assessments and subsequent designs
and, on the other hand, for generating or maintaining public confidence
in the face of significant environmental pressures.

Interface with other factors

There are many obvious and fundamental interfaces between this
chapter and others. For example, in site investigation (Chapter 4) and in
the consideration of rehabilitation options (Chapter 6), hazards will have
critical roles. In this chapter, hazards are considered within the principal
context of redevelopment of contaminated land, with the major emphasis
being on environmental rather than engineering factors. Thus, for
example, ground stability and engineering operations related to redevelopment are not given any detailed attention here.

Personnel involved

The importance of having a corporate approach to the redevelopment
of hazardous sites is emphasised. The effectiveness of such corporate
design teams is greatly enhanced if the individuals have an awareness of
the essential features of other disciplines involved in a particular project.
If the situation is otherwise, it can be much more difficult to develop
appropriate methods for abating a hazard or, more correctly, diminishing
the risk of a hazard occurring.

The range of principal personnel that could be involved in identifying
hazards and assessing their implications includes a chemist, an environmental scientist/engineer, an occupational hygienist, a geotechnical/civil
engineer, a structural engineer and a mining engineer. It is probable that
a suitably experienced chemist/environmental scientist and a geotechnical/
civil engineer will be capable of providing appropriate expertise in the
majority of situations. As in all complex situations, however, it is important to recognise when more comprehensive expertise is required (e.g.
radiology, toxicology, hydrogeology or microbiology).

Nature and contexts of hazards

A wide range of hazard types exists and there are several different target
groups which are vulnerable to these hazards. In simplified terms these are
categorised in Table 3.1.

The contexts in which any of these hazards might arise include a
preliminary site visit, the demolition of contaminated structures, a site

with fugitive organic vapours, and a maintenance worker installing new pipework in a redeveloped site. In each example, the lack of awareness that an actual or potential hazard can exist, could have a critical influence on the consequential effects.

Nature of hazards

Toxicity. The effect of exposure to a toxic substance is dependent on a number of factors, including the size of dose, the chemical properties of the substance, and the manner in which the dose is administered (e.g. by inhalation, ingestion or via skin absorption (percutaneous)). Toxic effects can generally be divided into those that result from short-term (i.e. acute) exposure to a substance and those due to doses administered over a longer period of time (i.e. chronic exposure). The *Registry of toxic effects of chemical substances* published for the US National Institute for Occupational Safety and Health (NIOSH) (ref. 3.1) is a useful source of data on ingestive toxicity. Data on inhalation toxicity of gases, fumes and dusts are compiled in *Occupational exposure limits 1989* (ref. 3.2), guidance note EH40/89 of the Health and Safety Executive (HSE).

In ref. 3.1, human adult oral toxicities are generally presented as the lowest published lethal dose (LDL_o) expressed as weight of toxic agent per unit body weight (mg/kg). Where no human oral toxicities are known, published data on experimental animal toxicity are often used to determine the possible toxicity to humans. However, there are inherent difficulties in applying information about lower animals to humans, because different species may respond differently to toxic substances.

Occupational exposure limits (OELs) are prescribed under the Control of Substances Hazardous to Health (COSHH) Regulations, 1988. These limits (formerly threshold limit values (TLVs)) have two components, long term exposure limits (LTELs) and short term exposure limits (STELs). Extensive information is published on OELs and STELs (ref. 3.2). These are expressed as time-weighted averages (TWAs), usually over an 8-hour period in the case of LTELs and a 10-minute period for STELs. Both LTELs and STELs could be considered as maximum permissible concentrations which should not normally be exceeded, and exposure to all toxic substances should be kept as low as is reasonably practicable at all times. The exposure limits are applicable to airborne concentrations of single substances. The effect of synergism should be considered when a species is exposed to two or more compounds.

In the context of contaminated land redevelopment, useful information is given by the Interdepartmental Committee on the Redevelopment of Contaminated Land (ICRCL) in *Guidance on the assessment and redevelopment of contaminated land* (ref. 3.3). This document includes two tables giving tentative threshold values for a number of principal contaminants.

Threshold values are divided into two sections: trigger threshold values (TTVs) and action threshold values (ATVs). Concentrations below the TTV represent a risk no greater than is normally accepted and so the land can be treated as uncontaminated. Concentrations in excess of the TTV require the use of professional judgement to assess the risk of a hazard arising. Levels in excess of the ATV are likely to represent an explicit hazard and some remedial action should be taken.

Carcinogenicity. The WHO International Agency for Research on Cancer (IARC) define carcinogenesis as the induction of cancer (i.e. malignant tumours), a definition adopted by the DoE (ref. 3.4). A comprehensive (but not exhaustive) list of current proven, or probable, human carcinogenic chemicals and proven animal carcinogens is presented in Annex 1 of the DoE's waste management paper 23 (ref. 3.4), with the substances categorised according to their degree of risk. Examples of proven and probable human carcinogens include arsenic (III) oxide, asbestos, benzene, beryllium (particulate), cadmium oxide, coal tars (PAH), mustard gas and nickel salts. In all, Annex 1 (ref. 3.4) shows 140 examples of materials that DoE recommend should be considered as presenting a carcinogenic risk to humans.

Corrosivity. In the context of redevelopment, the principal hazards associated with the corrosivity of chemical contaminants are damage to human tissue and degradation of building services and materials.

Tissue damage can be caused by inhalation, ingestion and skin contact and will vary according to the nature and form of contaminant and, of course, the duration of contact. Effects can range from allergenic sensitisation, to mild skin irritation through to permanent physical damage. Children and site investigation/demolition workers are the principal target groups in this category. Corrosive materials include acids; alkalis; phenols; coal-tar creosote; compounds of fluorine, phosphorus, potassium and sodium; toluene and xylene/xylenol, and many other organic solvents.

Tissue damage is generally associated with short term exposure; limits for airborne substances as given in *Occupational exposure limits 1989* (ref. 3.2) apply, and NIOSH is a useful source of information on corrosivity and skin irritation.

Substances which are corrosive, directly or indirectly, to building materials include those mentioned previously and also sulphates, sulphides, chlorides and a range of organic compounds. Concrete, ferrous metal pipes and structures, and plastic pipework are all potential targets (ref. 3.5).

Combustibility. A combustible material can be defined as a substance that is capable of burning or being set alight. The calorific value (CV) and ash value are the main criteria for determining the potential combustibility of a substance. Generally it is accepted (refs 3.6, 3.7) that materials whose CV exceeds 10 MJ/kg are almost certainly combustible, while those with values below 2 MJ/kg are unlikely to burn. Combustible materials can be in the form of a solid, liquid or gas, and the actual form of the material can govern its combustibility. There are many metals in powder or flake form that will ignite and burn rapidly, whereas these compounds may be far less combustible as bulk solids. Similarly, cellulose is combustible in the form of a textile fabric, and paper lint is inflammable as fine fibres.

Sources of combustion are a critical consideration and, in most relevant contexts, the source will probably be an external agent rather than spontaneous combustion. The latter source is considered to be extremely rare and many reported instances in landfilled sites are now generally believed to have originated in a surface fire.

The main hazards associated with combustible materials, if ignited, are

- o production and release of toxic, asphyxiant or noxious gases
- o physical damage to humans, buildings and services; creation of underground cavities or subsidence conditions (through ground-mass loss).

Inflammability and explosiveness. Inflammability relates to the ease with which a material (gas, liquid or solid) will ignite, either spontaneously (pyrophoric) from exposure to a high temperature (auto-ignition) or to a spark or open flame. (Flash point is the temperature at which a volatile substance gives off a vapour sufficient to form an ignitable mixture with the air.)

Inflammability will depend on the concentration of the gas in air and the concentration of oxygen present.

Explosiveness generally relates to the rapid propagation of a flame in a confined space. The consequent effects are due to the high energy generated. (An explosion is, strictly, the result of a sudden release of energy.)

Asphyxiation. An asphyxiant gas causes unconsciousness and death by depriving an organism of oxygen. Some gases (e.g. carbon dioxide) can be both toxic and asphyxiant: which of these properties is critical will depend on concentration and exposure period. A 5% concentration of CO_2 would have a chronic toxic effect (with relatively little oxygen depletion), whereas a 20% concentration would have a profound effect on oxygen levels.

Physical. Physical hazards can be in two forms, namely ground stability and personal contact. Many hazardous sites can be very unstable when excavations are made, and so present the hazards of (a) workers falling into excavations and (b) excavations collapsing on workers within. Further forms of hazard relate to demolition processes and sharp objects such as hypodermic needles, glass and sharp metallic materials. Also structural instability can be created through ground settlement or voids, whether resulting from biodegradation or the effects of combustion. The excavation of sites with live electricity cables or gas mains may also present hazards.

Contexts of hazards

As shown earlier, the principal groups affected directly, or otherwise, by the identified hazards are

- o investigation workers
- o demolition and construction workers
- o after-users of site, particularly children
- o maintenance workers
- o animals and plant life, including aquatic life
- o building structures.

Humans clearly represent the most critical group and can be affected not only directly but also indirectly through material failures (e.g. from explosions or degradation) or consumption of water, plant and animal life.

Many hazardous substances exhibit warning signs such as distinctive odours, colours or physical forms (e.g. dusts). Others can be less than obvious, although in some instances these can give rise to physiological symptoms which can alert one to the presence of a hazard (e.g. breathing difficulty or headaches suggesting asphyxiant conditions). Generalised comments are given in Table 3.2 on the potential hazards during different project phases, bearing in mind that there are some obvious overlaps in the hazards (e.g. combustion and inflammability). Also, there must be a reasonable presumption that gross obvious contamination, such as by 'oily' wastes, does not normally exist openly on developed sites.

An example of a risk increased by indiscriminate demolition is shown in Fig. 3.1.

Fig. 3.1. Indiscriminate demolition can increase risks: transformer oil spillage containing PCBs

Table 3.2. Principal hazards during project phases

Investigation phase

Toxicity. Unlikely to be critical but inhalation of dusts, vapours or gases can be most undesirable and in extreme cases a critical build-up could occur in an unventilated space such as a pit. Examples of toxic gases include CO_2, H_2S and HCN. Ingestion is unlikely to be critical, particularly if hygiene procedures are followed.

Carcinogenicity. Unlikely to be critical in the large majority of instances due to the short term nature of exposure, but this does not reduce in any way the need for proper protection and precautions.

Corrosivity. Can arise through handling of liquids in particular, and the ground-mass in general; vapour emissions or splashing can also be relevant. Effects can vary from dermic response to severe tissue damage. Common examples include phenols, acids, spend oxide and coal tars.

Combustibility. Not normally a direct critical hazard (unless, of course, all normal obvious warning signs are ignored).

Inflammability and explosiveness. A wide-ranging hazard depending on the physical contexts prevailing (e.g. gas migration into a site hut or pit, or being doused in a highly inflammable material, or encountering an underground tank).

Asphyxiation. Unlikely to occur except in a confined unventilated space such as a trial pit (which should not be entered without due testing and precautions) or existing structure/tunnel.

Physical. Ground stability problems are most likely to occur on domestic waste and similar sites or where combustion has taken place, leaving loose conditions, underground tanks, chambers or manholes with weak covers; buried live services (e.g. gas mains and electricity cables) may also pose a potential risk.

Demolition/construction phase

In this phase the duration of potential interactions with some hazardous substances is likely to be greater and more intense than for investigation workers (e.g. dealing with tanks containing liquids).

Toxicity. Unlikely to be critical but, as for investigation workers, inhalation of toxic dusts, vapours or gases might be a problem in confined spaces (e.g. pits and trenches), and if fires are lit on a contaminated site (e.g. burning of treated timber may give rise to unacceptable levels of As_2O_3).

Carcinogenicity. Unlikely to be critical due to the usual short-term nature of exposure. However, specialist site clearance workers may suffer an increased risk through repeated exposure (e.g. asbestos-strippers).

Corrosivity. Potential risks similar to those for investigation workers, but they can usually be greatly reduced by use of protective clothing.

Combustibility. Potential risk usually only when surface fires are lit.

Inflammability and explosiveness. Contexts similar to those for investigation workers but increased risks if using tools which could induce ignition.

Asphyxiation. Contexts similar to those for site investigation workers.

Physical. Contexts similar to those for site investigation workers, but profoundly greater risks from structures, cavities and sharp objects.

Table 3.2. (Continued)

Site occupation/use
This phase involves the most sensitive and longer term targets if no ameliorative measures have been taken. Clearly, in such circumstances, profound hazards can occur under all categories.

Toxicity. Potential hazard through ingestion of soils, plants or water; particular problem for 'pica' children (who habitually eat non-foods such as soil), or in households where vegetables are grown and eaten extensively; chronic toxicity effects mainly associated with metals such as lead, arsenic and cadmium, and some organic compounds; phytotoxic effects on plant life.

Carcinogenicity. Potentially critical for sensitive after-uses such as housing.

Corrosivity. Except for gross contamination, unlikely to be critical through handling shallow contaminated soil (i.e. corrosiveness may have been 'stripped'). Problems may arise due to the aggressive nature of some substances to building materials and services (e.g. sulphate is corrosive to concrete, while phenols and coal tars may degrade plastic pipework (and contaminate drinking water supplies)).

Combustibility. Likely to be a critical hazard if bonfires are lit on former waste sites, for example, which have a considerable fraction of combustible materials (there might also be consequences of toxic gases).

Inflammability and explosiveness. Potentially critical if buildings are constructed on or near former landfill sites without adequate gas control systems; particular hazards in confined spaces.

Asphyxiation. Unlikely to be a critical hazard, except in confined spaces where, for example, oxygen deficiency or high carbon dioxide concentrations can occur.

Physical. Hazards likely to be non-critical, except possible subsidence where buildings are constructed on former landfill sites, or in areas of mine shafts.

Maintenance works
Maintenance workers can be critically affected through, for example, possible lack of awareness of residual hazards following rehabilitation.

Toxicity. Potential hazard from the inhalation of dusts or gases in service ducts or pipes.

Carcinogenicity. Unlikely to be critical due to short term of exposure.

Corrosivity. Potential hazard associated with the handling of corrosive soils, principally at depth; also the designed protective mechanisms of services and pipes might not be reinstated correctly.

Combustibility. Non-critical hazard to workers but some operations might induce combustion (e.g. heat application to pipe repairs).

Inflammability and explosiveness. Potential build-up of explosive concentrations of gases in confined spaces, service ducts or manholes.

Asphyxiation. Confined spaces present the primary hazardous context.

Physical. Unlikely to be a critical hazard except for mining shafts or sharp objects.

The hazards outlined can also relate to off-site regimes, where the local neighbourhood is affected by, for example, dust or asbestos migration during demolition, gas migration, water regime contamination, explosion effects and combustion effects. As with on-site situations, the significance of such hazards is dependent on the magnitude of the source and the sensitivity of the 'receiver'. Landfill gas migration is probably the most common direct hazard, together with leachate effects on groundwater supplies.

Sources and forms of hazard
Sources of hazard
Examples of sites on which contaminants are likely to be found include

- o   landfills and other waste disposal sites
- o   gasworks, coal carbonisation plants and ancillary by-product works
- o   chemical works
- o   railway land (especially large sidings and depots)
- o   oil refineries, petroleum storage and distribution sites
- o   metal mines, smelters, foundries, steelworks and metal-finishing installations
- o   munitions production and testing sites
- o   asbestos works and ship-breaking
- o   tanneries and plating works
- o   paper and printing works
- o   industries making or using wood preservatives
- o   scrap-yards.

Particular examples are shown in Figs 3.2 and 3.3.

Forms of hazardous substances
The form of hazardous substances will vary on each site depending on the former site processes, and may include gaseous, solid or liquid phases. In addition, many sites have physical hazards such as instability.

Gases/vapours. The principal hazard from gases or vapours is usually in the build-up of concentrations within confined spaces such as cavities, basements, small rooms, trenches, drains and manholes. Landfill gases (mainly methane and carbon dioxide) are particularly common but gases or vapours can also arise from

- o   biodegradation processes (e.g. CO_2, CH_4, H_2S)
- o   spontaneous combustion (e.g. PH_3)
- o   combustion of waste materials (e.g. HCN, SO_2, H_2S, As_2O_3)
- o   chemical reactions in soil through increased acidity (e.g. HCN, H_2S).

Volatile organics can also exist on sites with relevant spillages, storage or disposal areas.

Solids. The principal direct hazard with solid substances is associated with ingestion, directly or indirectly. The indirect route implies that some of the toxic fraction is either soluble or 'available' so that leaching into

Fig. 3.2. Some hazards can be encountered unexpectedly, in this instance a phosphorus waste

water supplies or uptake by plants is possible. For example, the aggressiveness of 'solid' sulphate compounds is fundamentally related to their solubility (i.e. capacity to produce acidic conditions).

Liquids. The principal hazard associated with liquid contaminants is their corrosive or aggressive nature and their potential for water pollution. Toxicity is also an obvious potential, but consumption of such liquids is rare. Splashing of exposed skin by some substances may lead to toxicity problems via percutaneous absorption. Phytotoxicity is, however, a real hazard.

Dusts and fumes. The principal hazard associated with dusts and fumes is from inhalation. This is generally likely to be a short term exposure risk and actually can be created by demolition and removal of wastes from site (e.g. asbestos dusts), or through the burning of contaminated material on site (e.g. Ni fumes) or exposure to organic solvents. Also, some gases form acidic corrosive aerosols in the presence of water (e.g. H_2S, SO_2, PH_3).

Pathogens. A further form of contaminant to be considered is that of pathogens. In this regard the main hazard is probably to site investigation workers on former landfill sites and where sewage sludge or hospital wastes have been deposited. Disease-producing (pathogenic) organisms such as bacteria, viruses, or eggs or cysts of parasites may be present. Sewage treatment significantly reduces numbers of pathogens present and the incidence on old sites is likely to be small. An increasing cause for concern is the highly hazardous Weil's disease that can result from infections of cuts and abrasions and is transmitted by rat urine; tetanus is a further disease of particular concern. Site workers and investigators are, therefore, most at risk.

Fig. 3.3. The visual (and olfactory) evidence of tarry wastes is often obvious

Radioactivity. In general terms, radioactivity is unlikely to be a significant hazard; moreover, in protecting against general waste deposits, by covering systems for example, the risks are usually significantly decreased.

Data on specific hazards

Set out in Table 3.3 are some relevant factors relating to a range of hazardous substances that might be encountered on a large number of contaminated sites. These substances have been grouped, for ease of reference, into gases, metallic compounds, inorganic compounds, organic compounds, and others. Strictly speaking, cyanides should be in the organic group. Also, acids/alkalis should be in a separate section, but it is invariably the inorganic group that is of concern.

There are many sources of useful information on the substances considered. The four major references to which the reader's attention is drawn are the *Occupational exposure limits 1989* (ref. 3.2); the ICRCL trigger values (ref. 3.3); the DoE's waste management paper 23 (ref. 3.4); and the *Encyclopaedia of occupational health and safety* (ref. 3.8).

text continues on page 59

Table 3.3. Specific hazards

___

GASES
Effective ventilation (i.e. dilution) can eliminate all risks from gases, whether toxic, asphyxiant or explosive.

Carbon dioxide (CO_2)
General characteristics
Colourless, odourless gas
Denser than air (specific gravity 1·53)
Present in air at 0·03% (300 ppm) by volume
Dissolves in water to form carbonic acid
Non-combustible

Relevant sources
Natural occurrences (acids on limestone)
Produced on landfill sites by aerobic and anaerobic decomposition of organic
    matter or as a product of combustion

Principal effects on humans
Toxic and asphyxiant by inhalation
Concentration > 3%: laboured breathing and headaches result
Concentration 5–6%: these symptoms become severe
Concentration 12–25%: victim becomes unconscious
Concentration > 25%: death can occur
Occupational exposure limits 5000 ppm (8 h), 15 000 ppm (10 min)

Principal effects on plants
Variable toxicity

Principal human targets
Workers in poorly ventilated trenches or tunnels (e.g. investigation and
    clearance demolition workers), as CO_2 is denser than air and capable of
    accumulating in deep pits or excavations
After users of site (see 'landfill gases' below)

Principal materials affected
Metals and concrete could degrade where strong solutions form

Carbon monoxide (CO)
General characteristics
Colourless, almost odourless gas
Slightly soluble in water
Burns with a violet flame
Produced during incomplete combustion of organic materials

Relevant sources
Underground combustion

Principal effects on humans
Highly toxic by inhalation
Highly inflammable
Has an affinity for blood haemoglobin that is over 200 times that of oxygen,
    causing hypoxia in victims
Concentration > 200 ppm: headache after 50 min
Concentration > 500 ppm: headache after 20 min
Concentration 1000–10 000 ppm: headache, dizziness and nausea in 13–15 min;
    death if exposure continues for 10–45 min
Concentration 10 000–40 000 ppm: death within a few minutes

Table 3.3. (Continued)

Occupational exposure limits 50 ppm (8), 300 ppm (10 min)
Combustion possible at 12–75%

Principal effects on plants
Phytotoxic

Principal human targets
Redevelopment workers (in confined spaces)
Site users (in buildings)

Hydrogen cyanide (HCN)

General characteristics
Colourless and has a faint odour of bitter almonds
Soluble in water
Highly inflammable
White liquid at temperatures below 26·5°C

Relevant sources
Combustion of complex cyanides in soil (e.g. spent oxides at gas works sites)
or acidification of cyanide salts in soil

Principal effects on humans
Highly toxic by inhalation, ingestion and skin absorption
Fire and explosion risk
Inhibits enzyme systems, especially the enzyme cytochrome oxidase, resulting in
the prevention of oxygen uptake by living tissue
Concentration < 18 ppm: poisoning symptoms exhibited
Concentration 18–36 ppm for several hours: causes slight weakness, headache,
confusion and nausea
Concentration > 100 ppm for several minuites: causes collapse, respiratory
failure and possible death
Concentration > 300 ppm: immediately fatal
Occupational exposure limit 10 ppm (10 min)
Lower explosive limit 6% in air

Principal human targets
Site investigation workers (in confined spaces)
Site users (in buildings)

Hydrogen sulphide (H$_2$S)

General characteristics
Colourless gas
Distinctive offensive odour of rotten eggs (odour threshold 0·5 parts per billion
(i.e. 10^9))
Dulls olfactory senses (creating impression of concentration abatement)
Sweetish taste
Soluble in water

Relevant sources
Microbial action on sulphate salts (e.g. gypsum) under anaerobic conditions
Plasterboard discarded in landfill sites
Kraft paper mill sites, oil refineries, coal carbonisation sites and chemical works
Acid soil conditions may produce H$_2$S where high sulphide concentrations exist

Principal effects on humans
Highly toxic by inhalation
Highly inflammable

Table 3.3. (Continued)

Highly malodorous
A strong irritant to the eyes and mucous membranes
Concentration > 20 ppm: causes loss of smell, thus toxic limits reached without
    odour warning
Concentration 20–150 ppm: causes sub-acute effects (i.e. irritation of the eyes and
    respiratory tract)
Concentration > 400 ppm: toxic effects occur
Concentration > 700 ppm: life-threatening
Occupational exposure limits 10 ppm (8 h), 15 ppm (10 min)
Lower explosive limit 4·5% in air

Principal effects on plants
Phytotoxic

Principal human targets
Site investigation and construction workers in trenches and drains
Site users in confined unventilated spaces
Neighbourhood

Methane (CH$_4$)
General characteristics
Colourless, odourless, tasteless gas
Lighter than air (specific gravity 0·55)
Inflammable; lower explosive limit in air 5%; upper explosive limit in air 15%

Relevant sources
Decaying vegetation in swamps and marshes (CH$_4$ produced naturally)
Natural gas and coal gas
Microbial anaerobic degradation of organic matter, principally in landfill sites

Principal effects on humans
Severe explosion risk when present in concentration range 5–15% in air
Asphyxiant as it replaces air, but non-toxic in itself

Principal effects on plants
Causes root die-back by replacing oxygen
May be oxidised to CO$_2$ by soil bacteria

Principal human targets
Site investigation workers in unventilated pits and trenches
Inhabitants of buildings on or adjacent to landfill sites

Principal effects on plants
Affects vegetation on restored landfill sites and adjacent areas

Phosphine (PH$_3$)
General characteristics
Colourless gas
Garlic-like odour
Denser than air (specific gravity 1·85)
Spontaneously inflammable in air (usually with the highly visible phosphorus
    pentoxide vapour (Fig. 3.2))

Relevant sources
Deposits of phosphorus compounds

Principal effects on humans
Highly toxic by inhalation
Fire and explosion hazard

Table 3.3. (Continued)

Symptoms of inhalation include headache, fatigue, nausea, vomiting, jaundice and ataxia
Strong irritant
Odour threshold 2 ppm
Occupational exposure limits 0·3 ppm (8 h), 1 ppm (10 min)
Ignites at room temperature where impurities exist
Principal human targets
Site investigation workers
Redevelopment workers

Sulphur dioxide (SO$_2$)
General characteristics
Colourless gas with a sharp pungent odour
Denser than air (specific gravity 1·43)
Soluble in water to form sulphurous acid
Non-combustible
Strong oxidising and reducing agent
Relevant sources
Burning of sulphurous materials such as coal and oil
Released during the combustion (accidental or deliberate) of contaminated materials (e.g. spent oxide) on former gasworks sites
Principal effects on humans
Toxic by inhalation
Strong irritant to eyes and mucous membranes, causing a variety of respiratory effects depending on concentration and individual susceptibility (bronchitis sufferers more severely affected)
Concentration 0·3–1·0 ppm: detectable by most individuals
Concentration 6–12 ppm: becomes an irritating gas
Occupational exposure limits 2 ppm (8 h), 5 ppm (10 min)
Principal effects on plants
Phytotoxic
Principal effects on materials
Corrosive where sulphurous acid is formed
Principal human targets
Site occupiers
Neighbourhood residents
Principal affected materials
Concrete and metals can degrade where acid forms

Landfill gas
The composite gas produced by the decomposition of biodegradable materials in most landfilled waste sites is covered in the text

METAL COMPOUNDS
Arsenic (As)
General characteristics
Elemental As is a silver–grey, brittle crystalline solid that darkens in moist air
Forms organic and inorganic compounds which are solid and may/may not be soluble in water

Table 3.3. (Continued)

Arsine (AsH_3) is a colourless gas which is soluble in water and is flammable

Relevant sources
Soil contamination as a result of mining and smelting of the metal, and
  extensive use of agricultural preparations such as pesticides and herbicides
Burning of preserved wood on building sites produces harmful levels of As_2O_3
  (ash may contain up to 5% As, which may be water-soluble)

Principal effects on humans
Solid compounds highly toxic by ingestion, skin contact and dust inhalation
Ingestion results in severe diarrhoea and vomiting; 70–180 mg arsenic trioxide
  (As_2O_3) represents a fatal dose
Skin contact causes dermatitis; As_2O_3 linked with skin cancer (20 years latency)
Inhalation of As compounds irritates mucous membranes of the respiratory
  system; AsH_3 gas highly toxic by inhalation (55 times more toxic than
  cyanide)
Poisoning is acute or chronic according to exposure concentration and
  duration
Occupational exposure limit As and compounds except arsine and lead
  arsenate 0·2 mg/m^3 (8 h)
ICRCL trigger values (threshold) (see Chapter 5) As (total) 10 mg/kg (gardens),
  40 mg/kg (parks, playing fields)

Principal effects on livestock
Poisoning through ingestion of contaminated herbage and As-rich soils

Principal effects on plants
Toxicity depends on oxidation state and form of the element; arsenite more
  toxic than arsenate
Reduced growth occurs before toxic levels reached within plant
Accumulation in edible plants may present a hazard to humans

Principal effects off-site
Water pollution possible; arsenite or arsine may be predominant species if
  reducing conditions develop

Principal human targets
Risk to site investigation workers and demolition/clearance workers through
  inhalation of dusts, and gases in unventilated spaces
Risk to site after-users through ingestion of soils, plants or water; 'pica'
  children especially at risk

Principal livestock targets
Animals grazing on contaminated vegetation

Principal plant targets
Vegetables have reduced yield and are contaminated

Boron (B)
General characteristics
Elemental B is a black hard solid or brown amorphous powder which is highly
  reactive; it is soluble in water; dust ignites spontaneously in air
Forms organic and inorganic compounds which may be solid, liquid or gaseous
  and may or may not be soluble in water
Compounds of interest include halogenated boron, boron hydrides, boric oxide
  and sodium metaborate

Table 3.3. (Continued)

Relevant sources

Manufacturing wastes of certain petrochemical (e.g. nylon) or other industries (e.g. washing powders)

Wastes containing B compounds in glass, ceramics, porcelain and enamelware are not in an ingestible form unless presented as powders

Principal effects on humans

Elemental B is non-toxic

Boron dust is a fire and explosion hazard

Compounds mentioned under 'General characteristics' may irritate or be corrosive to the skin, nasal mucous membranes, the respiratory tract and eyes

Occupational exposure limits boron tribromide (BBr_3) 1 ppm (8 h), 3 ppm (10 min)

Occupational exposure limits boron oxide (B_2O_3) 10 mg/m^3 (8 h), 20 mg/m^3 (10 min)

Principal effects on plants

Phytotoxic effects

Grasses more resistant

ICRCL trigger value (threshold) water-soluble boron 3 mg/kg (soil)

Toxicity increased in acidic soils

Principal human targets

Unlikely to be a critical hazard, but inhalation of dusts by site investigators and demolition/clearance workers may cause ill effects

Little hazard from consumption of contaminated vegetation

Principal plant targets

Most non-grasses

Cadmium (Cd)

General characteristics

Elemental Cd is a soft blue–white malleable metal or grey–white powder; inflammable in powder form

Forms organic and inorganic compounds which are solid and soluble in water

Relevant sources

Mining and smelting, pigments, paints, electroplating, PVC stabilisers, fungicides, batteries, photocells, alloys and solders

Landfill is the major outlet for Cd-bearing wastes

Principal effects on humans

Highly toxic via inhalation of Cd metal or oxide as fumes or dust

Inhalation of Cd at a concentration of 1 mg/m^3 for 8 hours may lead to chemical pneumonitis

Soluble compounds are toxic by ingestion; a concentration of Cd of 15 mg/ml produces food-poisoning symptoms, but emetic action reduces poisoning risk

Long term effects include hypertension and prostatic cancer; Cd accumulates in the liver and kidney, causing renal damage and disturbed metabolism

Occupational exposure limit Cd and Cd compounds 0·05 mg/m^3 (8 h)

Occupational exposure limits cadmium oxide fume 0·05 mg/m^3 (8 h and 10 min)

Occupational exposure limits cadmium sulphide pigments 0·04 mg/m^3 (8 h)

ICRCL trigger values (threshold) Cd (total) 3 mg/kg (gardens), 15 mg/kg (parks, playing fields, open spaces)

Table 3.3. (Continued)

Principal effects on plants
Phytotoxic in high concentrations
Leafy plants take up more metal, causing food contamination

Principal effects on livestock
Poisoning through ingestion of Cd-contaminated herbage and soils

Principal effects off-site
Water pollution by soluble compounds may occur

Principal human targets
Acute hazard to site investigators, redevelopment workers, Cd workers
Long-term hazard to site after-users through ingestion of Cd-contaminated
    food from gardens and water supplies; children particularly vulnerable

Principal plants targets
Any vegetation

Principal livestock targets
Animals grazing on contaminated vegetation

Chromium (Cr)
General characteristics
Elemental Cr is a hard, brittle, grey metal
Compounds have strong and varied colours
Hexavalent compounds (e.g. chromic oxide, chromyl compounds, chromates,
    and dichromates) are of most relevance; all are soluble in water and/or acids
Landfill is the major outlet for Cr-bearing wastes

Relevant sources
Natural occurrences; smelting and mining operations; hexavalent compounds
    within wastes from Cr-plating, anodising, metal surface preparation,
    chemical industries, pigment manufacture

Principal effects on humans
Elemental Cr and trivalent compounds are relatively non-toxic
Hexavalent compounds have an irritating and corrosive effect on tissue,
    producing ulcers and dermatitis on prolonged skin contact; irritation of the
    respiratory tract and ulceration of the nasal septum from inhalation
Particulate inhalation linked with bronchogenic carcinoma
Occupational exposure limit Cr $0.5\,mg/m^3$ (8 h)
Occupational exposure limit Cr (II) (i.e. divalent) $0.5\,mg/m^3$ (8 h)
Occupational exposure limit Cr (III) $0.5\,mg/m^3$ (8 h)
Occupational exposure limit Cr (VI) $0.05\,mg/m^3$ (8 h)
ICRCL trigger value (threshold) Cr (VI) $25\,mg/kg$ (all uses)
ICRCL trigger values (threshold) Cr (total) $600\,mg/kg$ (gardens/allotments),
    $1000\,mg/kg$ (parks, playing fields, open spaces)
Concentration $> 1\%$ calcium chromate in dusty or friable waste regarded as
    'special' waste

Principal effects on plants
Phytotoxic
Uptake causes food contamination

Principal effects off-site
Pollution of water supplies is possible as ammonium, lithium, magnesium,
    potassium and sodium chromates and dichromates and chromic acid are very
    soluble in water

Table 3.3. (Continued)

Maximum permissible concentration in potable water is 0·05 ppm (Cr (VI))

Principal human targets
Long-term effect on site after-users through skin contact and ingestion of
  contaminated vegetables and water supplies
Low risk to site investigators and redevelopers due to short-term contact —
  unless exposed to chromic acid, dust and mist, which may cause perforation
  of nasal septa

Principal plant targets
Vegetation growing on contaminated sites

Copper (Cu)
General characteristics
Elemental Cu is a malleable, ductile, reddish-coloured metal; non-combustible
  except as a powder
Forms many organic and inorganic compounds, some soluble in water and
  some not
Commonly occurs as sulphates, sulphides and carbonates in the soil

Relevant sources
Smelting of Cu ores
Waste from electroplating, chemical and textile industries
Wastes from the manufacture of pesticides, pigments and antifouling paints

Principal effects on humans
Toxic by inhalation of dusts and fumes of Cu salts, and by by ingestion and
  skin contact
Inhalation causes congestion of the nasal and mucous membranes, ulceration/
  perforation of the nasal septum, and fume fever
Ingestion of soluble salts causes nausea, vomiting, diarrhoea, sweating, coma,
  and death if very large doses consumed
Skin contact causes irritation
Eye contact causes corneal ulcers
Occupational exposure limit Cu (fume) 0·2 mg/m^3 (8 h)
Occupational exposure limits Cu (dusts and mists) 1·0 mg/m^3 (8 h), 2 mg/m^3
  (10 min)

Principal effects on plants
Phytotoxic, especially at low soil pH and low organic matter
ICRCL trigger value (threshold) Cu (total) 130 mg/kg (where plants are to be
  grown)

Principal effects on materials
Corrosive to rubber

Principal human targets
Little risk to site investigators and redevelopers
Chronic toxicity rare

Principal plant targets
Any vegetation, but some tolerant species/cultivars exist

Lead (Pb)
General characteristics
Elemental Pb is a heavy, ductile, soft grey solid, insoluble in water (slowly
  soluble in water containing a weak acid)

Table 3.3. (Continued)

Present in a divalent state in most of its inorganic compounds
Lead divalent salts, lead oxides and lead sulphide have low solubility in water (except for the acetate, chlorate and nitrate)

Relevant sources
Natural occurrence
Mining and smelting operations
Batteries, scrap metal, petrol additives, pigments, paints, glass manufacture

Principal effects on humans
Toxic principally by inhalation but also by ingestion
Central nervous system, blood and kidneys affected
Symptoms range from sickness, fatigue and loss of appetite to damage to the brain and other organs, and death
Behavioural disorders in children
Serious effects usually the result of cumulative exposure
Soluble lead compounds more dangerous
Concentration 30% inhaled Pb and 10% ingested Pb enters the blood stream
Occupational exposure limit Pb (except tetraethyl) $0 \cdot 15 \, mg/m^3$ (8 h)
Occupational exposure limit tetraethyl Pb $0 \cdot 1 \, mg/m^3$ (8 h)
ICRCL trigger values (threshold) Pb (total) 500 mg/kg (gardens, allotments), 2000 mg/kg (parks, playing fields, open spaces)

Principal effects off-site
Water supplies may be contaminated in soft-water areas where Pb piping dissolves

Principal human targets
Children who ingest Pb dust due to 'pica' habit
Inhabitants ingesting Pb contamination from garden vegetables (on surface of plants and taken up by plants) (also close to Pb works and heavy traffic)
Inhabitants of soft-water areas with old Pb piping

Mercury (Hg)
General characteristics
Elemental Hg is silvery, extremely heavy and insoluble in water; highly volatile
Forms inorganic and organomercury compounds and amalgams with many other metals
Inorganic Hg converts to methyl Hg in soil

Relevant sources
Wastes from manufacture or formulation of Hg compounds (e.g. process wastes)
Wastes from the use of Hg compounds (e.g. slurries from the chlor-alkali, paint, agriculture and pharmaceutical industries)

Principal effects on humans
Metallic, inorganic and organic Hg highly toxic by ingestion, skin absorption or inhalation
Alkylmercurials most hazardous
Inorganic Hg toxicity on swallowing depends on solubility
Causes denaturation of proteins, inactivation of enzymes, severe disruption of any tissue
Skin contact causes burns and blistering
Absorption results in digestive and nervous symptoms
Occupational exposure limits alkyl Hg $0 \cdot 01 \, mg/m^3$ (8 h), $0 \cdot 03 \, mg/m^3$ (10 min)

Table 3.3. (Continued)

Occupational exposure limits Hg and compounds $0.05\,mg/m^3$ (8 h), $0.15\,mg/m^3$ (10 min)

ICRCL trigger values (threshold) Hg (total) 1 mg/kg (gardens, allotments), 20 mg/kg (parks, playing fields, open spaces)

Principal effects on plants
Phytotoxic
Uptake causes food contamination

Principal effects off-site
Possible contamination of water supplies by soluble Hg compounds

Principal human targets
Low risk to site workers
Greater risk from long-term ingestion of contaminated food (i.e. vegetables from contaminated areas), and drinking contaminated water or eating fish therefrom

Principal plant targets
Any vegetation, but some tolerant species exist

Nickel (Ni)
General characteristics
Elemental Ni is a malleable, silvery metal, inflammable as a dust or powder
Inorganic compounds of interest include nickel oxide (NiO), nickel hydroxide ($Ni(OH)_2$), nickel subsulphide (Ni_3S_2), nickel sulphate ($NiSO_4$) and nickel chloride ($NiCl_2$)

Relevant sources
Refining of impure nickel oxide
Wastes from metal finishing processes including electroplating, alloy and stainless steel manufacture, enamel and battery production

Principal effects on humans
Elemental Ni toxic
Compounds toxic by skin contact (allergic dermatitis) and inhalation (rhinitis, nasal sinusitis and chronic pulmonary irritation)
Carcinogenic effects from long-term inhalation of Ni dust and fumes, and $Ni(CO)_4$
$Ni(CO)_4$ inhalation also produces immediate symptoms of nausea, vertigo, headache, breathlessness and chest pain
Occupational exposure limit Ni $1\,mg/m^3$ (8 h)
Occupational exposure limits Ni (soluble compounds) $0.1\,mg/m^3$ (8 h), $0.3\,mg/m^3$ (10 min)
Occupational exposure limits Ni (insoluble compounds) $1\,mg/m^3$ (8 h), $3\,mg/m^3$ (10 min)
Fire risk with Ni dust or powder

Principal effects on plants
Phytotoxic, especially in acid soils
ICRCL trigger value (threshold) Ni (total) 70 mg/kg (any uses where plants are to be grown)

Principal human targets
Carcinogenic effects associated with occupational exposure and site after-users, especially children

Table 3.3. (Continued)

Risks to site workers are increased if fires are lit on heavily contaminated sites, as these can produce toxic fumes

Principal plant targets
Any vegetation, but some tolerant species/cultivars exist

Selenium (Se)
General characteristics
Elemental Se is an amorphous red powder, becoming black on standing
Forms organic and inorganic compounds, some soluble in water and some not

Relevant sources
By-product from the smelting and refining of copper, nickel, silver and gold ores
Waste from the manufacture and reconditioning of 'xerox' drums, the pigments industry and the production of paints containing cadmium orange

Principal effects on humans
Elemental Se is harmless
Compounds are toxic, absorbed through the lungs, intestinal tract or damaged skin
Soluble compounds (e.g. SeO_2) are most toxic
Inhalation causes pulmonary oedema
Skin contact causes burns
General symptoms of absorption include a garlic odour to the breath, pallor, lassitude, irritability, vague gastro-intestinal symptoms and giddiness
Occupational exposure limit Se and compounds $0.2\,mg/m^3$ (8 h)
Occupational exposure limit SeF_6 $0.2\,mg/m^3$ (8 h)
ICRCL trigger values (threshold) Se (total) 3 mg/kg (gardens, allotments), 6 mg/kg (parks, playing fields, open spaces)

Principal human targets
Construction workers

Zinc (Zn)
General characteristics
Elemental Zn is a shining white metal with a bluish-grey lustre; Zn dust may form explosive mixtures with air
Most simple salts of Zn are soluble in water (although the oxide, hydroxide, carbonate, sulphide, phosphate and silicates are insoluble or only slightly soluble)

Relevant sources
Smelting of ore
Wastes from metal-finishing, and battery, pigment, plastics, fire-retardant and cosmetics manufacture

Principal effects on humans
Fire and explosion risk from Zn dust in damp conditions
Zn compounds relatively non-toxic by ingestion, although large doses of soluble salts may cause vomiting and diarrhoea
Poisoning by inhalation of ZnO fumes and dust causes metal-fume fever (i.e. shivering, sweating, nausea, thirst, headache, painful limbs)
$ZnCl_2$ and ZnO corrosive to skin, causing dermatitis
Zn chromate carcinogenic

Table 3.3. (Continued)

Occupational exposure limits $ZnCl_2$ (fume) $1 mg/m^3$ (8 h), $2 mg/m^3$ (10 min)
Occupational exposure limits ZnO (fume) $5 mg/m^3$ (8 h), $10 mg/m^3$ (10 min)

Principal effects on plants
Phytotoxic, synergistic effect with Cu, Ni, especially at low pH
ICRCL trigger value (threshold) Zn (total) 300 mg/kg (any uses where plants
   are to be grown)
ICRCL trigger value (threshold) Zn (equivalent) 280 mg/kg (any uses where
   plants are to be grown)

Principal human targets
Low risk to site investigators, redevelopment workers and after-users

Principal plant targets
Any vegetation, but some tolerant species/cultivars exist

INORGANIC COMPOUNDS
Acids and alkalis (pH)
General characteristics
Acids are a large class of chemicals whose water solutions have a pH value less
   than 7, have a sour taste, turn litmus dye red, and react with certain metals
   and bases to form salts
Inorganic acids include sulphuric (H_2SO_4), nitric (HNO_3), phosphoric (H_3PO_4),
   hydrochloric (HCl) and hydrofluoric (HF) acid
Organic acids include carboxylic and acetic acid, fatty acids, amino acids
Alkalis are caustic substances which in water solution have a pH greater than
   7, have a bitter taste and turn litmus dye blue
Alkalis include ammonia (NH_3), ammonium hydroxide (NH_4OH), calcium
   oxide (CaO), calcium hydroxide ($Ca(OH)_2$), sodium carbonate (Na_2CO_3),
   sodium hydroxide (NaOH)

Relevant sources
Inorganic acids in wastes from the fertiliser and chemical industries, metal
   surface preparation and finishing, plastics manufacture
Organic acids in wastes from acetate preparation, nylon manufacture, surface
   metal treatment, the food industry
Natural inorganic/organic acids
Alkalis in wastes from the glass, chemical, and paper industries, fertiliser
   manufacture

Principal effects on humans — inorganic acids
Fire and explosion risk if in contact with certain other chemical substances or
   combustible materials; flammable hydrogen evolved on contact with metals
Corrosive, especially at high concentration; tissue damage at 0·6% nitric acid,
   1% sulphuric acid
Skin contact causes severe burns
Eyes readily damaged
Inhalation of vapours/mists causes respiratory-tract irritation
Ingestion causes severe irritation of the throat and stomach, destruction of
   internal organ tissue, possible death
Occupational exposure limits nitric acid $5 mg/m^3$ (8 h), $10 mg/m^3$ (10 min)
Occupational exposure limit sulphuric acid $1 mg/m^3$ (8 h)
ICRCL soil trigger value (threshold) pH < 5 (gardens, allotments, landscaped
   areas)

Table 3.3. (Continued)

ICRCL soil trigger value (action) pH < 3 (gardens, allotments, landscaped areas)

Principal effects on humans — organic acids
Irritant to eye, respiratory system and skin
Degree of effect determined by acid dissociation and water solubility; tissue damage at 10% acetic acid concentration
Occupational exposure limits acetic acid $25\,mg/m^3$ (8 h), $37\,mg/m^3$ (10 min)

Principal effects on humans — alkalis
Corrosive to tissue whether in solid form or concentrated liquid solution; tissue damage at 0·1% sodium hydroxide, 10% ammonia solution
Severe destruction of skin and eye tissue, irritation of the respiratory tract
Occupational exposure limits sodium hydroxide $2\,mg/m^3$ (8 h), $2\,mg/m^3$ (10 min)

Principal effects on plants
Acidity in soils will increase the availability of certain toxic metals (e.g. Zn, Cu, Ni)

Principal effects on materials
Acids will cause degradation of building materials (i.e. metals, concrete, limestone)

Principal effects off-site
Contamination of water supplies possible

Principal human targets
Site investigators, redevelopment workers and site users

Principal plant targets
Vegetation generally

Principal materials affected
Building materials generally

Cyanides (CNs)
(HCN — see 'Gases')

General characteristics
The 'simple' salts and their solutions present the greatest risk to humans (e.g. potassium or sodium cyanide)
Crystalline complex CNs present lesser risk (e.g. sodium and potassium ferri- and ferrocyanides)
Thiocyanates are important CN compounds

Relevant sources
Simple salts from plating works, heat treatment works
Complex CNs from photography and pigment manufacture, gasworks sites (spent oxide)
Thiocyanates from gasworks sites

Principal effects on humans
Simple CNs
  Moderately toxic
  Absorbed from all entry routes
  Causes inhibition of enzymes required for cell respiration, preventing oxygen uptake by the tissues; death by asphyxia if 50–100 mg ingested
  Chronic exposure to very low levels causes dermatitis, nose irritation
Complex CNs

Table 3.3. (Continued)

Relatively non-toxic
Ferricyanide is more toxic than ferrocyanide
Skin contact with > 50 g/kg spent oxide causes skin irritation
Thiocyanate
  Low acute toxicity
  Large doses cause vomiting and convulsions
  Sodium thiocyanate at > 50 mg/kg is lethal
Chronic exposure causes skin eruptions, dizziness, cramps, nausea, vomiting,
  nervous-system disturbances
Occupational exposure limit cyanides (except HCN, cyanogen, cyanogen
  chloride) 5 mg/m^3 (8 h)
ICRCL trigger values

	Threshold	*Action*
Free CN		
Gardens, allotments, landscaped areas	25 mg/kg	500 mg/kg
Buildings, hard cover	100 mg/kg	500 mg/kg
Complex CN		
Gardens, allotments	250 mg/kg	1000 mg/kg
Landscaped areas	250 mg/kg	5000 mg/kg
Buildings, hard cover	250 mg/kg	No limit
Thiocyanate		
All proposed uses	50 mg/kg	No limit

EEC drinking water criterion 50 mg/l

Principal effects on plants
Free and complex CN phytotoxic
Phytotoxic levels for spent oxides in soil approx. 5g/kg, equivalent to 250 mg/kg
  complex CN
Uptake causes food contamination

Principal effects on fish
Concentration > 0·001 ppm may cause fish toxicity
Concentration 0·1 ppm may cause chronic effects

Principal effects off-site
Possible groundwater pollution, as CN salts are soluble

Principal human targets
Site investigators and redevelopment workers where simple CN dumped
Particular danger where CN and acids in close proximity; may react to form HCN
  gas
Site after-users where vegetables are contaminated; children particularly
  susceptible

Principal plant targets
All vegetation

Sulphur (S) compounds
(Hydrogen sulphide, sulphur dioxide — see 'Gases'; sulphuric acid — see 'Acids
  and alkalis')
Sulphates, sulphides and sulphur are of most importance

Relevant sources
Sulphates from acid rain, dumping of S-containing wastes (e.g. gypsum),
  gasworks wastes (may be up to 20% sulphate)
Sulphides from metal ores, wastes from pigment manufacture, ceramics

Table 3.3. (Continued)

Sulphate-reducing, sulphide-oxidising conditions (by bacterial action)
Sulphur native to volcanic regions
Principal effects on humans
Toxic effects vary according to metal salt
Amount of sulphate/sulphide ion ingested itself of no significance
Ferrous sulphates more toxic than ammonium sulphate
Ingestion of small doses of ferrous sulphate (>7.8 g) may be fatal to a 'small'
    child
Gastro-intestinal irritation from high sulphate levels in drinking water
Inhalation of sulphur dust causes respiratory inflammation and
    bronchopulmonary disease after several years
Skin contact with sulphur results in eczematous lesions
ICRCL trigger values

Sulphate	Threshold	Action
Gardens, allotments, landscaped areas	2000 mg/kg	10 000 mg/kg
Buildings	2000 mg/kg	50 000 mg/kg
Hard cover	2000 mg/kg	No limit
Sulphide		
All uses	250 mg/kg	1000 mg/kg
Sulphur		
All uses	5000 mg/kg	20 000 mg/kg

Principal effects on plants
Phytotoxic effects, although plants differ in their ability to withstand high
    sulphate/sulphide levels
Phytotoxicity more marked in acid soils
Soil sulphate $>200–300$ mg/kg considered to be of concern for plant growth
Possible microbial transformation of sulphate to toxic sulphide salts in
    anaerobic, waterlogged soils
Principal effects on materials
Sulphate is corrosive to building materials (e.g. concrete); sulphide-oxidising
    bacteria can create highly acid conditions; cast iron piping is particularly
    affected by sulphides generated by sulphur-reducing bacteria (SRB)
Principal effects off-site
Possible contamination of water bodies with soluble sulphates and sulphides
Principal human targets
Little risk to site workers, investigators, redevelopment workers
Children and inhabitants of contaminated-water areas at risk
Principal plant targets
Some vulnerable species
Principal materials affected
May require sulphate-resisting cement and/or protective coatings where
    sulphate levels greater than 0·2% in soil, 300 mg/l in water; no effect below
    these levels (see BRE digest 250 (ref. 3.9))

ORGANIC COMPOUNDS
Coal tar
General characteristics
Black viscous liquid with naphthalene-like odour and sharp burning taste
Combustible

Table 3.3. (Continued)

Only slightly soluble in water

Highly complex and variable mixture containing up to 10 000 compounds

Relevant sources

Derived from the coal carbonisation process

Gasworks sites may contain up to 60% coal tars in waste

Principal effects on humans

Effects dependent on components

Risk via inhalation and skin contact

Inhalation of low-molecular-weight (i.e. volatile) aromatics presents toxicity
   hazard — benzene and toluene have narcotic properties

Inhalation of polyaromatic hydrocarbon (PAH) content may cause cancer

Skin/eye contact causes severe irritation, cancer (from PAH contact)

Ingestion hazards not significant — a 20 kg child would need to ingest 100 g of
   material containing 10 g coal tar per kilogram to present a poisoning risk

ICRCL trigger values (expressed as polyaromatic hydrocarbons (PAHs))

	Threshold	*Action*
Gardens, allotments, play areas	50 mg/kg	500 mg/kg
Landscaped areas, buildings, hard cover	1000 mg/kg	10 000 mg/kg

Principal effects on plants

Phytotoxicity at 1–10 g/kg

Uptake causes food contamination

Principal effects on materials

Plastic piping attacked chemically

Principal effects off-site

Odour; soil discoloration

Contamination of drinking water, causing tainting and odour

Principal human targets

Critical groups are children and gardeners who have regular contact with
   contamination

Volatile substances could present a short-term risk to investigators or workers on
   a site

Principal plant targets

Vegetation generally

Principal materials affected

Plastic piping

Phenols

General characteristics

A class of aromatic organic compounds that have a characteristic odour and an
   acrid burning taste

The simpler compounds are soluble in water

Relevant sources

By-products of the coal carbonisation industry

Present in wastes from gasworks sites (in coal tars), ammoniacal liquors,
   pentachlorophenol, pharmaceuticals, dyes, indicators

Principal effects on humans

Toxic by inhalation, skin contact and ingestion; strong irritant to tissue

Tissue damage at > 1%

Table 3.3. (Continued)

Ingestion causes intense burning of the mouth and throat, abdominal pain,
   nausea and vomiting, diarrhoea, dizziness, central nervous system damage;
   dose 10–30 g is fatal
Skin absorption causes above symptoms, skin blistering and necrosis
Inhalation causes above effects, but low vapour pressure reduces risk
Occupational exposure limits 5 ppm (8 h), 10 ppm (10 min)
ICRCL trigger values

	Threshold	*Action*
Gardens, allotments	5 mg/kg	200 mg/kg
Landscaped areas, buildings, hard cover	5 mg/kg	1000 mg/kg

Principal effects on plants
Phytotoxic effects at > 1000 mg/kg

Principal effects on materials
Plastic water piping and rubber attacked
May affect concrete at > 5%

Principal effects off-site
Contamination of water supplies due to migration through plastic pipes; this will
   lead to the formation of unpleasant-tasting chlorinated phenols ('TCP' taste)
Imparts disinfectant odour to soils

Principal effects on fish
Toxic, especially in cold waters, causing paralysis and cardiovascular congestion
Taints fish flesh
Water quality criterion (fisheries): < 0·7 ppm phenols

Principal human targets
Site investigators and workers through direct contact
Site after-users who ingest contaminated food and water

Principal plant targets
Vegetation generally

Principal materials affected
Plastics, rubber, concrete

Polychlorinated biphenyls (PCBs)
General characteristics
A group of organochlorine compounds
Clear, pale yellow, liquid, viscous or solid products, their consistency increasing
   with their chlorination percentage
Mild aromatic odour; low solubility in water
Use is restricted to closed systems

Relevant sources
Transformers, capacitors, coolants, hydraulic fluids, lubricating oils (closed systems)
Previous use as pesticides
> 1% PCB classified as 'special' waste

Principal effects on humans
Toxic, inhibits many enzymes
Suspected carcinogen
Skin and mucous membrane changes
Occupational exposure causes chloracne
Irritation of upper respiratory tract on inhalation when PCB oils heated
Ingestion causes abdominal pain, anorexia, nausea, vomiting, coma and death

Table 3.3. (Continued)

Occupational exposure limits $C_{12}H_7Cl_3$ (42% Cl) $1·0\,mg/m^3$ (8 h), $2\,mg/m^3$ (10 min)

Occupational exposure limits $C_6H_2Cl_3$ (54% Cl) $0·5\,mg/m^3$ (8 h), $1\,mg/m^3$ (10 min)

Principal effects on ecosystem
Highly persistent
Accumulation in birds feeding on aquatic organisms leading to eggshell thinning
Some aquatic organisms killed at low concentrations (e.g. freshwater shrimps at 0·001 ppm)

Principal human targets
Occupational exposure to PCB, especially through skin contact
Site investigators and redevelopers where leakage from or break-up of transformers; use of gloves and disposable protective clothing reduces risk

Principal ecosystem targets
Organisms at higher trophic levels (i.e. carnivores) most at risk due to accumulation within the food chain and high persistence

Solvents
General characteristics
Organic liquids used industrially to dissolve a large number of substances
Nine groups exist: hydrocarbons, halogenated hydrocarbons, aldehydes, alcohols, ethers, glycol derivatives, esters, ketones, and miscellaneous solvents

Relevant sources
Wastes from industry (e.g. printing, oil extraction, degreasing, dry cleaning)

Principal effects on humans
Fire and explosion hazard with most industrial solvents
Volatile inflammable solvents form explosive mixtures with air
Toxic, mainly by inhalation, causing narcosis
Chronic poisoning affects the liver and kidneys
Skin absorption may occur, associated with localised skin injury

Principal human targets
Site investigators and redevelopment workers
Residents on or close to waste solvent sites

OTHER HAZARDOUS MATERIALS
Asbestos
General characteristics
A group of impure magnesium silicate minerals which occur in fibrous form
Three common types: chrysotile (white asbestos), crocidolite (blue asbestos) and amosite (brown asbestos)
Chemically inert, heat resistant, mechanically strong

Relevant sources
Wastes from previous use in pipe insulation, boilers, heating elements, wall insulation, ceiling tiles, brake linings, ship building and breaking, railway carriage breaking, asbestos factories

Principal effects on humans
Carcinogenic and irritant
Hazard mainly associated with confined spaces

Table 3.3. (Continued)

Asbestos inhalation can cause respiratory diseases including asbestosis, bronchial cancer and mesothelioma

No 'safe' level of exposure but different risk associated with type; blue greater than brown greater than white for likelihood of mesothelioma development; latency period 20–30 years

Control limits (4 h) (ref. 3.10) crocidolite and amosite 0·2 fibre/ml, chrysotile 0·5 fibre/ml

Principal human targets

Workers with asbestos waste where fibres are released to the air (e.g. site investigation and redevelopment workers); different risks (friability, structure, content) associated with different methods of handling and stripping of wastes; asbestos cement less likely to generate dust than other products; more risk with insulation and sprayed asbestos; HSE may approve ball and chain demolition for asbestos-cement products as lesser risk to workers from generation of dust and asbestos fibres than dismantling of sheets

Inhabitants of areas close to disposal sites at risk if fibres become airborne

Pathogens

General characteristics

Organisms capable of causing disease to man, animals and plants

Include bacteria, moulds and fungi, viruses, parasites

Relevant sources

Sewage (pathogens may or may not be destroyed by treatment; eggs or cysts of parasites are highly resilient)

Hospital waste

Laboratory waste

Biodegradable domestic waste

Principal effects on humans

Disease

Symptoms vary widely according to organism involved

Principal effects on livestock

Disease

Danger from parasitic eggs/cysts where sewage sludge dumped on land

Principal effects off-site

Disease

Contamination of water supplies (e.g. from sewage discharge)

Spread from waste sites by insects, birds, etc.

Principal human targets

All groups

Radioactivity

General characteristics

Energy of the process emitted as alpha or beta particles or gamma rays

Alpha particles cannot penetrate the skin but are 20 times more harmful than an equivalent amount of beta or gamma radiation if inhaled or swallowed; stopped by a sheet of paper

Beta particles can pass through skin and penetrate the body; stopped by a fairly thin sheet of lead or aluminium

Gamma rays are extremely powerful and penetrating; stopped by thick sheets of lead, many feet of concrete or water

Table 3.3. (Continued)

Radioactivity not affected by the physical state or combination of the element

Radioactivity of a nuclide is characterised by the nature of the radiation, its energy, and the half-life of the process (i.e. the time required for the activity to decrease to one half of the original)

Relevant sources

Hospital waste: mainly short-lived beta- and gamma-emitters (e.g. ^{125}I, 60-day half-life; ^{99}Tc, 6-hour half-life)

Laboratory waste: mainly short-lived beta-emitters, although ^{14}C has a 5000 year half-life

Mining wastes: uranium ore wastes contain long-lived alpha- and beta-emitters (e.g. ^{238}U, half-life 4510×10^6 years; ^{226}Ra, half-life 1620 years)

Natural (phosphorus; granite areas) (e.g. long-lived alpha- and beta-emitters of the uranium and thorium decay series)

Principal effects on humans

Low doses induce carcinogenic and genetic damage which takes many years to emerge

Leukaemia, and thyroid, breast and lung cancer may be induced

Genetic effects involve changes in the number or structure of chromosomes, and mutation of the genes themselves

High doses may kill cells, damage organs, and cause rapid death; damage becomes evident within hours or days

Reproductive organs and eyes particularly sensitive

Occupational exposure limits: ICRP dose limits (1977) (ref. 3.11) 50 millisievert*/year (workers), 1 millisievert/year (public, mean annual), 5 millisievert/year (public, short periods); NRPB guidance limits (1987) (ref. 3.12) 15 millisievert/year (workers), 0·5 millisievert/year (public)

Principal human targets

All groups

Physical hazards

General characteristics

Instability from excavations, old mineshafts, sewers, trial pits, underground cavities and tanks

Hazards from demolition processes

Hazards from sharp objects (e.g. glass, hypodermic needles, metallic objects)

Relevant sources

Mining areas, industrial waste land, waste disposal sites

Ground settlement/voids resulting from biodegradation or the effects of combustion

Principal effects on humans

Physical injury (direct or indirect through structural failure)

Principal effects on materials

Physical damage

Principal human targets

All groups, particularly investigation and demolition and clearance workers

Principal materials affected

All types, particularly rigid members

---

*The sievert is a unit of dose equivalent which takes account of the absorbed dose and the damage potential of the particular type of radiation.

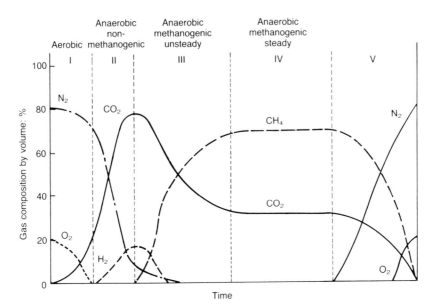

Fig. 3.4. Phases in the generation of landfill gas

Landfill gas

The principal gases produced in the large majority of landfill sites are methane (CH_4) and carbon dioxide (CO_2). These gases can migrate into buildings or confined spaces and may accumulate to explosive, asphyxiant or toxic concentrations. They can also affect vegetation. Other landfill gases include hydrogen sulphide, hydrogen, hydrogen cyanide and various organic gases and vapours depending on refuse composition. This range of gases is greatly extended if a site is combusting; in such conditions sulphurous gases and carbon monoxide, for example, may be included. The likely range of gaseous products where organic substances other than lignin and cellulose products are involved is clearly dependent on the particular conditions. Also, the range is related to both combustion and pyrolitic processes.

Gas generation and composition

The generation of gas progresses through a number of stages and is dependent on a number of critical factors such as biodegradability, moisture content, pH, temperature and oxygen supply. These factors are in turn influenced by waste density and permeability, and climatic conditions. The early decomposition stages are usually dominated by CO_2, the latter stages by CH_4 (Fig. 3.4). These changes are due to the amount of air available in the decomposition zone: CO_2 dominates while conditions are aerobic and CH_4 where they are anaerobic. Generally, during the aerobic phase CO_2 may form up to 80% of landfill gas, while in the anaerobic phase it may form 30–50%, with CH_4 forming 50–70%.

The average start-up time for CH_4 production is extremely variable since one of the main controls relates to landfilling operations — for example, the time taken for the initial deposits to be covered such that air ingress is inhibited. The presumption must be that critical gases can arise in a matter of weeks, but clearly the volumes involved would be dependent on the waste masses.

Hazards

The dangers of CO_2 and/or CH_4 accumulation have been outlined earlier. The major hazards relate to the danger of explosion. Depending on the circumstances, people may be knocked over, shocked, injured, burned or killed, and buildings may be burned or suffer structural damage (with potential human consequences). Factors influencing hazards arising from the migration through and from the landfill site mass can be related principally to gas pressure and ground permeability. Gas pressure within the landfill can be greatly affected by movements of the water table. Pressure gradient, rather than diffusion or buoyancy effects, is the major flow determinant (although landfill gas mixtures are not particularly buoyant, temperature effects apart). Gas migration from landfill sites through the surrounding ground presents an ever-increasing problem and gas is known to travel considerable distances at critical concentrations. Such distances cannot be reasonably generalised due to the fundamental local variations, such as fissured or stratified rocks, mining activities or gravel/sandy strata.

Where gas enters a building or other confined space, such as an unventilated trench, a greater explosion risk exists. This is because there can be a reduced potential for dilution within the building, and because the physical effects of an explosion can be greater. The main routes of gas entry to buildings are through cracks or discontinuities in the floor or walls, around service pipes or in service ducts. The ultimate objective of controls should be to prevent such gas ingress.

Landfill gas may also cause vegetation die-back. CH_4 and CO_2 can cause a deficiency in oxygen in the plant root environment, while CO_2 can itself be toxic to some plants. In addition, CH_4 may be oxidised by soil bacteria, causing both a depletion of oxygen and an increase in CO_2. This phenomenon is highly exothermic and so elevated ground temperatures usually result.

Protective and monitoring systems

The preceding pages outline the wide variety of chemical hazards that may exist within the working and general environments of contaminated sites. In addition, potential physical hazards exist for normal engineering practices. Protection from such hazards is of the utmost importance for investigation and redevelopment workers and, of course, the ultimate users. It is not appropriate here to discuss the measures needed on grossly contaminated sites that may require highly specialised skills. Rather, it is more appropriate to address conditions that are likely to prevail on sites where the most hazardous substances have been removed, leaving some residual risks that must be countered. Equally there are many sites that investigations have shown to have hazards of modest scale which might harbour hot-spots. Thus, the following advice relates to circumstances where most of the hazards are likely to be encountered during trenching works and other ground-mass excavations.

The hazardous chemicals of interest can be present in all three physical forms: solid, liquid or gaseous. Thus they can be harmful via inhalation, ingestion or physical contact, or through their inflammability or explosiveness, and there is a wide range of protective measures that are necessary. Such measures involve the use of protective equipment together with carefully constructed safety and emergency procedures.

Protective equipment

Protection for workers can be provided in the form of suitable clothing, and personal hygiene and safety equipment. Each site must be assessed individually in the light of known historical and chemical data, but the potential for encountering unexpected hazards should be recognised.

The simplest forms of protective clothing are overalls, boots, gloves and helmets. These measures may have to be enhanced from time to time as increased robustness or durability is required in specific circumstances. Overalls or boiler suits should be made of polyester, or polyester and cotton. Steel-protected wellington boots are recommended, although liquid organic contaminants may reduce their protective integrity. PVC-coated gloves offer adequate protection under most circumstances, although they are not fully resistant to some organic compounds.

Personal hygiene offers further protection against hazardous chemicals. Risks are reduced by hand-washing before eating and by avoiding hand-to-mouth contact. Thus, suitable washing facilities must be provided and washing must be carried out effectively. The use of suitable barrier creams applied to clean hands will protect against casual interaction with contaminants and aid the protection of any cuts and abrasions. However, cream is not a substitute for gloves.

Showers can be essential on contaminated sites; drench showers provide effective and rapid dousing when necessary. Eating facilities should be sheltered from contaminated dusts, and boots and protective clothing should not be brought into such buildings if heavily soiled. A ban on smoking will obviously be necessary where the risk of an explosion exists (e.g. in trenches) and where this habit will increase the risk of ingestion of contaminated soil through hand-to-mouth contact.

Safety equipment will include

o   face masks and filters
o   breathing apparatus
o   safety harness and lanyards
o   safety torches
o   fire extinguishers
o   first aid.

Face masks may be simple dust masks, or respirators with filters attached (chosen to match a specific hazard). Breathing apparatus may be self-contained or remote. Such apparatus may be necessary in confined and unventilated spaces where a build-up of gases is likely to occur, although it should be stressed that the provision of adequate ventilation will help prevent such a hazardous situation arising in the first place. Safety harnesses and lanyards are needed when people are entering a trench to effect a rescue. Harnesses should be simple enough to be donned in an emergency. First-aid measures include a first-aid box, the size and contents being prescribed by the HSE, and the presence of an experienced first-aider on site. It is essential that safety and monitoring equipment is properly stored and maintained in accordance with the manufacturers' instructions.

Hazard monitoring

Hazard monitoring will alert site investigators to any potential dangers. This relates largely to airborne fractions and involves the use of visual and olfactory senses or detection devices.

Gas monitoring can be carried out either by automatic gas detectors or, for example, by Draeger tubes (which operate on a similar principle to that of a breathalyser). In either case, specific or generic gas types must first be listed, account being taken of site history, the conditions observed or analysed, and any relevant experience on other contaminated sites. Instruments for measuring inflammability and oxygen concentrations are appropriate on all sites.

A practical approach might be to select gases that can act as indicators (directly or indirectly) for other gases; for example, carbon dioxide in high concentrations can be indicated indirectly by a reduction in oxygen. However, it must be recognised that a 5% concentration of CO_2 (which is a serious hazard causing severe headaches and laboured breathing) could result in only a 1% reduction in oxygen concentration (which in itself would not normally be a cause for concern), together with a 4% reduction in nitrogen concentration.

Automatic gas detectors with multiple gas sensors should have clear audible alarms and should be placed in a zone where a source of hazard is most likely to occur. Monitoring should be carried out before workers enter confined spaces, for example; this is a policy that should apply to all construction sites, particularly where deep trenches or sewers are involved.

Safety procedures

Safety procedures must present a balance between safety, reasonableness and practicability. At the centre of any safety policy, the relevant workers must be made aware of the types of hazard that exist and the degrees of risk associated with them. The safety policy and procedures should be clearly outlined to site staff, and the safety and monitoring equipment demonstrated. A widely used working procedure is the 'permit to work' system whereby only workers with valid permits are allowed to enter or work in 'restricted areas'. Suitable protective clothing will be required for entry into these and other contaminated areas.

Where hazardous materials have to be removed in order to ensure worker and neighbourhood safety, specialist advice must be sought, especially where drums or volatile organics are encountered.

Preparations before the start of work will reduce the scale of any emergency. These include informing the local emergency services of the works being carried out, the nature of possible hazards, and location of access points; the establishment of telephone numbers of emergency services; the arrangement of easy access to a telephone on site; and keeping vehicular access routes clear.

References

3.1. US Department of Health, Education and Welfare. *Registry of toxic effects of chemical substances.* US Dept of Health, Education and Welfare, Cincinnati, Ohio, USA.

3.2. Health and Safety Executive. *Occupational exposure limits 1989.* HMSO, London, 1989, HSE guidance note EH 40/89.

3.3. Interdepartmental Committee on the Redevelopment of Contaminated Land. *Guidance on the assessment and redevelopment of contaminated land.* Department of the Environment, London, 1987, 2nd edn.

3.4. Department of the Environment. *Special wastes: a technical memorandum providing guidance on their definition.* HMSO, London, 1981, waste management paper 23.

3.5. Barry D.L. *Material durability in aggressive ground.* Construction Industry Research and Information Association, London, 1983, report 98.

3.6. Interdepartmental Committee on the Redevelopment of Contaminated Land. *Notes on the fire hazards of contaminated land.* Department of the Environment, London, 1986, 2nd edn, ICRCL 61/84.

3.7. Building Research Establishment. *Fire and explosion hazards associated with the redevelopment of contaminated land.* BRE, Garston, 1987, information paper IP2/87.

3.8. Parmegiani L (ed.). *Encyclopaedia of occupational health and safety.* International Labour Office, Geneva, 1983, 3rd edn.

3.9. Building Research Establishment. *Concrete in sulphate-bearing soils and groundwater.* HMSO, London, 1981, BRE digest 250.

3.10. Health and Safety Executive. *Asbestos: control limits, measurement of airborne dust concentrations and the assessment of control measures.* HMSO, London, 1988, HSE guidance note EH 10.

3.11. Sowby F.D. (ed.). *Recommendations of the International Commission on Radiological Protection.* Publication No. 26, Annals of the ICRP, **1**, No. 3, 1977 (Pergamon Press, Oxford).

3.12. National Radiological Protection Board. *Interim guidance on the the implications of recent revisions of risk estimates and the ICRP 1977 Como statement.* HMSO, London, 1987, NRPB–GS9.

| **4** | **Site investigation** |

JOHN McENTEE, BSc, CEng, FICE
Chief Engineer, Wimpey Laboratories Ltd

The investigation of a site on contaminated and derelict land is essentially similar to an investigation at a site underlain by natural materials. It comprises four basic stages

- o desk study
- o identification of materials underlying the site
- o measurement of geotechnical and chemical properties of these materials
- o recommendations for development of the site.

The desk study is generally confined to an inspection of the available geological records.

The soils or rocks underlying the site will have resulted from their mode of deposition and subsequent weathering, glaciation and tectonic movements. The ground investiagtion should therefore be designed to establish the number of soil or rock types present and to delineate the boundaries between them. The type of investigation will also be dependent upon the proposed development. Mechanically excavated trial pits will usually be sufficient for a housing or light industrial development, whereas a large office block or a power station may require an extensive number of deep boreholes.

The scope of the investigation has thus evolved on the principle that having identified the soils or rocks underlying the site — by inspection of the materials recovered from the boreholes and exposed in trial pits or trenches, and by simple laboratory tests — further tests are carried out to establish their geotechnical properties.

In theory, the results of in situ tests made at one or more locations, or laboratory tests carried out on samples taken from these locations, will provide information on the properties of all the material of a similar composition that underlies the site.

The type of test has been derived from the general principle that a form of undisturbed sample can be obtained from cohesive soils from which specimens can be prepared for tests to measure shear strength and settlement characterisitics. Such samples cannot easily be obtained for granular soils, and thus a variety of in situ penetration tests have been evolved, the results of which can be evaluated to provide information on strength and settlement.

Guidance on the investigation of natural sites is given in BS 5930 (ref. 4.1), ICE *Specification for ground investigation* (ref. 4.2) and the CIRIA *Site investigation manual* (ref. 4.3). Guidance on the range of laboratory and in situ tests is given in BS 1377 (ref. 4.4) and by Head (ref. 4.5).

Notwithstanding the guidance in refs 4.1–4.5, many investigations are carried out for lightly loaded housing or industrial units and the money available for such investigations is all too often sparse. The scope of these investigations is thus often confined to sinking boreholes and carrying out standard split-barrel or cone penetration tests in granular soils and laboratory undrained triaxial compression tests on specimens extruded from so-called undisturbed samples of clayey soils.

However, over the past 50 or so years, a general concept has been established for lightly loaded structures. Where such structures are under-lain by cohesive soils, a simple bearing capacity calculation is made based on the results of a laboratory quick undrained triaxial compression test carried out on 37·5 mm diameter or 100 mm diameter specimens tested at a given rate of strain in accordance with the specification given for Test 21 in BS 1377. A saftety factor of 3 is used in the calculation and a design bearing pressure is evaluated, an assessment being made of the variations in test results due to the effects of weathering and fissuring of the test specimen and disturbance due to sampling and subsequent handling, storage and preparation of the test specimen. For most UK soils, the settlement of lightly loaded structures designed on the basis of strength criteria is to all intents and purposes of a tolerable order.

A similar situation has occurred with granular soils, where the results of the standard penetration tests are assessed using the work of Peck *et al.* (ref. 4.6) and the evaluation of bearing pressure is made on the basis that the structure will tolerate a settlement of 25 mm. As in the case of cohesive soils, the settlements are generally acceptable.

However, in reality there is very little available information on the actual settlements that have occurred. The fact that a given structure shows no evidence of ground movement may indicate that the safety factor is far in excess of 3, in which case the design was not economic. There are also differences in the types of building materials. The softer bricks and low-strength sand–lime mortars used 50 or so years ago would tolerate a higher range of differential movement than the currently used brittle bricks and high-strength sand–cement mortars. There are known instances of structural damage affecting the latter type of construction where the differential movement has been in the order of 5 mm.

When carrying out the investigation of a derelict or contaminated site, the general scope, type of equipment, and in situ and laboratory tests are derived from the procedures adopted for a site that is underlain by natural soil or rock. There are, however, a number of factors that must be considered. The materials underlying the derelict and contaminated site have in one way or another been placed or affected by human activities. They will often be heterogeneous in composition over small variations in horizontal and vertical deposition. Furthermore, they may be deleterious to human life and construction materials. The investigation of such sites must therefore be modified to provide the information that will be necessary for their efficient and safe redevelopment.

Derelict and contaminated land
Problems

The major problems associated with derelict and contaminated sites may be divided into the following groups

- o   assessment of geotechnical properties
- o   assessment of chemical properties
- o   presence of buried foundations and obstructions
- o   emission of methane and landfill gas.

Types of site

Derelict sites may generally be divided into two broad categories

- o   sites of manufacturing and processing works
- o   mineral abstraction sites.

There is no clear-cut distinction between these two categories, but a typical range of activities will comprise

- o   chemical processing (e.g. asbestos, paper works, tanneries, gas works)
- o   oil refining and petroleum processing
- o   sewage treatment
- o   heavy engineering
- o   use for scrap-yards
- o   monitoring, production and testing
- o   mineral abstraction followed by landfill and waste disposal
- o   radioactive processing and manufacturing.

Investigation

The main difference between the investigation of a contaminated site and a green-field site is that the former will rarely comprise a single-stage investigation. The work will be carried out in a series of phases dependent on the problems associated with the particular site. Furthermore, the efficient investigation will be supervised by geotechnical, chemical and environmental health personnel.

General guidance on the scope of investigation, the frequency of sampling and the hazards associated with the various types of site is given in the following publications

- o   British Standards Institution DD 175 (ref. 4.7)
- o   *Problems arising from the redevelopment of gas works and similar sites* (ref. 4.8)
- o   ICRCL papers (refs 4.9–4.15)
- o   HMIP waste management paper 27 (ref. 4.16)
- o   BRE report, *Measurement of gas emissions from contaminated land* (ref. 4.17).

Consideration is now given to specific stages of the investigation

o   desk study
o   evaluation of geotechnical properties
o   chemical analysis
o   measurement of methane emission.

Desk study

The importance of undertaking a thorough desk study prior to the field-work stage of the investigation cannot be overstressed. The results of the study will provide information for the protection of construction personnel and the future occupiers of a contaminated site. There are instances where the site investigation personnel have worked on sites with no knowledge whatsoever of the chemical hazards affecting the site, and consequently have taken no precautions for their own safety.

The main sources of information are given in DD 175 (ref. 4.7). For times prior to 1850 the major source of information will be old regional maps, often held at central libraries and archives, and for times after about 1880 the various editions of Ordnance Survey maps. The old editions of the geological scale maps are based on surveys carried out in the period 1870–1890, and often show topographical details of that era.

A number of sites have gone through a series of different developments, each of which has left its own imprint on the site. A typical example is the multi-stage development of a site in the West Midlands, shown in Figs 4.1–4.3. The site was affected by the construction of a canal with three loading basins on the northern boundary, and then by a colliery. On completion of the coal extraction, this was replaced by a brickworks, extracting Keuper marl to a depth of 19 m. The pit was subsequently infilled with a variety of materials, including toxic slag from metal refineries, and the site was finally occupied by a succession of engineering works. A second canal in a cutting was also constructed on the western boundary. When offered for redevelopment, the site had been cleared to become a generally level piece of land.

Sites that have been occupied over a long period by the same company or type of manufacturing process may also have been subject to a succession of enlargements and extensions, often bearing no relation to later layouts on the site.

When dealing with infilled pits used for the extraction of clay or sand and gravel, the major problem is to delineate the boundaries. Such workings that were undertaken for periods longer than 20 years may be recorded on the old Ordnance Survey maps. Extractions which were completed within 5–10 years may have taken place between the periodic re-surveys carried out by the Ordnance Survey, and thus may not have been recorded.

Recently-infilled pits and quarries that were open or being worked after the early 1950s may have been included in aerial surveys. If coverage is available from a survey flown at or near the cessation of an extraction working, it may be possible to obtain a contoured plan of the site taken from a pair of stereoscopic aerial photographs. Such a plan is shown in Fig. 4.4, for a 25 m deep sand pit in Surrey, which ceased work in 1950.

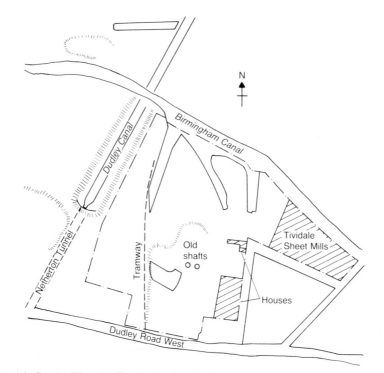

Fig. 4.1. Site in West Midlands showing development in 1887

All too often when a site has ceased production, the records are either destroyed or moved to a location within a large company complex, often not the owner of the original site, and are then subsequently lost or destroyed.

By the time of the investigation the structures that occupied the site may have been removed to ground level and a capping of fill placed to tidy up the site. The only available sources of information may then be a local inhabitant or worker and the Ordnance Survey maps or aerial photographs which will at least indicate the outline of the buildings.

Scope of ground investigation

The ground investigation must take into account the variations that can occur in the composition of the materials underlying an infilled site, and the presence of buried foundations and obstructions.

In many instances the material contained in an infill site will vary over very small distances, especially if it has been carted to site from a variety of sources. In these circumstances, the conventional 150 mm diameter shell-and-auger borehole, with a cross-sectional area comparable to the area of a page from this book, will provide only minimal information on the composition of the materials underlying the site. Furthermore, the variety of materials may be such that the results of conventional in situ

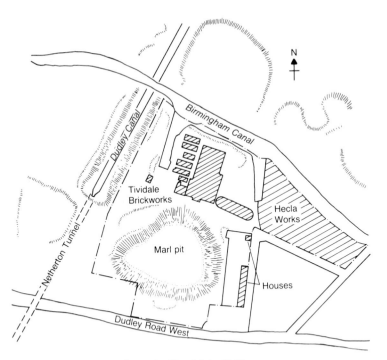

Fig. 4.2. Same site as that shown in Fig. 4.1 in 1919

tests and laboratory tests will be of little value in assessing their geotechnical properties.

The basic concept of the investigation must therefore be to provide the maximum information on the composition of the fill and to ascertain the settlement characteristics of the material in relation to the imposed intensity of loading and the size of the proposed structures. It must also cover the problems associated with toxic materials and gases which may be present on the site.

Trial pits

The use of mechanical excavators will allow the inspection of large volumes of fill and where necessary the trial pit can be extended into a trial trench. The conventional wheeled mechanical backhoe will, depending upon the operator, be capable of excavating to depths of about 3.5 m, which can be increased to some 5 m with extending-boom machines. A similar depth can be achieved by tracked machines, which also are capable of handling large pieces of concrete and metal.

On occasion, a depth of 10 m can be attained using benching techniques and additional plant to remove the spoil. Such excavations may be required, for example, to ascertain the state of backfill to a known worked shallow-depth coal seam, or the composition, state of compaction and presence of voids in old fill placed in the bottom of a mineral working.

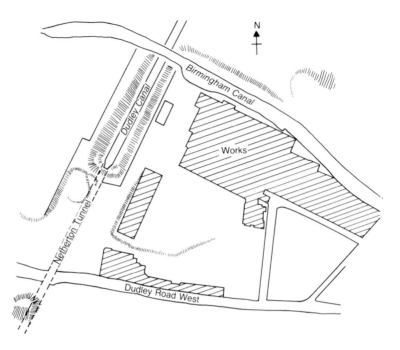

Fig. 4.3. Same site as that shown in Fig. 4.1 in 1964 with canal basin and brick pit infilled

It may on occasion be necessary to use two machines, one using a concrete-breaker to break out concrete hardstandings, floor slabs and old foundations.

Shoring equipment is rarely provided for the preliminary stage of the ground investigation, and safety precautions must be observed. An unsupported trial pit must not be entered where the depth of excavation exceeds 1·2 m.

Where buried tanks, chambers or workings are encountered and broken open they must never be entered without the provision of gas detectors, breathing apparatus and safety harness, together with a winch and safety line operated by independent personnel.

The inspection of the trial pits should identify materials which may have an adverse effect on the future development of the site. The presence of pieces of timber will restrict the use of vibro-placement techniques, while large pieces of concrete will affect the penetration of pile foundations. Old rubber tyres, often placed in landfill sites, may effectively preclude the use of piles or dynamic compaction techniques.

The descriptions of the materials encountered should be detailed, and should include all the items observed, with comments where feasible on the numbers of the different items in relation to the volume of excavated materials, and on emitted odour.

Fig. 4.4. Plan of 25 m deep sand pit based on stereoscopic aerial photographs

Boreholes

Where the depth of fill exceeds the reach of mechanical excavation it will be necessary to prove the depth of the fill by means of boreholes. Conventional shell-and-auger holes will be required to provide information on the underlying natural materials for the design of deep pile foundations.

In the case of a deep infilled pit, where the results of in situ tests indicate that it may be feasible to adopt shallow foundations, it will be necessary to prove the existence of any voids at depth, which may in future collapse and cause ground movement.

This type of probing may be achieved by using small-diameter rotary percussive drilling methods on say on an initial 15 m or 20 m grid. The non-return and drop in pressure of the flush medium, air or water, and the sudden drop of the drill stem will be indicative of the presence of a void. The subsequent grouting of the borehole will also indicate voids when the volume of grout exceeds the volume of the borehole.

Table 4.1. Minimum number of sampling points for
investigation of a contaminated or derelict site (ref. 4.7)

Area of site: ha	Minimum number of sampling points
0·5	15
1·0	25
5·0	85

Choice of inspection and sampling locations

The number of boreholes or trial pits sunk for the investigation of a natural site, apart from cost considerations, will be largely dependent upon the size of the proposed development, modified by variations in the deposition of the underlying soils.

The number of trial pits for the investigation of a contaminated or derelict site is dictated by the need to identify the variety of materials present and also to provide sufficient samples for chemical analysis. Here the criterion is to obtain sufficient data to statistically identify the highest levels of contamination and to delineate the distribution of contamination both in plan area and vertically. DD 175 (ref. 4.7) suggests that the minimum number of sampling points should be as shown in Table 4.1.

For gas works and similar sites, the DoE (ref. 4.8) suggests sampling densities of 20–50 trial pits per hectare in suspected hot spot areas, and 5–10 pits per hectare in areas not suspected of significant contamination. Smith and Ellis (ref. 4.18), in an empirical study on a gas works site, found no significant difference in conclusion from sampling-grid sizes in the range 6·25 m to 25 m, and grid spacings above 50 m were judged to be satisfactory.

Sampling

Due to the variation in composition of man-made materials, it is usually not possible on derelict or marginal sites to obtain undisturbed samples for conventional laboratory strength tests, and thus the majority of samples are obtained for chemical analysis.

Guidance on the size of sample for testing for civil engineering purposes is given in BS 1377 (ref. 4.4): the volume or weight of the sample must be sufficient for the various types of test apparatus.

The criterion for chemical analyses must be to provide a meaningful answer. The sample must therefore be representative—the problem is, representative of what? In a typical heterogeneous *mélange* of materials exposed in a trial pit, a sample may be taken of a particularly bright coloured chemical. The chemical may be very toxic, but if only present in a very small volume, will it have a severe deleterious effect in comparison with the overall chemical behaviour of all the other materials that surround it? Also, should a cadmium-plated screw, a lead soldier or battery plate be included in the sample? If these objects are present as isolated occurrences, they could possibly be ignored, although they must be listed in the description of the materials revealed in the trial pit. However, if lead or mercury batteries have been dumped at a specific location, then possibly they should be sampled in preference to other objects or materials that may be present.

Again, the importance must be stressed of assessing the number of individual items exposed when assessing the dangers associated with an individual toxic material. Sampling thus depends very much on the judgement of the personnel carrying out the investigation.

Guidance on the sampling of contaminated sites is given in DD 175 (ref. 4.7), which recommends a minimum of three samples per location, taken at the following depths

o   near surface (ground level to 150–200 mm)
o   greatest depth of concern
o   random intermediate sample.

For most purposes, glass or plastic bottles or jars will provide suitable containers. Often the container will be the time-honoured 300 ml (12 oz) glass jam jar.

All containers must be cleaned and dried before use, and should be placed in a waterproof storage area when filled. When sampling materials that are subject to deterioration, especially water and liquid samples, the site personnel must be adequately briefed on the percautions to be adopted. Again, the samples must be adequately protected during transport to the testing laboratory.

In situ testing

The geotechnical characteristics of the materials underlying a derelict site must be determined in order that the foundations for the proposed redevelopment may be designed. An accurate assessment of these characteristics will establish whether the proposed structures can be supported on shallow-depth foundations placed within the fill, or whether the foundations can be taken through the fill and placed in the underlying competent natural materials.

Unlike natural soils, where the foundations for lightly loaded structures may be designed on a knowledge of the shear strength characteristics of the underlying soils, the major design criteria for the infilled site are the settlement characteristics of the fill materials.

The infill material to a pit or quarry may be split into four major categories

o   household rubbish
o   industrial fill
o   chemical fill
o   a variable mixture of the above three types.

The overall composition of household rubbish is largely time-dependent, with a change marked by the clean air act coming into effect in the 1950s, together with the arrival of natural gas and the rise in central heating and attendant fall in open coal fires. Household rubbish placed

Table 4.2. In situ loading tests

Thickness of fill: m	Type of test
Ground level to 5 m	Simple skip loading test
5–10 m	Full-scale skip loading test
Greater than 10 m	Trial embankment

before the 1960s contained little organic matter and a large proportion of ash and clinker: this material often behaves as a granular material, albeit the individual grains comprise bottles and tin cans. Household rubbish placed after the 1960s contains a high proportion of putrescible organic material, which can give rise to the generation of landfill gases.

Industrial fill is variable by composition, but it often contains a high proportion of natural materials, especially if emanating from construction sites.

Chemical fill is again variable and may be placed, sometimes illegally, as granules, powders or liquids.

To obtain an assessment of the settlement characteristics of a fill material, the test must reflect the behaviour of the proposed structure in relation to ground conditions. Whereas with conventional plate bearing tests carried out on natural soils the settlement of the full-size foundation can be mathematically equated to that of the small-size test plate, this approach cannot be adopted for the variable materials likely to be encountered on an infilled site.

If a foundation is to be placed in the fill, there is the problem of knowing how the foundation will behave. A commonly adopted type of house foundation for use in this situation is the reinforced concrete slab with downstand edge beams. Does this foundation act as a wide strip footing with a stressed zone extending to a depth below the foundation approximately equivalent to the width of the edge beam, or conversely does it behave like a form of raft foundation, with the stressed zone extending to a depth equivalent to the width of the structure?

Further considerations affecting the type of in situ test are the depth of fill, and the characteristics of the underlying natural materials.

In general terms, the in situ loading test may be of one of three types, depending on the thickness of fill material (Table 4.2). The divisions shown in Table 4.2 are obviously only general, and each site must be considered separately. For example, a site with a thickness of fill in the order of 3 m may be underlain by soft organic alluvial soils, in which the full size test would be appropriate.

Simple skip loading test

The base width of the average rubbish skip is about 1·6 m, which is comparable with the width of the downstand edge beam of a typical slab foundation. When filled with spoil, the loading intensity of a single skip is in the order of 45 kN/m², which is approximately equivalent to the loading intensity imposed on the edge beam by a typical two-storey house.

Table 4.3. Precautions to be taken in skip loading test

1. The test site should be cleared and levelled.
2. The skip should not be placed directly on the ground.
3. The skip should not be placed directly on a layer of sand. Variations in the thickness of the sand layer and also in the compaction of the sand may result in differential settlements, which are not induced by settlement of the underlying fill.
4. Settlement measurements should be obtained by use of a precise engineering level, in conjunction with an invar staff. The survey should be referred to a competent bench-mark, remote from the test location and not affected by the movement of site plant.
5. The top sides of the skip should not be used as a levelling station.
6. The skip should be positioned on a concrete block placed directly on to the cleared test site. The dimensions of the block should be smaller than the base dimensions of the skip. The block may be either cast in situ or precast. In the latter case, the block can also be handled by the skip lorry.
7. The levelling stations should be cast directly into the concrete block and may consist of lengths of scaffolding or reinforcing bar.
8. The skip should be positioned centrally over the concrete block.
9. There should be constant checking that the level is in adjustment.

Two skips placed one above the other will induce a loading on the soil which is about twice that of the actual house loading. For deeper fill, two skips placed side by side may be employed to obtain a deeper zone of loading intensity.

The advantage of this form of test is that the skip can be accurately weighed at a public weighbridge and can then be positioned on site by the skip transporter lorry, which obviates the use of kentledge and the necessary cranage. Furthermore, the load is constantly applied, whereas for a conventional loading the hydraulic jacks used must be supervised to maintain the intensity of test pressure.

To obtain meaningful results from a skip loading test, the precautions listed in Table 4.3 should be observed.

The test procedure comprises levelling the concrete block prior to installation of the loaded skip, and then monitoring the movement of the skip daily for a week and then at weekly intervals for a minimum period of 2–3 months.

A typical test arrangement is shown in Fig. 4.5. A twin skip test is shown in Fig. 4.6.

Full-scale skip loading test

Where the thickness of the fill and possible underlying soft alluvial soils is greater than the depth of the zone of loading intensity imposed by the single or double skips, it is necessary to consider a full-scale test which reflects the dimensions of the proposed development.

In the case of housing development this will require a levelled test area with dimensions equivalent to the plan area of a typical house. An in situ concrete slab is cast upon the test area and loaded skips are positioned

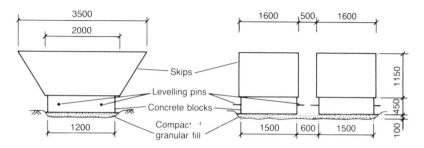

Fig. 4.5. Simple skip loading test (all dimensions in mm)

around the perimeter of the slab. The space in between the skips is then infilled with a material similar to that used to fill the skips. Shuttering is required between the skips to retain the infilling material. An alternative is to construct a reinforced blockwork perimeter wall. The enclosed area is infilled with compacted fill.

This type of test will have a depth of influence equivalent to that of the final structure. The intensity of loading is approximately equivalent to that of the structure and the distribution of loading over the foundation equates more to that of an evenly loaded slab, and not to edge beams carrying a greater intensity than the slab. However, as the actual behaviour of this type of foundation lies between that of a strip footing and a plate raft, the results of the full-scale test may represent an upper limit.

A typical arrangement of such a test, using eight skips located around the perimeter of the test slab, is shown in Fig. 4.7. A blockwork wall test is shown in Figs 4.8–4.10.

Fig. 4.6. Skip loading test

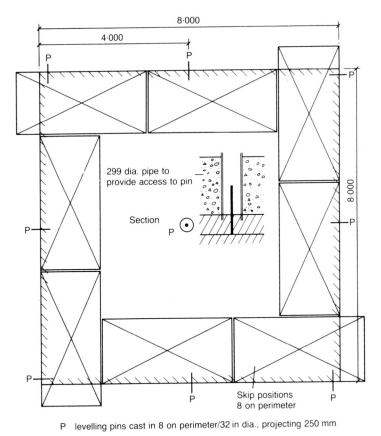

P   levelling pins cast in 8 on perimeter/32 in dia., projecting 250 mm

Fig. 4.7. Large-scale loading test using eight skips (all dimensions in mm)

Trial embankment

In the case of sites that are underlain by fill to depths in the order of 5 m, an alternative to the adoption of shallow foundations is to use vibro-replacement or vibro-compaction techniques to install stone columns down to the underlying natural competent soil and to improve the density of the fill, provided that timber and other obstructions are not present within the fill. Where the thickness of fill is in the order of 10 m, the alternative to shallow foundations may be the use of dynamic compaction to improve the density of the fill, or the installation of pile foundations into the underlying compacted soil or rock.

For infilled pits, where the depth of infilling may exceed 20 m, there may be no alternative to shallow foundations.

To assess the settlement characteristics of such a depth of fill it is necessary to consider the use of trial embankment. The dimension of the embankment may be chosen such that the zone of loading intensity will extend to the full depth of the fill. The height of the embankment can be

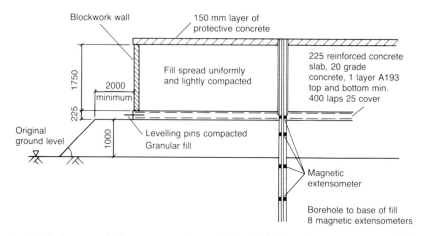

Fig. 4.8. Large-scale loading test using reinforced blockwork perimeter walls (all dimensions in mm)

designed not only to achieve a loading of 2–3 times the design load, but also to assess the effects of preloading the site prior to the construction of the proposed development.

Measurements of the settlement of the top and the ground adjacent to the embankment may be obtained by surveying levelling stations. Further measurements directly below the base of the embankment can be achieved by the installation of horizontal profile tubes. Movement of the profiler relative to a fixed concrete datum is obtained by pulling a probe through the tube and recording the level of the tube relative to the datum at 1 m intervals using a mercury manometer.

Fig. 4.9. Compaction of infilling for large-scale loading test

Fig. 4.10. Large-scale loading test using blockwork perimeter walls

Settlement of the fill at depth can be obtained by installing magnetic extensometers in boreholes located below the base of the embankment, prior to construction, and extending the boreholes upwards as the height of placement increases. The bottom magnet, positioned in competent natural ground, acts as a datum. The movement of the magnets relative to the datum show the settlement of the fill with respect to depth below the embankment. A layout of such an embankment is shown in Fig. 4.11.

Typical results, obtained from the three types of test described above, are shown in Figs 4.12–4.15.

Analysis of samples

Published guidance on the methods of chemical analysis to be carried out is limited. Apart from certain tests for soil samples given in BS 1377 (ref. 4.4), methods of most general applicability are related to the analysis of water samples and sludge samples. The relevant references are BS 6068 Part 2 (ref. 4.19), *Methods for the examination of waters and associated materials* (ref. 4.20) and *Methods for the determination of hazardous substances* (ref. 4.21).

ICRCL guidance note 59/83 (ref. 4.9) suggests the following selected inorganic contaminants: arsenic, cadmium, chromium (hexavalent and total), lead, mercury, selenium, boron (water-soluble), total copper, total nickel and total zinc.

For coal carbonisation and similar sites, the DoE (ref. 4.8) suggests the following contaminants: polyaromatic hydrocarbons, phenols, free cyanide, complex cyanide, thiocyanate, sulphate, sulphide and pH.

Such lists are useful for guidance but do not obviate the need for desk studies to identify other potential pollutants of significance.

Specific analyses will be required where the desk study reveals that

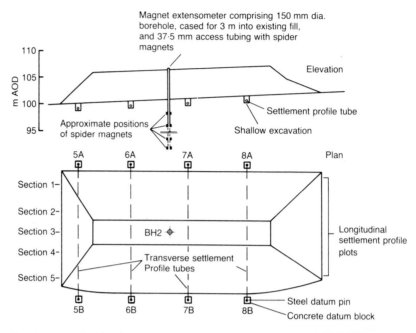

Fig. 4.11. Trial embankment underlain by 25 m of fill

special contaminants may be present on a site. For example, a munitions factory or weapon testing ground may require consideration to be given to explosive residues or specific heavy metals associated with high-explosive detonators. Where ash, clinker or coal is present within a fill material, the organic and carbon contents and a determination of the calorific value will be required to assess the potential for combustion.

In the absence of a specification for most of the above analyses, the

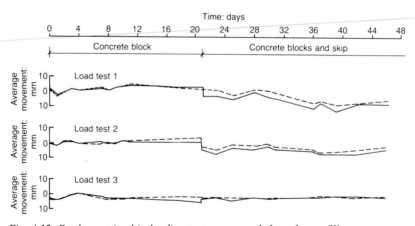

Fig. 4.12. Settlement in skip loading tests on regraded sandstone fill

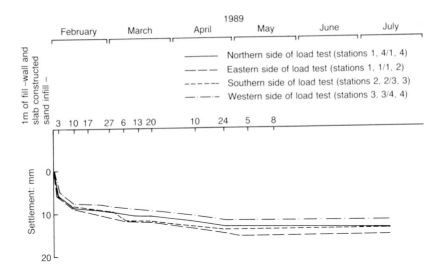

Fig. 4.13. Settlement in large-scale loading test using reinforced blockwork walls on 20 m of 60 year old backfill to brick pit

report on the investigation must include details of the methods of treatment and analysis employed, together with the method adopted for the preparation of the test samples.

The object in preparing the test specimen is to reduce the sample to a form that is acceptable to the particular analysis and also to reduce the effects of random error and bias. The latter effect may be induced by the presence of a cadmium-plated screw, or by volatilisation or oxidation during the preparation treatment.

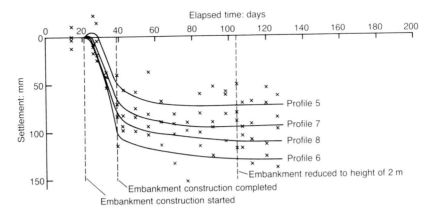

Fig. 4.14. Settlement of base of trail embankment underlain by infill to 25 m deep sand pit

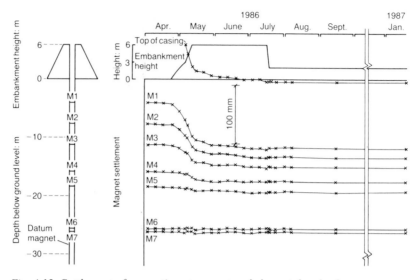

Fig. 4.15. Settlement of magnetic extensometers below trial embankment underlain by infill to 25 m deep sand pit

The usual initial method of preparation is to grind the test sample down to a size that is less than 1 mm. Fine grinding down to less than 0·15 mm is suggested by some sources (ref. 4.18) in an attempt to reduce the statistical coefficient of variation. However, in view of the reported range (ref. 4.8) of 100% to 50% in the coefficient of variation for analyses carried out on samples of nominally the same material, the extra fine grinding may not be effective.

In assessing the errors due to the preparation of test specimens and the subsequent analyses, DD 175 (ref. 4.7) indicates that the errors associated with analytical methods are usually insignificant in relation to those associated with sampling and subsequent preparation of the test specimen.

Sample preparation procedure is specified in DD 175 (ref. 4.7). Guidance on the preservation and preparation of samples taken from gasworks sites is also given by the DoE (ref. 4.8 tables 4.5 (a) and (b)).

Very few standards are available. Some may be obtained from the Community Bureau of Reference of the Commission of the European Communities.

Laboratory control of precision will normally require each laboratory to prepare its own series of reference materials. Care must be taken in the case of determinations of labile or unstable substances such as phenol or cyanide.

Methane

By reason of its behaviour, methane is by far the most emotive material to be encountered on contaminated and derelict sites. The end effect of the presence of methane on a site is liable to be sudden and disastrous, as illustrated by the explosions that occurred at Abbeystead and Loscoe (ref. 4.22).

Methane may result from the anaerobic decomposition of organic material or from the thermal decomposition of hydrocarbons in the geological environment. Where present at a specific location, it may have emanated from one of at least five sources

o   sewage
o   natural organic strata
o   leakage from a natural gas supply service pipe
o   relict methane, associated with coal measure rocks, which has migrated through rocks
o   gas from a landfill site.

The gases from these sources, while having in common their explosive potential under certain circumstances, may, however, vary with respect to their other properties such as chemical composition and physical age. An examination of these other properties will in some cases allow a distinction to be made between various potential sources.

While the presence of methane at a given site poses an obvious hazard, further investigation, measurement and analysis may be required not only to quantify the hazard and suggest possible remedial measures but also to cover the legal and insurance aspects.

Landfill sites are often located in areas of the country that are underlain by or are adjacent to coal measure rocks and thus the methane encountered near to these sites may have two sources of origin.

At the time of production of this book the state of knowledge regarding the generation and migration of methane is imprecise.

On a landfill site, methane is one of the products resulting from the degradation of organic or biodegradable material. The end product of the degradation which occurs in an oxygen-free or anaerobic condition is a mixture of gases comprising methane (up to 65%) and carbon dioxide (up to 35%) together with traces of the slightly heavier hydrocarbons ethane and propane, hydrogen sulphide, and a range of organic components which may depend in part on the nature of the waste materials.

The migration process is very dependent upon fluctuations in atmospheric pressure. During periods of high pressure, the migration of methane from the landfill site may be retarded; conversely, during periods of low pressure, and especially with a rapid rate of change of pressure, generation appears to be enhanced (ref. 4.22).

The investigation techniques currently available to ascertain the presence of methane comprise

o   in situ identification
o   in situ flow measurement
o   laboratory analysis of gas samples
o   carbon-14 dating.

Guidance on the measurement of gas emissions from contaminated land is given in a BRE report (ref. 4.17) and in HMIP waste management paper 27 (ref. 4.16).

In situ measurements

There is a large number of portable instruments available for carrying out site measurements of methane and other components of landfill gas. It must be noted that the gases may affect the sensing elements of the various instruments, and that these effects, together with the individual limitations of the particular instrument, may create difficulties when comparing the results.

The available types of instrument comprise

o   catalytic oxidation detectors
o   thermal conductivity detectors
o   combined catalytic and thermal detectors
o   infra-red analysers
o   flame ionisation instruments
o   gas indicator tubes.

Comments on the various types of instrument and their limitations are give in refs 4.16 and 4.17.

In situ measurements of the rate of flow of a gas, not necessarily methane, can also be carried out using a hot-wire anemometer, or a bubble flowmeter for low rates of flow.

Gas monitoring stations

Initial measurements for the presence of landfill gas can be made at the first stage of the ground investigation by use of a portable detector during the installation of a borehole or in trial pits. The measurements will only provide a guideline because of the disturbance caused during the formation of the borehole or trial pit and also the effects of wind on the trial pit.

Accurate measurements require the installation of standpipes, similar to those used for groundwater measurements. The standpipes may be installed in boreholes or trial pits, although in the latter instance there will be problems in achieving an efficient seal around the tube.

Alternatively, a driven probe may be used. A typical form comprises a steel outer tube and a detachable end cone. It can be driven into the ground by means of a hammer acting upon a drive head, or pushed by the bucket of a mechnical excavator. This form of installation is limited to loose or soft fill material. For harder materials, penetration can be achieved by use of a special adapter attached to a hydraulically operated concrete-breaker. When the outer tube has been driven to the required depth, a perforated plastic inner tube is inserted into the probe and screwed to the shank of the cone, and the outer tubing is removed.

It is essential to provide an adequate vandal-proof cover to the assembly and also to accurately identify its location. It is embarrassing to make a periodic visit to a site and discover a metre-high growth of grass and weeds completely covering up the monitoring stations.

When instruments are used which pump a sample of gas from a probe or borehole, a laboratory test should be made to ascertain the number of pumping strokes required to bring the gas up to the instrument from the depth being sampled. Also a collection bottle should be provided in the line to prevent groundwater from being sucked into the instrument.

All measurements must be accompanied by an observation of the atmospheric pressure. All records should clearly state the type of measurement being made: conventionally this will be the percentage explosive limit (LEL), or for high readings the volume in per cent per million.

Laboratory analysis

To accurately measure the various constituents of the gas which is present on a site it is necessary to obtain samples from a borehole or probe. The gases are drawn into a sample container by means of a manually operated aspirator or pump. The container may be a sealed metal tube which can store 200–300 cm^3 of gas, or a plastic bag with a storage volume of 0·5–1 litre. When taking samples, cognisance must be taken of the volume of the monitoring standpipe in order to avoid dilution of the sample when drawn into the standpipe by the process of sampling. Even when all precautions are taken, the measurements of concentration made may significantly underestimate the true concentration in the ground. This is particularly true when flow rates are low.

Analysis of the samples is made by means of gas chromatography, using thermal conductivity or flame ionisation detection as appropriate, to identify the proportions of the five common constituents of landfill gas: oxygen, nitrogen, carbon dioxide, methane and possibly hydrogen sulphide. If it is necessary to establish the prime source of the gas, other measurements may be required, such as ethane and propane measurements and possibly carbon dating.

Carbon-14 dating

Carbon dating may be necessary to establish the source of methane. The technique is based on the properties of the radioactive carbon-14 isotope, which has a half-life decay period of some 5700 years. The carbon present in a landfill gas is very much younger than that which is present in natural or relict mine gas. However, there is evidence to suggest that methane can be produced by the degradation of petroleum products that may have been placed in landfill site. The resultant carbon dating of the methane can then be confusing, especially if the site is in the vicinity of coal measure rocks.

Aerial thermography

Aerial thermography is a technique using an infra-red form of camera to measure the heat emission from the ground surface. The instrument scanner is mounted either on an aircraft or on a ballon which is towed across the site. The scanner transmits pictures to a video monitor. The recorded pictures can then be analysed to delineate temperature differences of 0·2°C. The survey must be carried out at night to avoid interference from the sun and it requires suitable atmospheric conditions. Apart from the excess heat caused by the emission of landfill gas at higher than ambient temperature, the temperature effects which this type of survey measures may be due to other events such as an underground fire. The distance from source over which this technique may be used to detect gas emissions from the ground is not established. It will in part depend on the gas flow rate and the loss of heat which occurs during migration. It is often useful in delineating areas within which further ground investigations might be concentrated.

References
4.1. British Standards Institution. *Code of practice for site investigation.* BSI, London, 1981, BS 5930.
4.2. Institution of Civil Engineers. *Specification for ground investigation.* Thomas Telford, London, 1989.
4.3. Weltman A.J. and Head J.M. *Site investigation manual.* Construction Industry Research and Information Association, London, 1983.
4.4. British Standards Institution. *Methods of test for soil for civil engineering purposes.* BSI, London, 1975, BS 1377.
4.5. Head K.H. *Manual of soil laboratory testing.* Pentarch, London, 1980 (vol. 1), 1982 (vol. 2), 1986 (vol. 3).
4.6. Peck R.B. *et al. Foundation engineering.* Wiley, New York, 1953.
4.7. British Standards Institution. *Draft for development: code of practice for the identification of potentially contaminated land and its investigation.* BSI, London, 1988, DD 175.
4.8. Department of the Environment. *Problems arising from the redevelopment of gas works and similar sites.* HMSO, London, 1987, 2nd edn.
4.9. Interdepartmental Committee on the Redevelopment of Contaminated Land. *Guidance on the assessment and redevelopment of contaminated land.* Department of the Environment, London, 1987, 2nd edn, ICRCL 59/83.
4.10. Interdepartmental Committee on the Redevelopment of Contaminated Land. *Notes on the redevelopment of landfill sites.* Department of the Environment, London, 1988, 7th edn, ICRCL 17/78.
4.11. Interdepartmental Committee on the Redevelopment of Contaminated Land. *Notes on the redevelopment of gas works sites.* Department of the Environment, London, 1986, 5th edn, ICRCL 18/79.
4.12. Interdepartmental Committee on the Redevelopment of Contaminated Land. *Notes on the redevelopment of sewage works and farms.* Department of the Environment, London, 1983, 2nd edn, ICRCL 23/79.
4.13. Interdepartmental Committee on the Redevelopment of Contaminated Land. *Notes on the redevelopment of scrapyards and similar sites.* Department of the Environment, London, 1983, 2nd edn, ICRCL 42/80.
4.14. Interdepartmental Committee on the Redevelopment of Contaminated Land. *Notes on the fire hazards of contaminated land.* Department of the Environment, London, 1986, 2nd edn, ICRCL 61/84.
4.15. Interdepartmental Committee on the Redevelopment of Contaminated Land. *Asbestos on contaminated land.* Department of the Environment, London, 1985, ICRCL 64/85.
4.16. Her Majesty's Inspectorate of Pollution. *The control of landfill gas.* HMSO, London, 1989, HMIP waste management paper 27.
4.17. Crowhurst D. *Measurement of gas emissions from contaminated land.* Building Research Establishment, Garston, 1987.
4.18. Smith M.A. and Ellis A.C. An investigation into methods used to assess gas

works sites for reclamation. *Reclamation and Revegetation Research*, 1986, **4**, 183–209.

4.19. British Standards Institution. *Water quality — Part 2. Physical, chemical and biochemical methods.* BSI, London, 1983, BS 6068.

4.20. *Assessment of biodegradability: methods for the examination of waters and associated materials.* HMSO, London, 1981.

4.21. Health and Safety Executive. *Methods for the determination of hazardous substances.* London. (MDHS series)

4.22. *Report of the non-statutory public inquiry into the gas explosion at Loscoe, Derbyshire, 24 March 1986.* Derbyshire County Council, Matlock, 1988.

)

5 | Data analysis and interpretation

MICHAEL SMITH, BSc, CChem, FRSC, MICeram
Director, Clayton Bostock Hill & Rigby Ltd

Two separate but parallel assessments will be necessary on most sites

o   the geotechnical assessment
o   the contamination assessment.

Although they are likely to be carried out separately, indeed by different people and even by different organisations, they are not independent of one another: there are overlaps and interactions. For example, geological and hydrogeological information will be relevant in both assessments, and the presence of contamination may constrain the responses available to any geotechnical problems.

The generally favoured approach (ref. 5.1) to the assessment of contamination is to identify the principal hazards and targets and to concentrate on these: in dealing with these any secondary hazards may be adequately dealt with. An initial assessment of the contamination and the geotechnical investigation may enable a similar approach to be adopted. For example, if the most effective way of dealing with a geotechnical problem were to remove the fill, then the important facets of the contamination would be how it would affect the removal operation and disposal of the waste. Similarly, the contamination might be best dealt with by removing fill, thereby solving a geotechnical problem. Thus, although the contamination and geotechnical assessments may initially be carried out separately, they must eventually be brought together into an overall assessment. This will require a combined effort by the specialist assessors.

This chapter concentrates on the assessment of the results of contamination surveys, with particular emphasis on chemical contamination and gases (e.g. methane), although attention is also paid to combustibility. Biological and radioactive contamination receive brief mentions. The discussion of the geotechnical assessment draws heavily on the analysis presented in a recent CIRIA report (ref. 5.2).

The assessment and presentation of geotechnical and related data can be done within a well established framework and on the basis of considerable practical experience, although the inadequacies of much site investigation work have been apparent for decades (refs 5.3, 5.4). The assessment of the results of contamination surveys is more difficult: both formal guidance and practical experience is limited. And because of the long term nature and problems in diagnosis of, for example, possible health effects on exposed populations, there may never be practical evidence on which to base the judgements that must be made. In contrast, failures in geotechnical terms can be readily identified.

In talking about data analysis and interpretation it is necessary to assume that the data available are commensurate with the task in hand: that is, that site investigations in accordance with good practice (ref. 5.5) have been carried out (Chapter 4) and an appropriate analytical strategy has been employed (see below). In practice the assessor will on occasion be faced with situations in which, despite the best endeavours of the investigating team, further information will be required. There will also be times when the investigation has been totally inadequate. The assessor must resist any temptation to make a diagnosis on inadequate data. That way leads to both technical and professional failure — if not financial failure.

Sometimes the chemical data are obtained supplementary to a geotechnical investigation, perhaps as a prelude to a more comprehensive investigation for contamination. Provided that the sampling and data needs have been properly considered at the outset (Chapter 4) and the likely limitations recognised, then useful data can be obtained and a preliminary assessment may be possible. However, where there has not been an initial expert input, there is a high probability that such surveys will yield data of only limited value and the caution above — about making an assessment on inadequate data — must be observed.

Analytical considerations
Analytical strategy

As indicated above it is not possible to make a proper assessment of chemical contamination unless an appropriate analytical strategy has been followed in terms of deciding 'what to look for' and the analytical methods to be employed. Space does not permit a comprehensive discussion of this topic but a knowledge of some of the variables and limitations of present methodologies is important to an understanding of the difficulties of chemical assessment. Further guidance can be found in the British Standard draft for development DD 1975, *Code of practice for the identification of potentially contaminated land and its investigation* (ref. 5.5), and the topic is discussed at length by Lord (ref. 5.6). Selection of contaminants to be included in the programme should be based on the findings of the preliminary investigation and observations during sampling.

A comprehensive analytical programme is likely to include three components

o   ubiquitous contaminants such as lead, zinc, mineral oils
o   contaminants characteristic of the land use(s)
o   adventitious or not easily predicted contaminants.

It is important to consider each of these components for every site investigation. Many analytical houses offer 'standard packages' of analyses: these should not be used without their appropriateness being reviewed, together with the response to be made to the results of 'screen-

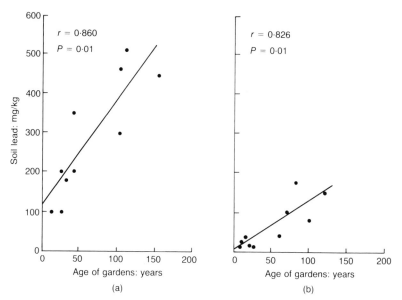

Fig. 5.1. Relationship of soil lead concentrations to age of gardens for two villages in Devon (after Davies (ref. 5.7)): (a) Bere Alston; (b) St Dominick

ing' or 'surrogate' methods (see below). Care should also be taken to ensure that the package is not limited by the capability of the laboratory: not all will be equipped to carry out the full range of analyses that might be required.

Ubiquitous contaminants

Elevated concentrations of contaminants such as lead, zinc and cadmium can occur for many reasons, and even rural garden soils can give elevated values (ref. 5.7) (Fig. 5.1) because of the deposition of domestic wastes, coal ash etc. over the centuries. It will therefore usually be advisable to look for such contaminants irrespective of the site history.

Similarly, mineral oils and other petroleum products may occur on many sites. In addition to any hazard they present themselves, they in turn may be contaminated with various additives including organo-lead compounds. Refuse and other gas-producing and combustible materials may be found irrespective of a specific history of waste disposal.

Other, more hazardous, chemicals are perhaps more commonly present than is usually suspected. For example, a wide range of solvents, degreasing agents and lubricants are used in the engineering industries. Extremely low concentrations (a few milligrams per kilogram) of some of these may be of concern but the analytical strategies commonly employed will not allow their detection.

Contamination and land use

The main clues to what to look for are provided by the site history. Knowledge of the processses operated or of the materials deposited can give a good indication of the chemical species likely to be present. It follows that it is possible to draw up tables relating land use to characteristic contaminants. For example, on a gasworks site one might expect to find complex cyanides, elemental sulphur, phenols and combustible carbonaceous residues among other contaminants. Such tables as those included in DD 1975 (ref. 5.5) and the descriptions available in other publications (refs 5.8–5.12) can be very useful (see in particular ref. 5.12), but need to be used with great care lest they induce a blinkered approach. Each and every site must be considered on its merits.

Unexpected contaminants: screening techniques
There are two main ways of finding the unexpected

o   from clues provided by careful observation in the field and laboratory, including the use of the analyst's 'nose'
o   from the use of 'broad-spectrum', or 'surrogate', 'screening' or 'non-specific' techniques.

Modern chemical analytical instrumentation — for example, inductively coupled plasma optical emission spectrophotometry (ICPOES) and X-ray fluorescence spectrometry (XRF) — enables a scan to be made for a wide range of elements (often 15 or more) at very little cost over and above that of looking for four or five elements or by other less sophisticated techniques. This may often lead to accumulation of a lot of 'negative' data (and possibly accusations that unnecessary analysis has been carried out at unjustified expense), but when it matters it will reveal the unexpected high concentration of unusual, but highly toxic, elements such as beryllium.

The use of broad-spectrum analyses and surrogate methods for organic species is not well developed in the UK, although frequently employed in other countries, particularly the USA, for screening mixtures of organic chemicals. However, these methods are becoming more widely available with the wider use of gas chromatography and mass spectrometry systems. The principle in the use of such screening or surrogate techniques is to cascade down to a more detailed examination in a controlled way.

The simplest variants are the frequently employed toluene or cyclohexane extracts. Properly used these simply provide an indication of the need to look in more detail at the composition of the extracts (e.g. to look specifically for mineral oils or coal tar chemicals). It is important to note that the sensitivity of these methods is low. The detection level may be 500 mg/kg, whereas the concentrations of the organic species of concern may be only 100 mg/kg, or even less than 10 mg/kg. The methods commonly employed may cause the loss of the more volatile, and frequently more hazardous, components. In addition, there is no standard method, so that results obtained by different laboratories may differ by a factor of 2 or more (even the temperature of extraction is not standardised). If not used with care, such measures can give a false sense of security.

More specific and reliable screening techniques might cover classes of organic compounds such as long-chain fatty acids, chlorinated hydrocarbons, polyaromatic hydrocarbons (PAHs) or 'total phenols'. In the USA, where such techniques are employed for examining stockpiles of unidentified drummed materials, the process is highly developed (ref. 5.13) and allows for the compositing of samples from a number of drums to reduce the number of analyses required. The presence of chlorinated hydrocarbons in a composite from ten drums would indicate a need to look at each drum individually. Greater analytical sensitivity is required when compositing as the procedure results in dilution of contaminants.

At a more mundane level, it is common practice to determine 'total phenols' in the first instance, and only if these exceed a set value to seek to determine the nature of the phenols present. Similarly, a determination of 'total cyanides' may precede determination of 'simple' or 'free' cyanide, and one may determine 'total sulphur' or individual sulphur species such as sulphate or sulphide. This process of progressive speciation is sometimes carried further to attempt to determine the amount of a contaminant 'available' to a particular component of the environment, such as plants.

'Totals' v. 'availables'

A single element may occur in different forms exhibiting different physical properties such as solubility and volatility, and different toxicity. Thus lead may be present in the crystal structure of a silicate mineral, as a sulphate or sulphide, as organo-lead or as a plumbate. Arsenic may be present as arsenide, arsenate or arsenite (the last generally considered the most toxic form). Thus a decision has to be made, for example, whether to attempt to determine the 'total' amount of lead present or only that which is 'water-soluble' or 'soluble in the digestive juices of a small child'.

Some chemical forms are not particularly stable, and under the influence of weathering, including microbial action, one form may be transformed to a more soluble or less soluble form, to a more toxic or less toxic form, to a more volatile or less volatile form; indeed, over time, with changing pH and redox conditions, an element may cycle between forms (i.e. speciation may be a transient phenomenon). Thus in the first instance it will usually be best to determine the 'total' concentration and then, if this exceeds some critical value, to carry out further analysis either to determine the chemical form or to obtain an indication of the 'availability' to some component of the environment (e.g. to plants) using an empirical selective extraction technique. A 'total' determination provides the best indication of the overall potential hazard from a contaminant over a period of decades or even centuries. More specific analyses often refer only to a point in time and do not usually refer to 'absolute' quantities. For example, the 'availability' of zinc for plant uptake will be influenced by pH and the amount of organic matter in the soil, both usually variable with time.

The civil engineer is familiar with this approach in relation to sulphate attack on concrete. BRE digest 250 (ref. 5.14) refers to determination of acid-soluble sulphate, and water-soluble sulphate (an empirical method). It shows how the former may often indicate a greater need to take precautions than the latter because of the greater solubility of some sulphates in acid than in water. However, as discussed below, the assessment becomes much more difficult when other factors such as acidity and the presence of other, transmutable, sulphur species (elemental sulphur, sulphide, thiosulphate etc.) must be taken into account, as they must on a gasworks site.

A word of caution is required about 'total' determinations for lead, zinc etc. These are not always what they purport to be. They are usually based on extraction with a strong mineral acid or combination of mineral acids which may still leave an 'insoluble residue' in which some contaminant remains. Special techniques must be employed to achieve total solution, and these are not always available because of associated health and safety hazards and their time-consuming nature (techniques such as X-ray fluorescence may have an advantage here in not requiring dissolution of the sample). Experience has shown that strong-acid extractions are adequate for most purposes, but their effectiveness does vary with different matrices and it is important that any analytical report indicates the method employed. The practice in silicate chemistry (e.g. cements) of reporting the amount of insoluble residue could usefully be encouraged for contaminated soils.

Sample preparation

Analysis can only be done once the sample has been prepared. This usually means size reduction and drying (usually at room temperature or slightly above). As with other procedures, this requires consideration in relation to each investigation, lest the process of sample preparation leads to erroneous results (refs 5.5, 5.6, 5.15). Of particular concern is the loss of volatiles during drying (e.g. organics, mercury) or change of chemical form (e.g. sulphide to sulphate). It may be that samples must be analysed in an 'as received' condition, even though this is likely to lead to greater variability in the analytical results. This seems to be general practice in the USA, where greater emphasis is placed on 'organics' than has generally been the case in the UK to date.

A visual examination of the sample should be made during the preparation stage and any unusual features should be noted and reported to the analyst.

When the sample is unstable and cannot be readily stabilised, it is vital that preparation and analysis should be carried out as soon as possible.

Presentation of analytical results

There are many standardised methods for the analysis of water and related materials both in the UK and in other countries. There are, however, few standardised methods for 'soils' or the wide range of contaminated solid materials that may be found on contaminated sites. All reports of analyses of contaminated sites (this applies to microbial, biological, radioactivity assays etc. as well as chemical investigations) should contain a statement of the methods used, the expected precision

Table 5.1. Concentrations of some metals and metalloids in igneous and sedimentary rocks (from Thornton (ref. 5.16))

Element	Concentration (range and mean): mg/kg					
	In basaltic igneous rocks	In granitic igneous rocks	In shales and clays	In black shales	In limestones	In sandstones
As	0·2–10 2·0	0·2–13·8 2·0	– 10	– –	0·1–8·1 1·7	0·6–9·7 2·0
Cd	0·006–0·6 0·2	0·003–0·18 0·15	0–11 1·4	<0·3–8·4 1·0	– 0·05	– 0·05
Cr	40–600 220	2–90 20	30–590 120	26–1000 100	– 10	– 35
Co	49–90 50	1–15 5	5–25 20	7–100 10	– 0·1	– 0·3
Cu	30–160 90	4–30 15	18–120 50	20–200 70	– 4	– 2
Hg	0·002–0·5 0·05	0·005–0·4 0·06	0·005–0·51 0·09	0·03–2·8 2·5	0·01–0·22 0·04	0·001–0·3 0·05
Pb	2–18 6	6–30 18	16–50 20	7–150 30	– 9	<1–31 12
Mo	0·9–7 1·5	1–6 1·4	– 2·5	1–300 10	– 0·4	– 0·2
Ni	45–410 140	2–20 8	20–250 68	10–500 50	– 20	– 2
Se	– 0·05	– 0·05	– 0·6	– –	– 0·08	– 0·05
Zn	48–240 110	5–140 40	18–180 90	34–1500 100	– 20	2–41 16

and accuracy, and the quality control and quality assurance procedures employed (refs 5.5, 5.6).

Chemical contamination

A comprehensive investigation of even a site of modest size is likely to produce thousands of data. The assessor has two tasks: to make sense of the data in a technical sense; and to present the data as a whole, and the technical assessment in particular, in a way that is readily understood by clients and others with an interest in the results of the investigation.

In making the assessment, it will therefore be necessary to manipulate the data and to present it in various ways, and to make comparisons with such guidance as is available on the response required to particular levels of contamination. In some cases the guidance may be authoritative and long established (e.g. the requirements of concrete to withstand sulphate attack); in other cases the assessor may need to develop site-specific criteria (e.g. when unusual contaminants are present not covered by established guidance).

In most cases a large measure of professional judgement will be required (for example in application of the ICRCL 'trigger values'). Judgement will usually have to be made on the highest levels of contamination recorded rather than on average values etc. In addition, the response required will vary with the use to which the land is to be put: different uses expose different 'targets' to different degrees to the risks posed by particular contaminants. Judgements may also have to be made on the current and long term 'availability' of contaminants (including chemical stability) to different components of the environment. Given the many uncertainties and lack of knowledge, a conservative approach will usually be required.

When is a soil contaminated?

The question that must be answered first is whether a soil is, or is not, contaminated. 'Contamination' is the presence of a substance where it should not be: this means essentially that it is present in concentrations above 'natural background levels'. What matters is its presence: whether it is a 'problem' (i.e. whether the land can be considered polluted) is a separate question.

In the case of toxic metals, comparison can readily be made with published data on the levels to be found in natural soils, or with background levels established locally as part of the investigation, using well established statistical techniques. Data are available on both agricultural soils and on soils from urban areas. Organic substances such as polyaromatic hydrocarbons (PAHs), polychlorinated biphenyls (PCBs), phenols and dioxins present greater difficulty, although more data are gradually becoming available.

The natural range of many metals in soils is very wide. Soils reflect the chemical composition of their parent materials (Table 5.1), though the total contents and forms are modified to varying degrees by soil-forming processes which may lead to the mobilisation and subsequent redistribution of metals both within the soil profile and between neigh-

Table 5.2. *Common ranges and typical levels of trace elements in cultivated surface soils (mg/kilogram dry soil) (from Berrow and Burridge (ref. 5.17))*

Element	Total content		Extractable content — normal range	
	Normal range	Typical level	Using 0·5 mol/l acetic acid	Using 0·05 mol/l EDTA
Ag	0·01–5	0·1	–	–
Al	10 000–300 000	70 000	50–2600	50–2000
As	0·1–40	6	–	–
B	2–100	10	0·01–10*	–
Ba	100–4000	1000	–	–
Be	0·1–40	6	–	–
Cd	0·01–1	0·5	<0·01–0·3	<0·01–0·3
Co	1–40	15	<0·05–2·0	<0·05–4·0
Cr	5–1000	100	<0·01–1·0	0·1–4·0
Cu	2–100	20	<0·05–3·0	0·3–10
F	30–300	200	–	–
Fe	10 000–200 000	40 000	10–2000	100–3000
Ga	10–70	25	–	–
Ge	<1–50	1	–	–
Hg	<0·01–0·5	0·1	–	–
Li	5–200	50	–	–
Mn	100–4000	800	5–100	5–100
Mo	0·2–5	2	<0·004–0·03	<0·03–1·0
Ni	5–500	50	0·1–5·0	0·2–5·0
Pb	2–200	20	<0·002–4·0	1·0–10·0
Rb	20–600	100	–	–
Sc	<3–20	8	–	–
Se	0·1–2·0	0·5	–	–
Sn	<1–10	3	<0·02–0·2	<0·02–1·0
Sr	50–1000	300	0·2–10	–
Ti	1000–20 000	4000	<0·1–1·0	0·5–10
V	20–500	100	<0·05–1·0	0·2–5·0
Y	3–150	40	–	–
Zn	10–300	50	<2–30	<3–20
Zr	60–2000	400	–	–

*Soluble boron figure are amounts extracted by hot water.

bouring soils. Some data on 'normal' soils are given in Tables 5.2 and 5.3. In practice, because of geochemical concentration of elements and man's search for metals, some 'natural' soils may exhibit concentrations well outside the ranges shown. Naturally occurring levels of some elements may be deleterious to crops and stock; for example, nickel-rich ferro-magnesium minerals in soils from the basic igneous rocks in parts of Scotland have, when poorly drained, given rise to nickel toxicity in agricultural crops. Soils associated with Namurian black shales may give rise to excess molybdenum in cattle, resulting in hypocupraemia (low blood copper). The regional distribution of trace-element problems in Great

Table 5.3. Median trace element content of soils in England and Wales (from Archer (ref. 5.18))

	Element	Median	Range	Number of farms	Number of samples
Total: mg/kilogram air-dry soil	Boron	33	7–71	72	227
	Cadmium	<1·0	0·08–10	204	689
	Cobalt	8	<1·0–40	125	421
	Copper	17	1·8–195	226	751
	Lead	42	5–1200	226	752
	Mercury	0·04	0·008–0·19	17	53
	Nickel	26	4·4–228	226	752
	Selenium	0·6	0·2–1·8	34	114
	Zinc	77	5–816	225	748
Extractable with acetic acid: mg/litre air-dry soil	Nickel	1·0	0·12–22·7	198	647
	Zinc	6·6	0·4–97·6	204	664
Extractable with EDTA: mg/litre air-dry soil	Copper	4·4	0·5–74·0	201	662
	Selenium	0·04	0·01–0·59	32	112
Extractable with hot water: mg/litre air-dry soil	Boron	1·0	0·1–4·7	153	493

Britain, both those due to excess and those due to deficiencies, has been reviewed by Thornton and Webb (ref. 5.19). It is important to recognise that elevated levels of cadmium, arsenic etc. may be due to natural causes (see Table 5.4): this does not, of course, make them more acceptable. Metal levels are typically high in soils from old metal-mining areas (Table 5.5).

Anomalous values can be distinguished on a local basis from background levels by application of statistical technniques. If a number of 'uncontaminated' soils are collected from a single source material and mean values and standard deviations (s.d.) calculated, then a 'normal' range can be calculated on the basis that

- o   68·3% of values will be in the range ±1 s.d.
- o   95·5% of values will be in the range ±2 s.d.
- o   99·7% of values will be in the range ±3 s.d.

Thus, with varying degrees of confidence, any value greater than the mean ±3 or ±2 standard deviations can be regarded as anomalous.

If, during collection, it is not possible to distinguish between normal and contaminated soils, another statistical technique is available. For a given element, cumulative percentage frequency is plotted against class intervals on probability graph paper. For a unimodal, normal population the points lie on a straight line (a smooth curve if the distribution is log-normal).

Table 5.4. Trace elements in soils derived from normal and geochemically anomalous parent materials (from Thornton (ref. 5.16))

Element	Content in normal soil: mg/kg	Content in metal-rich soil: mg/kg	Sources	Possible effects
As	<5-40	Up to 2500 / Up to 250	Mineralisation / Metamorphosed rocks around Dartmoor	Toxicity in plants and livestock; excess in food and crops
Cd	<1-2	Up to 30 / Up to 20	Mineralisation / Carboniferous black shale	Excess in food crops
Cu	2-60	Up to 2000	Mineralisation	Toxicity in cereal crops
Mo	<1-5	10-1000	Marine black shales of various ages	Molybdenosis or molybdenum-induced hypocuprosis in cattle
Ni	2-100	Up to 8000	Ultra-basic rocks in Scotland	Toxicity in cereal and other crops
Pb	10-150	10000 or more	Mineralisation	Toxicity in livestock; excess in foodstuffs
Se	<1-2	Up to 7	Marine black shales in England and Wales	No effect
Zn	25-200	10000 or more	Mineralisation	Toxicity in cereal crops

Table 5.5. Analyses of agricultural soils from metalliferous mining areas (from Davies and White (ref. 5.20))

Area	Number of samples	Total Pb: mg/kilogram dry soil		Total Cd: mg/kilogram dry soil	
		Mean	Range	Mean	Range
Derbyshire	25	2414	99–19 693	8·6	2·4–67·0
Halkyn	260	886	35–47 995	6·1	0·4–540·0
Minera	23	870	74–6944	1·9	0·5–8·5
Mendips	69	390	31–11 236	4·4	0·6–116·0
Ystwyth	17	1419	90–2900	2·5	1·2–4·0
Tamar	58	110	20–522	1·8	0·7–4·5

Intersecting lines (or curves) imply more than one population, and the lowest point is taken as that class interval that separates normal from anomalous soils (Fig. 5.2).

Further sensitivitiy can be obtained by consideration of the ratios between elements (e.g. Cd : Zn), which tend to be fairly constant in samples from any particular source (see Fig. 5.3).

Urban soils

Urban soils (including gardens soils) are frequently contaminated with metals such as lead, cadmium and zinc as a result of aerial deposition, disposal of ash and soot, flaking lead-based paints, breakdown of galvanising, and burning of domestic refuse on bonfires. Rural garden soils can also be contaminated, the degree of contamination reflecting the age of the property (Fig. 5.1). Various surveys have been made of urban soils

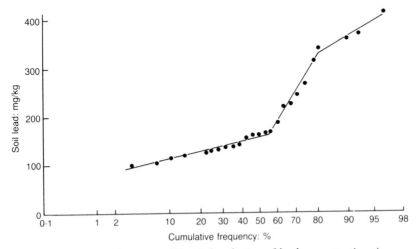

Fig. 5.2. Cumulative frequency (% <) distribution of lead concentrations in surface soils from urban site

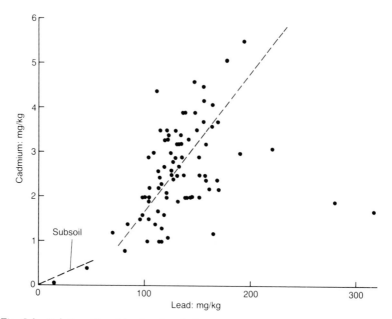

Fig. 5.3. Relationship of lead and cadmium concentrations in topsoil and subsoil from sewage farm

in an attempt to characterise them in terms of different categories of land use (e.g. ref. 5.21; Table 5.6) or density and type of urban development. The Joint Unit for Research on the Urban Environment of Aston University provided data on lead, zinc, copper, cadmium, thallium, selenium, mercury, nickel, barium and antimony (see Tables 5.7–5.9). Data on city-centre industrial areas and the hinterland of Glasgow were collected to provide background data in connection with the use of dredgings from the Clyde in the manufacture of a topsoil substitute (it should be noted that this was done only after an extensive feasibility study, including assessment of the contamination levels in the silt (ref. 5.23)). The results are summarized in Table 5.10. The wide range of values for the hinterland is explained by the fact that it included 50% farmland and that the

Table 5.6. Available trace metals (mg/kg) in soils in different land use categories on Merseyside (from Parry et al. (ref. 5.21))

Land category	Available copper:* mg/kg	Available zinc: mg/kg	Available lead: mg/kg	Available cadmium:† mg/kg
Gardens/allotments	0·8–346	1·7–2730	0·1–64·7	0·01–4·2
Parkland	1·6–545	2·4–258	0·1–63	0·1–3·3
Agricultural grassland	0·5–116	1·3–182	<0·1–25·2	<0·01–1·3
Agricultural arable	0·4–289	1·4–461	<0·1–51·5	<0·01–5·4

* Cu extracted in 0·05 mol/l di-ammonium EDTA.
† Zn, Pb and Cd extracted in 0·5 mol/l acetic acid.

remainder of the samples came from residential road verges, recreational areas, wasteland, and hospital and railway sites.

Organic substances

As stated above, the information available on the background levels of organic chemicals is much more limited than for trace elements. There are many reasons for this, including the extremely large numbers of chemicals

Table 5.7. *Classification of area types used in the 'state of the environment' report for the West Midlands (ref. 5.22)*

Road density	Land use
A (high)	1. Mostly commercial; small amounts of industry and residential land. 2. Mostly residential but with a considerable mix of industry and/or commercial areas. 3. Mostly residential; small proportions (less than 20%) of recreational or vacant land.
B	1. Mostly residential; small proportions of industry and recreational land. 2. Broadly even mix of residential and industrial land. 3. Mostly residential but also small commercial areas. 4. Mostly residential but also noticeable amounts of recreational land and/or some vacant land.
C	1. Almost all residential; a very small amount of vacant or recreational land or small shopping areas. 2. Broad mix of industry and residential land. 3. Mostly residential; some vacant land, possibly associated with industry. 4. Mostly residential but significant amounts of recreational and/or agricultural land.
D	1. Mainly industrial, but also vacant land and residential areas. 2. Even mix of residential and recreational land. 3. Mostly residential but substantial presence of vacant land; also some industry. 4. Agricultural/residential mix, with agricultural land predominant.
E (low)	1. Industrial, vacant and recreational land, broadly mixed. 2. Mostly recreational, but mixed with substantial residential areas. 3. Mostly agricultural, but noticeable amounts of residential land. 4. Mostly usually agricultural, but mixed with substantial recreational land. 5. Almost entirely agricultural.

Table 5.8. Mean metal concentrations in the 20 area types in West Midlands (ref. 5.22)

Land use classification	Metal*	Mean metal concentration:† mg/kg				
		Road density A	Road density B	Road density C	Road density D	Road density E
1	Zn available	359	83	87	183	94
	Cu available	133	33	50	36	57
	Pb total	184	151	131	131	274
2	Zn available	73	147	201	60	38
	Cu available	85	46	141	16	10
	Pb total	172	473	219	99	74
3	Zn available	242	78	39	117	21
	Cu available	44	24	18	38	9
	Pb total	297	160	49	49	149
4	Zn available	–	61	79	70	38
	Cu available	–	21	37	24	26
	Pb total	–	97	88	137	25
5	Zn available	–	–	–	–	31
	Cu available	–	–	–	–	10
	Pb total	–	–	–	–	48

* 'Available' metals on medium acetate/EDTA extract; 'total' metals on nitric acid/perchloric acid extract.
† There is a wide variation associated with the means (see Table 5.9).

that might be of concern and the difficulty (and expense) of many of the analyses required. However, in order to provide an indication of the concentration of some of the chemicals that are frequently mentioned in contamination surveys, data from a few studies are summarised below. It is important to recognise that some of these, such as polyaromatic hydrocarbons (PAHs) are likely to be very common, albeit at low concentrations, in the urban environment because of the wide range of sources, particularly the burning of fossil fuels. Many man-made chemicals are now also present in measurable concentrations in the rural environment.

Polychlorinated biphenyls (PCBs). PCBs are compounds with the general formula $C_{12}H_xCl_y$ where $x = 0$–9 and $y = 10 - x$. There are 209 such compounds. Commercially supplied PCBs contained a mixture of compounds in varying proportions. Analysis is therefore difficult and various strategems are thus employed to enable an estimate of PCB concentrations in a sample to be made (ref. 5.24).

Creaser (ref. 5.25) and colleagues have studied PCBs in a wide range of soils. An account of their work (ref. 5.26) written in 1987 includes the following results.

Table 5.9. Comparison of results for a range of metals from different area types in the West Midlands (ref. 5.22)

Metal	Metal concentration: mg/kilogram dry weight				
	Area type A_2	Area type B_2	Area type C_2	Area type D_4	Area type E_5
Lead total	27–307	35–2000	59–780	37–404	38–100
Lead available	10–125	23–292	25–230	21–171	6–76
Cadmium total	0·5–6·3	0·8–5·8	0·5–8·60	0·2–3·2	0·2–0·8
Copper total	28–4000	22–1104	23–1400	12–500	10–100
Copper available	3–360	9–128	10–850	3–100	3–55
Zinc available	5–160	9–235	17–990	7–165	6–88
Antimony total	Overall range 15–23				
Arsenic total	Overall range 2–41				
Mercury total	Overall range 1–4				
Selenium total	Overall range < 1–3				
Thallium total	Overall range 2–8				

o PCBs were detected in all 99 surface (0·30 mm) soil samples analysed.
o The range was 2·3–444 μg/kg.
o Less than 10% exceeded 20 μg/kg.
o The median was 7·2 μg/kg.
o The mean value was 22·8 μg/kg.

It was considered that background levels could be described as being close to the median value.

Badsha and Eduljee (ref. 5.27) also looked at PCB levels in soil from rural and urban areas. The average PCB concentration for rural areas was 8 μg/kg (range 1–23 μg/kg), for urban areas 43 μg/kg (range 11–141 μg/kg), and for industrial locations 41 μg/kg (range 20–67 μg/kg).

Polynuclear aromatic hydrocarbons (PAHs). There is an extremely large number of compounds within the general grouping of PAHs. The practice, therefore, is usually to restrict the analysis to a package of, say, 6–12 of the more common/toxic PAHs and occasionally to use just one or two as a general indicator of contamination levels.

The occurrence of PAHs in soils in the UK has been studied by Jones (ref. 5.28). PAHs are considered to be mutagenic and carcinogenic. Formed during combustion, PAHs are released and dispersed whenever natural vegetation is burnt. However, the major sources are anthropogenic: burning of fossil fuels, waste incineration, stubble burning etc.

Analyses of stored soils at Rothamsted Experimental Station from a plot that had received no artificial amendments showed 'total PAHs' increasing from about 300 ng/kg in 1846 to about 1750 ng/kg in 1986 in the top 230 mm of the soil. The increase reflects increased use of fossil fuels. Although the enrichment was most marked in the ploughshare layer

(0–230 mm), increased concentrations also occurred in the subsoil (230–460 mm depth). Jones (ref. 5.28) reported the results on 'typical' surface (0–50 mm) soil samples from 49 study sites in Wales. The samples were 'typical' in not coming from grossly contaminated locations. Total PAH concentrations ranged from about 100 μg/kg to 54 000 μg/kg. The results of this study are summarised in Table 5.11.

Table 5.10. Baseline survey of Glasgow and its hinterland (Fleming et al. (ref. 5.23))

Metal		Baseline hinterland survey	Inner city survey	Industrial survey
As: mg/kg	Range	–	2·0–20·0	5·5–> 100·0
	Mean	–	9·35	20·95
	Median	–	9·25	11·00
Cd: mg/kg	Range	< 0·01–5·80	< 0·01–2·90	< 0·01–2·60
	Mean	0·39	0·86	0·76
	Median	< 0·01	0·9	0·65
Hg: mg/kg	Range	< 0·5–4·5	< 0·5–3·8	< 0·5–4·5
	Mean	0·7	0·6	1·4
	Median	< 0·5	< 0·5	0·5
Pb: mg/kg	Range	60–1900	20–800	65–3193
	Mean	294·2	276·5	496·7
	Median	200	222·5	320
Ni: mg/kg	Range	37·5–180·0	5·0–45·0	7·5–35·0
	Mean	82·6	16·0	17·2
	Median	82·5	14·0	15·8
Zn: mg/kg	Range	58–1180	28·4–496·0	64·8–1120
	Mean	248·4	191·1	420·0
	Median	187·0	161·6	264·4
Cu: mg/kg	Range	16–840	12·0–126·4	10·8–1110·0
	Mean	92·6	45·9	112·0
	Median	48·0	36·4	57·2
Cr: mg/kg	Range	12–640	6·7–68·8	8·9–92·8
	Mean	77·9	24·4	28·9
	Median	53·0	20·4	25·5
Mn: mg/kg	Range	120–1780	140–706	198–1028
	Mean	742·9	371·4	460·1
	Median	590·0	377·0	421·0
Fe: wt %	Range	1·18–9·90	0·87–1·92	0·71–3·26
	Mean	3·08	1·49	1·76
	Median	2·81	1·49	1·62

Data presentation

Table 5.12 shows a typical page from a report on the investigation of a contaminated site: it contains the results of 72 determinations on four samples taken from a single trial pit. On this particular site, 43 trial pits were dug on a 25 m grid, together with ten boreholes, from each of which a further five samples were taken. A total of 265 soil samples were taken and analysed, yielding 4770 items of data for appraisal. This presents a considerable problem of assimilation, both for the assessor and for the eventual readers of the report. Means of identifying and illustrating the important results are therefore required.

Some of the results in Table 5.12 are in bolder type. This is the simplest first step. Each value is tested against some criterion, for example the ICRCL trigger values (see below) and marked accordingly. If necessary this can be done by hand or it can be done automatically using modern computer spreadsheet systems.

The most common way of presenting the data is to produce some form of frequency distribution: based on either arbitrary class divisions or available guidelines (published or specially devised). This can be done for all the data from the site; or more commonly, the data from different zones and/or depths of sampling are grouped. This data analysis is usually presented in tabular form but it can be presented graphically (Figs 5.2–5.6). Reference has already been made to the use of graphical techniques to derive 'background' levels of contaminants. Finally, the data can be presented through maps, either showing the observed values or showing concentration contours. Various computer programs enable this to be done fairly easily but they are only likely to work effectively where the contamination follows some pattern.

The body of data obtained from a site investigation is rarely amenable

Table 5.11. PAHs in 'typical' Welsh surface soil samples (μg/kilogram dry weight) (from Jones (ref. 5.28))

Compound	Mean	Median	Range	s.d. $(n-1)$
Naphthalene	34·8	2·8	< DL*–1000	147·0
Acenaphthylene	4·8	< DL*	< DL*–130	18·9
Acenaphthene/fluorene	217·0	38·1	12·4–5500	815·0
Phenanthrene	273·0	28·7	7·7–6700	991·0
Anthracene	49·7	2·7	0·6–1500	217·0
Fluoranthene	514·0	54·0	16·8–11 600	1714·0
Pyrene	225·0	31·2	9·7–5650	816·0
1,2-dibenzathracene/chrysene	460·0	46·0	12·2–12 000	1738·0
Benzo(b)fluoranthene	207·0	26·5	7·0–4600	678·0
Benzo(a)pyrene	138·0	16·5	3·5–3700	534·0
1,2,5,6-dibenzathracene	64·7	11·0	< DL*–666	130·0
Benzo(ghi)perylene	137·0	43·5	< DL*–1600	274·0
Total PAHs	2325·0	301·5	108–54 250	7936·0

* Less than detection limit (varies between samples).

to statistical manipulation and analysis (other than in the ways already discussed). Even calculations of simple statistics such as means and medians are rarely of use, and indeed are to be avoided since the assessment of the site must be made on the highest values observed. However, a frequency distribution analysis (e.g. determination of the range limits of quartiles, deciles etc.) can be helpful in giving an overall impression of the qualitative nature of the contamination and indicating whether any particular (high) value is part of the overall pattern or represents a 'hot spot' that can be dealt with as such.

The problem of the sampling and assessment of the results of chemical analysis in relation to possible attack by sulphates on concrete is explicity discussed in BRE digest 250 (ref. 5.14) as follows.

Interpretation of analytical results. The results of all the individual chemical analyses should be available to the engineer to assist him in deciding on the precautions necessary. If classification is based solely on the analysis of groundwaters, it should correspond to the highest sulphate concentration recorded. If

Table 5.12. Typical page from site investigation report

Trial pit number 19

	Sample TP 19/3	Sample TP 19/4	Sample TP 19/7	Sample TP 19/8
Depth: m	0·5	0·7	1·1	2·0
pH value (40% extract)	7·4	7·9	8·0	8·2
Loss on drying at 105°C: %	1·1	7·6	1·0	0·6
Loss on ignition at 500°C: %	21·3	16·0	5·5	13·1
Moisture content: %	15·4	27·3	16·2	28·2
Total cyanide as CN: mg/kg	1·1	< 1	< 1	9
Toluene extract: mg/kg	600	< 500	< 500	1200
Coal tar derivatives: mg/kg	< 500	< 500	< 500	1000
Mineral oil: mg/kg	< 500	< 500	< 500	< 500
Total phenols: mg/kg	2·3	0·8	0·9	3·3
Acid-soluble sulphate (2% HCl): mg/kg	1900	12 000	370	1000
Sulphide as H$_2$S: mg/kg	90	NA	60	350
Total arsenic as As: mg/kg	**31**	**10**	**58**	**13**
Total cadmium as Cd: mg/kg	< 1	11	< 1	< 1
Total chromium as Cr: mg/kg	49	9·5	20	16
Total copper as Cu: mg/kg	**580**	**68 000**	**680**	**170**
Total lead as Pb: mg/kg	**2300**	410	360	**650**
Total nickel as Ni: mg/kg	65	**730**	32	42
Total zinc as Zn: mg/kg	**750**	**24 000**	**490**	**390**

Notes

All results except pH, loss on drying, loss on ignition, and moisture content are expressed as mg/kilogram of air-dried soil.

NA denotes not analysed due to insufficient volume of sample.

Values in bold type exceed ICRCL trigger values for domestic gardens etc. (see Tables 5.14 and 5.15).

classification is based on the analysis of only a small number of soil samples and the results vary widely, it may be worth while to take further samples for analysis.

When a larger number of results are available it is suggested that the site classification should be based on the mean of the highest 20 per cent of the results. When the soil samples have been combined before the analysis the selection should be more stringent.

Most simple statistical techniques assume that the values are 'normally' distributed or are otherwise related in some simple way. There is no reason to suppose that this will be the case on a site that has become

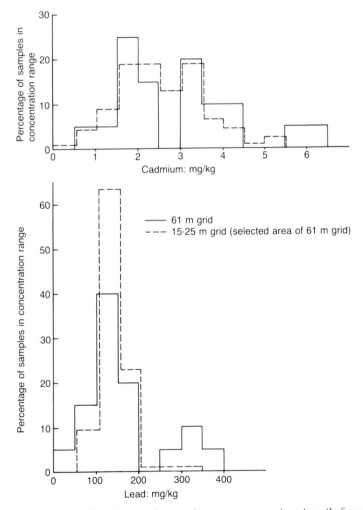

Fig. 5.4. Frequency distribution of trace element concentrations in soils from sewage farm

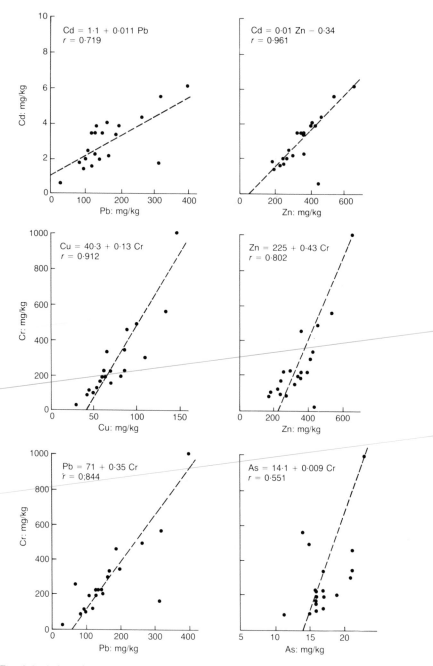

Fig. 5.5. Selected scatter diagrams showing correlations for various elements in soils from sewage farm

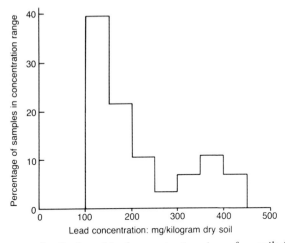

Fig. 5.6. Frequency distribution of lead concentrations in surface soils from urban site

contaminated as a result of numerous separate events (e.g. by the dumping of many loads of highly variable wastes), although there may be some basis for application of such statistics when the contamination originates from a more uniform process (e.g. the dumping of sewage sludge on land). The real questions must be (notwithstanding the power of modern ready-made computer programs) not only whether the effort devoted to carrying out a statistical analysis produces a 'valid' result, but whether the data once obtained are of any help in the decision-making process. The procedure may provide information of value in understanding the nature of the contamination process (if the statistics are valid), but not yield anything that is of help in deciding what to do about the site.

For example, Fig. 5.4 illustrates data obtained from part of a site that received sewage sludge over more than 60 years. A bimodal distribution of both lead and cadmium (trimodal) appears to be present: this may simply indicate that data from disparate parts of the site have been grouped together and might provide a basis for dividing the site into at least two zones. Fig. 5.5 shows that there can be strong relationships between contaminants derived from a single source.

Figures 5.2 and 5.6 illustrate a small urban site. The distinction between the background lead contamination (up to 250 mg/kg) and the areas of higher contamination is apparent.

One final word about information presentation in reports: where a notable value has been identified in the analytical results, the assessor is likely to be reassured if it proves possible to locate supporting evidence in the trial pit log (Fig. 5.7) or laboratory description of the sample.

Comparision with guidelines

When the intention is to determine the need for remedial action and to design appropriate remedial measures, emphasis should be placed on those samples with the greatest contamination (the maximum value itself may not be particularly important, since it may only indicate the presence of an isolated 'hot-spot'). Mean, modal or median concentrations are rarely a satisfactory basis for assessment: results from bulked or composited samples are never satisfactory.

Where different parts of the site have clear and justifiable differences in contamination levels, they may be judged separately provided that proper attention is paid to the possibilities for migration of contamination and to the practicable possibilities for discriminating between the different parts of the site when it comes to carrying out remedial action. Thus, the division is likely to be, at most, into a few broad areas rather than, say, on the basis of the results obtained from a single trial pit leading to a chequerboard pattern of action (although this has been done in a few special cases (ref. 5.29)).

A single analytical datum does not provide a basis for decision-making about the particular location from which the sample was taken. There are two main problems. The first is the reliability of the analytical result itself given the range of sources of error during the analysis and sample preparation in the laboratory (a reputable laboratory with proper quality control procedures should be able to indicate what these errors are likely to be). The second problem is that of variations arising from the site sampling process. These latter are likely to far outweigh the laboratory errors. Fig. 5.8 shows how altering the sampling position on a typical gasworks site by a metre or less can have a profound effect on the result. Table 5.13 shows the effect of different grid sampling sizes on the results.

Guidelines relating chemical factors to the need to take action, and the type of action to take, are part of the civil engineer's normal stock-in-trade, even if they exist only for a limited range of situations. The best known of these, the BRE guidance on concrete for use in sulphate-rich soils (now incorporated in BRE digest 250 (ref. 5.14)), has been around for over 30 years but is still sometimes not applied properly. These guidelines provide a good starting point for a consideration of guidelines, how they evolve, and the difficulties that there can be in their application. The recommendations in BRE digest 250 (and the guidance derived from them in BS CP 8110 and elsewhere) are based on a whole range of small- and large-scale laboratory tests, field tests and experience over many years. However, despite decades of work in many different centres of excellence, materials scientists still struggle with the difficult task of predicting the behaviour of concrete in service from the results of laboratory tests carried out on small cement-paste specimens tested in the laboratory under accelerated conditions. Nevertheless, the guidance appears to be soundly based: if it were not, one would expect to find evidence in the field of its shortcomings.

However, the guidance offered in digest 250 is very limited in scope: it is concerned only with a narrow range of pH's and with naturally occurring sulphates. It does not deal with the highly aggressive conditions sometimes found on old industrial sites and provides no advice on how to select the coating or protective membrane that is required for class V conditions and above. More recently, the former problem has been addressed by Harrison (ref. 5.30), who has provided guidance on how to assess these more aggressive conditions. In order to arrive at this guidance, however, a valuable measure of professional and scientific judgement has had to be used.

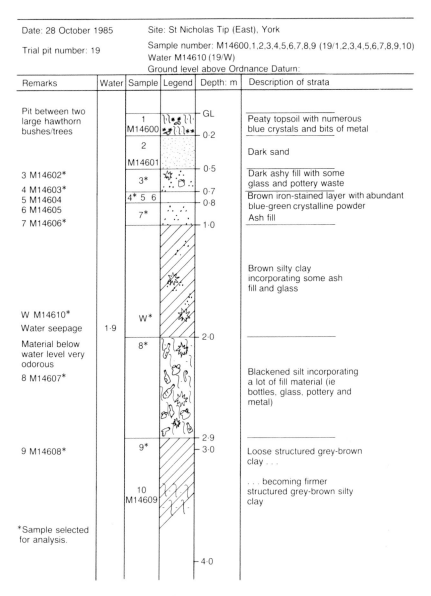

Date: 28 October 1985			Site: St Nicholas Tip (East), York		
Trial pit number: 19			Sample number: M14600,1,2,3,4,5,6,7,8,9 (19/1,2,3,4,5,6,7,8,9,10) Water M14610 (19/W) Ground level above Ordnance Datum:		
Remarks	Water	Sample	Legend	Depth: m	Description of strata
Pit between two large hawthorn bushes/trees		1 M14600		GL 0·2	Peaty topsoil with numerous blue crystals and bits of metal
		2 M14601		0·5	Dark sand
3 M14602*		3*		0·7	Dark ashy fill with some glass and pottery waste
4 M14603* 5 M14604 6 M14605 7 M14606*		4* 5 6 7*		0·8 1·0	Brown iron-stained layer with abundant blue-green crystalline powder Ash fill
W M14610* Water seepage	1·9	W*			Brown silty clay incorporating some ash fill and glass
Material below water level very odorous 8 M14607*		8*		2·0	Blackened silt incorporating a lot of fill material (ie bottles, glass, pottery and metal)
9 M14608*		9*		2·9 3·0	Loose structured grey-brown clay . . .
		10 M14609			. . . becoming firmer structured grey-brown silty clay
*Sample selected for analysis.				4·0	

Fig. 5.7. *Typical trial pit record*

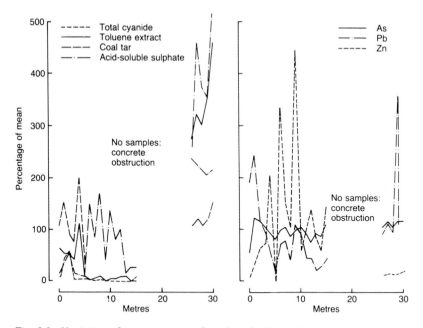

Fig. 5.8. Variation of contamination along length of trench

Table 5.13. Comparative results for different sizes of sampling grid on a gasworks site (from Smith and Ellis (ref. 5.15))

Data base	Grid size: m	Toluene extract: g/kg	Tars: g/kg	Sulphate: g/kg	Sulphide: mg/kg	Total cyanide: mg/kg	Free cyanide: mg/kg
Mean of all values	6·25	40·4	9·9	30·7	11	990	33
	12·5	32·7	8·8	25·3	53	980	40
	17·7	36·6	9·4	23·6	36	1060	33
	25	42·2	10·1	17·6	37	1360	37
	75	5·0	2·8	19·3	101	1060	3
Mean of 15–20% highest values	6·25	152·0	38·0	81·0	36	3320	85
	12·5	152·0	38·0	68·0	302	4400	134
	17·7	165·0	33·0	58·0	162	4000	133
	25	175·0	38·0	40·0	488	4570	153
	75	5·0	2·8	19·2	101	1060	3
Mean for area of 6·25 m grid only	6·25	40·4	9·9	30·7	11	990	33
	12·5	64·9	14·3	1·8	21	940	53
	17·7	5·3	3·6	25·5	19	170	46
	25	124·5	25·0	9·8	28	1820	83

The question of sulphate and acid attack has been discussed at some length because it illustrates the difficulty of drawing up guidelines where, although fairly simple chemical and physical processes are involved, the detrimental effects are likely to take a long time to manifest themselves and will be difficult to observe because the concrete in question is buried. The reader will appreciate how much more difficult it is to produce guidelines for biological and environmental systems, where, if one is working from first principles, it may be necessary to attempt to extrapolate from laboratory tests on small furry animals to possible effects on people 30–40 years ahead. This is not the place to discuss the derivation of individual guidelines; suffice it to say that they will generally have a basis in experimental studies, observations on exposed groups (e.g. in the workplace, and unplanned experiments such as accidental poisoning of groups of the population) and a considerable amount of professional and scientific judgement. It is also important to recognise that guidelines for contaminated land will often be secondary standards, having been derived by extrapolation from guidelines produced for other purposes. It should also be recognised that some of the possible effects of exposure of humans to chemicals are so intangible, when set against the variations in human well-being, that it will never, except in a few unfortunate cases, be possible to demonstrate a cause and effect relationship between exposure to a contaminated site and current, or more probably future, ill health. To ask to be shown a site where exposure to a particular level of contamination has caused harm is rarely a sensible question to ask. We do not, generally, have the tools or time available to answer it.

Guidelines in respect of health and the environment (soils)
The assessor requires three values in respect of any contaminant

o   a value A representative of background values
o   a 'trigger value B that indicates a need to consider action
o   a value C above which action is essential.

The value A provides a basis on which to judge whether the site is contaminated.
The values B and C provide the basis on which to judge whether this contamination matters. B and C will vary depending upon the risk that is being assessed and the route by which the risk is manifested (e.g. long term cadmium accumulation in humans from eating foods grown in or on contaminated soil, or acute poisoning from partial body contact with phenol in solution). Because different risks are associated with different land uses, different values of B and C can be derived for different land uses. This is the approach adopted in the UK in respect of a limited range of contaminants (mainly a few metals/metalloids (As) and contaminants associated with gasworks sites), resulting in the ICRCL 'trigger values' (Tables 5.14 and 5.15). In the Netherlands, however, the authorities have produced a wider range of ABC values (Table 5.16) but do not discriminate on land use. This is perhaps a reflection of their general policy on contaminated land which is to clean it up (i.e. to treat the soil to meet

Table 5.14. Tentative trigger concentrations for selected inorganic contaminants (ICRCL 59/83 (second edition))

Conditions

1. This table is invalid if reproduced without the conditions and footnotes.
2. All values are for concentrations determined on 'spot' samples based on an adequate site investigation carried out prior to development. They do not apply to analysis of averaged, bulked or composited samples, nor to sites which have already been developed. All proposed values are tentative.
3. (a) The lower values in group A are similar to the limits for metal content of sewage sludge applied to agricultural land. (b) The values in group B are those above which phytotoxicity is possible.
4. If all sample values are below the threshold concentrations then the site may be regarded as uncontaminated as far as the hazards from these contaminants are concerned and development may proceed. Above these concentrations, remedial action may be needed, especially if the contamination is still continuing. Above the action concentration, remedial action will be required or the form of development [will need to be] changed.

Contaminants	Planned uses	Trigger concentrations: mg/kilogram air-dried soil	
		Threshold	Action
Group A: Contaminants which may pose hazards to health			
Arsenic	Domestic gardens, allotments	10	*
	Parks, playing fields, open space	40	*
Cadmium	Domestic gardens, allotments	3	*
	Parks, playing fields, open space	15	*
Chromium (hexavalent) (note 1)	Domestic gardens, allotments	25	*
	Parks, playing fields, open space	–	–
Chromium (total)	Domestic gardens, allotments	600	*
	Parks, playing fields, open space	1000	*
Lead	Domestic gardens, allotments	500	*
	Parks, playing fields, open space	2000	*

Mercury	Domestic gardens, allotments	1	*
	Parks, playing fields, open space	20	*
Selenium	Domestic gardens, allotments	3	*
	Parks, playing fields, open space	6	*
Group B: Contaminants which are phytotoxic but not normally hazards to health			
Boron (water-soluble) (note 3)	Any uses where plants are to be grown (notes 2, 6)	3	*
Copper (notes 4, 5)	Any uses where plants are to be grown (notes 2, 6)	130	*
Nickel (notes 4, 5)	Any uses where plants are to be grown (notes 2, 6)	70	*
Zinc (notes 4, 5)	Any uses where plants are to be grown (notes 2, 6)	300	*

Notes

* Action concentrations will be specified in the next edition of ICRCL 59/83.
1. Soluble hexavalent chromium extracted by 0·1 M HCl at 37°C; solution adjusted to pH 1·0 if alkaline substances present.
2. The soil pH value is assumed to be about 6·5 and should be maintained at this value. If the pH falls, the toxic effects and the uptake of these elements will be increased.
3. Determined by standard ADAS method (soluble in hot water).
4. Total concentration (extractable by $HNO_3/HClO_4$).
5. The phytotoxic effects of copper, nickel and zinc may be additive. The trigger values given here are those applicable to the 'worst case': phytotoxic effects may occur at these concentrations in acid, sandy soils. In neutral or alkaline soils phytotoxic effects are unlikely at these concentrations.
6. Grass is more resistant to phytotoxic effects than are other plants and its growth may not be adversely affected at these concentrations.

Table 5.15. Tentative trigger concentrations for contaminants associated with former coal carbonisation sites (ICRCL 59/83 (second edition))

Conditions

1. This table is invalid if reproduced without the conditions and footnotes.
2. All values are for concentrations determined on 'spot' samples based on an adequate site investigation carried out prior to development. They do not apply to the analysis of averaged, bulked or composited samples, nor to sites which have already been developed.
3. Many of these values are preliminary and will require regular updating. They should not be applied without reference to the current edition of the report *Problems arising from the development of gas works and similar sites*.
4. If all sample values are below the threshold concentrations then the site may be regarded as uncontaminated as far as the hazards from these contaminants are concerned, and development may proceed. Above these concentrations, remedial action may be needed, especially if the contamination is still continuing. Above the action concentrations, remedial action will be required or the form of development [will need to be] changed.

Contaminants	Proposed uses	Trigger concentration: mg/kilogram air-dried soil	
		Threshold	Action
Polyaromatic hydrocarbons (notes 1,2)	Domestic gardens, allotments, play areas Landscaped areas, buildings, hard cover	50 1000	500 10 000
Phenols	Domestic gardens, allotments Landscaped areas, buildings, hard cover	5 5	200 1 000
Free cyanide	Domestic gardens, allotments, landscaped areas Buildings, hard cover	25 100	500 500

Complex cyanide	Domestic gardens, allotments Landscaped areas Buildings, hard cover	250 250 250	1 000 5 000 NL
Thiocyanate (note 2)	All proposed uses	50	NL
Sulphate	Domestic gardens, allotments, landscaped areas Buildings (note 3) Hard cover	2000 2000 (note 3) 2000	10 000 50 000 (note 3) NL
Sulphide	All proposed uses	250	1 000
Sulphur	All proposed uses	5000	20 000
Acidity (pH less than)	Domestic gardens, allotments, landscaped areas Buildings, hard cover	pH 5 NL	pH 3 NL

Notes
NL: No limit set as the contaminant does not pose a particular hazard for this use.
1. Used here as a marker for coal tar, for analytical reasons. See *Problems arising from the redevelopment of gasworks and similar sites* Annex A1.
2. See *Problems arising from the redevelopment of gasworks and similar sites* for details of analytical methods.
3. See also **BRE** digest 250: *Concrete in sulphate-bearing soils and groundwater.*

Table 5.16. Standards adopted in the Netherlands for soil contaminants: A, reference value below which soils are probably uncontaminated; B, value above which there is need for further investigation; C, value above which a clean-up is indicated (from Moen et al. (ref. 5.31))

Substance	Concentration in soil: mg/kilogram dry weight			Concentration in groundwater: µg/l		
	A	B	C	A	B	C
Metals						
Cr	100	250	800	20	50	200
Co	20	50	300	20	50	200
Ni	50	100	500	20	50	200
Cu	50	100	500	20	50	200
Zn	200	500	3000	50	200	800
As	20	30	50	10	30	100
Mo	10	40	200	5	20	100
Cd	1	5	20	1	2·5	10
Sn	20	50	300	10	30	150
Ba	200	400	2000	50	100	500
Hg	0·5	2	10	0·2	0·5	2
Pb	50	150	600	20	50	200
Inorganic pollutants						
NH (as N)	–	–	–	200	1000	3000
F (total)	200	400	2000	300	1200	4000
CN (total free)	1	10	100	5	30	100
CN (total complex)	5	50	500	10	50	200
S (total)	2	20	200	10	100	300
Br (total)	20	50	300	100	500	2000
PO (as P)	–	–	–	50	200	700
Aromatic compounds						
Benzene	0·01	0·5	5	0·2	1	5
Ethyl benzene	0·05	5	50	0·5	20	60
Toluene	0·05	3	30	0·5	15	50
Xylene	0·05	5	50	0·5	20	60
Phenols	0·02	1	10	0·5	15	50
Aromatics (total)	0·1	7	70	1	30	100

Polycyclic aromatic compounds (PCAs)	Naphthalene	0·1	5	50	0·2	7	30
	Anthracene	0·1	10	100	0·1	2	10
	Phenanthrene	0·1	10	100	0·1	2	10
	Fluoranthene	0·1	10	100	0·02	1	5
	Pyrene	0·1	10	100	0·02	1	5
	Benzo(a)pyrene	0·05	1	10	0·01	0·2	1
	Total PCAs	1	20	200	0·2	10	40
Chlorinated organic compounds	Aliphatic chlorinated compounds (individual)	0·1	5	50	1	10	50
	Aliphatic chlorinated compounds (total)	0·1	7	70	1	15	70
	Chlorobenzenes (individual)	0·05	1	10	0·02	0·5	2
	Chlorobenzenes (total)	0·05	2	20	0·02	1	5
	Chlorophenols (individual)	0·01	0·5	5	0·01	0·3	1·5
	Chlorophenols (total)	0·01	1	10	0·01	0·5	2
	Chlorinated PCA (total)	0·05	1	10	0·01	0·2	1
	PCB (total)	0·05	1	10	0·01	0·2	1
	EOCl (total)	0·1	8	80	1	15	70
Pesticides	Organic chlorinated (individual)	0·1	0·5	5	0·05	0·2	1
	Organic chlorinated (total)	0·1	1	10	0·1	0·5	2
	Pesticides (total)	0·1	2	20	0·1	1	5
Other pollutants	Tetrahydrofuran	0·1	4	40	0·5	20	60
	Pyridine	0·1	2	20	0·5	10	30
	Tetrahydrothiophene	0·1	5	50	0·5	20	60
	Cyclohexanone	0·1	6	60	0·5	15	50
	Styrene	0·1	5	50	0·5	20	60
	Fuel	20	100	800	10	40	150
	Mineral oil	100	1000	5000	20	200	600

A type criteria) before permitting its reuse (i.e. cover and containment solutions are not favoured).

The function of the threshold trigger or B value is to indicate that remedial action may be required. It is a matter of expert judgement as to whether to take action and then what action to take (i.e. a level above the threshold trigger value may be 'acceptable' on the basis of a site-specific judgement). Factors in addition to the general land use category which might be taken into account include the quality of the site investigation (e.g. amount of data), proportion of samples exceeding the trigger value, the range and amount of other contaminants (contaminants can have additive effects), presence of particularly sensitive targets, the margin of safety (confidence factor) that a particular trigger value offers (something the 'average' assessor will have to take at face value), the chemical form of the contaminant (some forms of a particular element will be more 'available', say, to plants, are more soluble and are more toxic (e.g. arsenite v. arsenate)), and the stability of the contaminant (e.g. it may be liable to be broken down to less harmful substances by microbial action or it may be liable to change into a more toxic form). In practice the scope for exercising sophisticated judgement in this way is limited. The data and knowledge available rarely justify it.

In general, a conservative approach should be adopted. In most cases when threshold trigger values are exceeded some form of action will be considered necessary. The big question is: When is it essential that action is taken? As already stated there is only limited formal UK guidance but use can also be made of the Dutch C values (Table 5.16). In the case of sensitive (in respect of human health) land uses (e.g. allotments, housing) one would not expect to exceed the trigger values by any great amount. In moving towards less sensitive uses (e.g. recreation) one might consider the probability of a future change of use and whether this could take place without undue risk (e.g. land used for an area of informal amenity grass within a housing estate should probably meet the same standards as the land for the adjacent housing). When considering whether to take remedial action one must also consider whether anything might happen in the future that might make conditions worse (e.g. rising water table, flooding, continued (or new) aerial deposition from nearby plant or road).

Guidelines for water

It is the nature of the UK approach to contaminated sites that the emphasis tends to be on soil analysis and the risk to targets that may come into contact, directly or indirectly, with that soil. However, the analysis of water is also important. In the case of surface water, or where disposal of water from the site is concerned, there are usually ready-made guidelines that can be applied (either in their own right or 'borrowed' from some other application). The potential effect on a neighbouring river or on the sewer system is likely to be direct and instantaneous; the question of whether harm will result is not usually the point at issue: the usual task will be to meet a standard and possibly, in the case of the sewer, pay the requisite amount of money.

Groundwater presents greater difficulties. Knowledge of composition in terms of naturally occurring, essentially inorganic, substances is quite extensive (ref. 5.32), and local water organisations will usually have the data available on which to judge whether a sample lies within the range of composition typically found for water from a particular source. Knowledge with regard to organic substances (naturally occurring and especially man-made) is more limited. If the water analysed comes from, or is only a short distance from, a well used to extract water for drinking purposes then the water abstractor or the environmental health authority (in the case of a private well) will make a judgement against established standards (public or internal as appropriate) about whether to continue to use the water and about any treatment that might be required.

In practice, things are rarely this simple. It is more likely that evidence of contamination of groundwater will be found remote from an abstraction point. It will then be necessary to predict when and if the contamination might reach an abstraction point. This is a specialist hydrogeological task.

It may be that the contaminated aquifer, or threatened aquifer, is not currently used for water abstraction, and what is at risk is a future resource.

Where water for abstraction is at risk the criteria to be met are those laid down by EEC directives, and the guidance from the World Health Organisation as adopted by the UK authorities. But it is not just water for abstraction that is at risk from migrating contamination. The contamination may pose a direct threat to adjacent properties and people either through aggressive attack on the materials of construction or through the release of toxic or flammable substances. Arriving at criteria to judge the extent of such hazards would be difficult even on a site-specific basis and is certainly not possible on a general basis. Although some attenuation would be expected as the contaminants move away from the source site, accumulation is also a possibility.

Demonstrated adverse health effect

Notwithstanding the comments above about the difficulty of proving health effects directly associated with contamination, it is useful to consider a couple of cases where such effects have been demonstrated — if only to make the point that fears about the potential hazards of contamination are real. The cases also illustrate the danger of guidelines, such as those discussed above, if they focus attention too much on a narrow range of possible contaminants. One case concerns thallium and the other a range of organic compounds, both forms of contamination not addressed by current ICRCL guidance.

Poisoning by thallium. Illness in a village in the South West Guizhou province of China was attributed (ref. 5.33) after investigation to thallium poisoning (the symptoms are fairly classic) but the authorities were puzzled because the village had existed for hundreds of years with no previous record of such endemic illness. The task was to identify the source of the thallium and also to find out, since the source was not immediately obvious, what changes there had been in and around the village that might explain the sudden onset of the problem. Investigation showed that the direct source was the consumption of cabbages (a major part of the diet) with elevated thallium levels. The cabbages had been grown in soils (up to 0·5 m deep) overlying slags from a previous era. The changed situation was that in recent years increased erosion following road construction had led to the spread of fertile alluvium over the pre-existing slags containing up to 106 mg/kg thallium. The village then expanded on to this new land. Ill health was observed in families with garden soils containing 28–60 mg/kg but not those with gardens with about 6–11 mg/kg. Background levels in garden soils in villages not affected by the slag were less than 0·02 mg/kg (a maximum of 8 mg/kg has been found in soils in the West Midlands (ref. 5.34)).

Love Canal. Love Canal, in New York State, USA, is probably the most famous uncontrolled hazardous waste (contaminated) site. Toxic wastes were sealed into a section of an uncompleted canal. They remained there for many years without apparently causing any problem until the top clay seal was disturbed, allowing water to enter. The canal eventually spilled over, contaminated water moving away from the site overland and along the channels of some buried streams or swales. The problem manifested itself when various organic substances began to emerge into the basements of houses.

After investigation the government authorities eventually bought up large numbers of houses and evacuated the people living close to the site of the old canal. Remedial action was taken in 1979 to prevent further entry of rain-water into the buried canal and the spread of contamination.

A health surveillance programme was mounted covering the population living near to the site. Various clinical effects were observed but it was difficult to demonstrate cause and effect using classical epidemiological techniques because many of the population had workplace exposure to the chemicals concerned and the absolute numbers showing adverse effects were small compared with the total population considered at risk on the basis of proximity to the site. In addition, comprehensive monitoring showed that there was a general level of air and groundwater pollution asociated with the local chemical industry. Good detective work, however, showed that there was a pattern of illness among those living close to the courses of the buried swales (i.e. just a small part of the population was subject to a high risk).

The general lesson is that more may be learned if the trouble is first taken to examine possible routes of exposure and identify those at greatest risk. However, the numbers may then be so low that it is not possible to demonstrate statistically beyond doubt that the few adverse effects observed could not have been caused purely by chance, such is the 'natural variation' to be expected (ref. 5.35).

Methane and other gases

An assessment of the results of a gas monitoring programme must usually answer two main questions: the possibility of immediate hazard either within the site itself or to the adjacent areas, and the propriety of building on the site.

The assessor will expect to have two basic sets of data on which to make these judgements

- o composition of the gas (e.g. concentrations of methane, carbon dioxide, and oxygen)
- o volume of gas being produced.

Information on the former will often be sufficient to say whether or not a potential hazard exists. Information on the latter is essential to the design of measures to control the movement of gas, or to the design of buildings to be erected on sites where gas is being evolved.

Two important qualifiers are necessary with respect to what follows. First, it is written largely in terms of methane — the explosion potential will usually be immediately recognised — but the assessor must also pay attention to the presence of other gases such as carbon dioxide and to the dangers of oxygen-depleted atmospheres, and will also want to be certain that the large-volume gases are not acting as carriers for small quantities of highly toxic substances.

The second qualifier is that although the criteria to be used in judging whether, and how, to build on a gassing site are discussed, the presumption should be against building on such sites: it is for the developer to justify such an action, not for the control authorities to justify refusing to countenance such a proposal.

Acceptable concentrations of gases

When the hazard is an immediate one, such as the explosion of methane, it is not too difficult to decide whether or not a potential hazard exists. When the question is long term exposure to some volatile organic compound, or more likely a cocktail of these, the setting of control limits can be more difficult.

It is important to recognise when setting control limits that there is a right and proper distinction to be drawn between the limits that might be set when dealing with an existing pollution problem and those that might be set for a new development. For example, if methane is found to be entering a factory, any concentration above the lower explosive limit (LEL) — about 5% — represents an immediate hazard which will probably require immediate evacuation. Thereafter, in designing the essential remedial actions, although the ideal will be to exclude the gas entirely, it may be acceptable to design remedial measures and install alarm systems on the basis of not exceeding some fraction of the LEL (e.g. 20% LEL, i.e. about 1% methane in air). On the other hand, if a new building were to be erected on the same site, the aim would have to be total exclusion of gas from inside the building, and if one were designing, for example, a ventilated undercroft, one might set a design target that the concentration within the void should never exceed some small fraction of the LEL — say 1/20 (about 0·25% methane). That is, in the design of a new building an additional margin of safety is required (an alarm system could, however, be geared to some higher concentration, e.g. 0·5% or 1·0% methane).

It is thus fairly easy to arrive at some control limits on the basis of judgement and rule of thumb for explosive hazards such as those for methane. Where the hazard is toxicity the problem is somewhat more difficult. The starting point will usually be occupational exposure limits (OELs) as set out by the Health and Safety Executive in respect of occupational exposure. But these are based on the requirement to protect reasonably healthy adults of working age on an assumed exposure of about 40 hours a week.

A control limit for the wider population has to take into account the exposure of more sensitive segments of the population (the old, young, infirm and pregnant), the longer exposure time (up to seven days (168 hours) a week), and the near impossibility of any systematic health surveillance. Thus it is customary to work on the basis of some small fraction of the OEL — no more than one thirtieth or one fortieth — but again the distinction must be made between an ongoing situation and the creation of a new situation. The aim in any new development must be to reduce any exposure to an absolute minimum: if there is any doubt then the only safe limit may be zero exposure — no development of the site.

There is one important additional, but unquantifiable, factor to take into account when considering exposure to organic substances. There is increasing concern about 'indoor air-pollution': the build-up of potentially toxic substances in the atmosphere of the home and office (as opposed to factory) as a result of emanations from modern furnishing and construction materials, coupled with lower ventilation rates introduced in the interests of energy efficiency. Thus, an individual's exposure to the site may be in addition to an exposure from the indoor environment.

Is there a methane problem?

There are two ways of approaching the question of what constitutes a gas problem. The first is to set simple control limits based on concentrations (as discussed above) or volumes (rates of production). The second is to set a design objective and then to back-calculate, applying such safety factors as might seem necessary, to decide what concentrations or emission rates would be acceptable in a particular situation: such specific solutions might then be generalised to give control limits.

Suggested limiting concentrations for the gases of major concern are given in Table 5.17.

Demonstration of risk from methane

If the concentration of methane in the ground exceeds the lower explosive limit (5% v/v air) a hazard exists. The risk involved will depend on the emission rate of the gas, whether there are any confined spaces, whether there are channels for transmision of the gas and whether there are sources of ignition. The last three are always likely to be present, although careful design can minimise their significance. The crucial factor is the rate of emission, and as any unventilated confined space in contact

Table 5.17. Limiting values for common gaseous contaminants

Contaminant	Limiting concentration for toxicity:* % v/v	Limiting concentration for flammability: % v/v	Trigger for potential hazard:† % v/v
Carbon dioxide	0·5	–	0·125
Carbon monoxide	0·005	12–75	0·00125
Sulphur dioxide	0·0005	–	0·000125
Hydrogen sulphide	0·001	4·3–45·5	0·0025
Methane	14‡	5–15	0·25
Petrol	0·1	1·4–7·6	0·025
Oxygen	Should never fall below 18% v/v		< 20

* Treat long term (8 h time-weighted average value) occupational limits as an absolute *maximum*. For highly toxic substances the acceptable concentrations may have to be set at no more than 1/30th or 1/40th of the long term occupational exposure limit to allow for longer exposure time and more vulnerable members of the community.

† Generally set at a quarter of lowest limiting concentration quoted (thus for highly toxic substances might be only 1/160th of long term occupational limit).

‡ More than 14% methane in air produces unacceptable oxygen-deficient atmosphere.

with the ground will eventually come into equilibrium with the gas in the ground, this reduces to the question, 'How long will it take for an unacceptable concentration of gas to build up?'

The calculation presented below is designed to show that under certain circumstances even very low methane emission rates can lead to a risk situation. There is no 'safe' limit. The calculation deals with the build-up of methane in a confined space. It must be remembered that the gas will usually enter at a point and, whatever the average concentration in the confined space, the concentration at the point of entry is likely to exceed an acceptable concentration. The calculation is thus only intended to illustrate the size of potential risk associated with a particular emission rate.

Consider the case of a confined space of $2·5\,m^3$ (2500 litres) — a reasonably sized broom cupboard of standard ceiling height.

The LEL for methane (5%) will be reached when 125 litres has entered the space. (This assumes uniform mixing throughout the space but in practice there will be at best a concentration gradient and at worst a distinct layering of the gas because of differences in density. In addition, the concentration at the point of entry will be high.)

If it is assumed that the cupboard remains undisturbed for 15 days (360 hours) — not an unreasonable holiday period — and that each incoming volume of gas displaces an equal volume of air (in practice the displaced gas will contain some methane if there has been thorough mixing), then an entry rate of methane of 0·347 l/h could lead to the LEL being reached uniformly throughout the cupboard atmosphere in that time (assuming a zero ventilation rate other than the displaced volume).

The model room has a floor area of 1 m² so the rate leading to the LEL in 15 days is 0·347 l/h per m².

However, a deliberate and known safety factor (as opposed to the unquantified factor offered by the assumption of zero ventilation rate) should be applied to allow for fluctuations in flow rate, lack of mixing etc. Using a factor of 5 (i.e. in 15 days one would not want an average concentration exceeding 1% methane), the 'maximum acceptable' flow rate reduces to 0·069 l/h per m² (1·16 ml/min per m²).

The dangers of even very low rates of gas emission are further illustrated by the case of a void forming beneath a floor slab because of settlement. A small house would have an area of about 40 m². Should all the gas collecting beneath the building enter a confined space within the building, for example around a service pipe, then the rate of build-up of gas would be 40 times that considered above in respect of the 2·5 m³ broom cupboard: this would lead to a 'maximum acceptable' flow rate of only 1·72 ml/h per m² (0·03 ml/min per m²).

The next question is now to relate this value to what is actually measured on site. In practice a number of boreholes are likely to have been installed at distances of up to 50 m apart and the data will be in terms of litres of methane per minute entering the borehole. Each borehole will have a finite catchment area. Assuming the overall diameter of the extraction system is 100–150 mm (50 mm central tube plus granular packing), it should be reasonably safe to assume a catchment area of just 1 m² (a circle of radius 0·564 m), which enables the acceptable rate calculated above to be related directly to that obtained from the borehole. This is a reasonable assumption since a problem is most likely to arise from gas emanating through a fissure or other easy route (which the borehole emulates) rather than from uniform emission through the surface of the site. A significantly more conservative approach is to assume a uniform emission rate through the surface of the site equivalent to that obtained from the borehole (this was the approach originally used in designing houses for Surrey Docks). The factor for a borehole of 100 mm effective diameter is 127 (1 m²/cross-sectional area of borehole). Applying this reduces the acceptable rate per borehole to just 0·014 ml/h.

The size of confined space of concern may be smaller than the rather generous 2·5 m³ used above. While the atmosphere in the broom cupboard might be ignited by the cleaner's cigarette, it could be that the ignition source is an electric spark in a meter switching box (no more than 0·5 m³); that is, it would not be totally unreasonable to apply a further factor of 5 to all the above figures. The maximum 'acceptable' rate becomes 0·34 ml/h or less entering the meter box.

In practice, the build-up of gas in the confined space will not occur in the simple way assumed above. If there is no ventilation other than through the connection to the larger source reservoir (the ground), then the two will eventually come to equilibrium (this is the situation of a capped borehole) and the concentration of methane in the 'confined space' will increase as illustrated in Fig. 5.9. The rate of change will initially be effectively linear (the case considered above). If the space is ventilated then

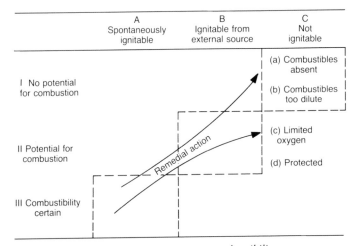

	A Spontaneously ignitable	B Ignitable from external source	C Not ignitable

I No potential
for combustion

(a) Combustibles
absent

(b) Combustibles
too dilute

II Potential for
combustion

(c) Limited
oxygen

(d) Protected

Remedial action

III Combustibility
certain

Fig. 5.9. Classification of sites with respect to combustibility

the concentration will asymptotically approach some other lower value dictated by the rate of ventilation. For example, if the pure methane is entering at 1 l/h and air is also supplied at 19 l/h, then (assuming uniform mixing) the average concentration of methane will gradually approach, but cannot exceed, the concentration in the combined entering gas streams; that is, 5%, or the LEL. It is thus possible, using well established procedures (ref. 5.36), to calculate ventilation rates required to keep the methane concentrations below a set limit if the rate of supply of gas and the composition of the gas is known. This is the basis of the design of systems for venting methane and other gases from beneath buildings.

Various safety factors have been introduced in the discussion above in order to make what may appear to be a conservative estimate of the risks. It is not overconservative. It must be remembered that gas emission rates will be influenced by many factors. Frozen or waterlogged surface soils around a building may force gas to exit beneath the dry or unfrozen soil beneath a building; a sudden increase in water levels (a flood situation) may force gas out of the ground; and, perhaps most importantly, a sudden drop in barometric pressure (perhaps a 1 in 100 year event) may induce a sudden increase in flow rates and the forcing open of cracks under the unusual pressure differential.

Carbon dioxide and oxygen-deficient atmospheres

Methane is not the only gas of concern. Carbon dioxide, which typically occurs in roughly the same proportion as methane in landfill gas, is of equal concern because of its toxic and asphixiant properties. In addition, oxygen-deficient atmospheres, generally inevitable if the concentrations of other gases are at significant levels, must be considered. The risks to occupants from both carbon dioxide and oxygen deficiency are both direct (toxicity and asphyxiation) and indirect through interference with the combustion of gas and other appliances, leading to the formation of carbon monoxide.

The maximum acceptable concentration of carbon dioxide is 0·5% (this implies a lower average concentration), equivalent to the long term (8 h time-weighted average) value for occupational exposure. This is half that suggested above as a maximum acceptable concentration for methane. Thus the acceptable emission rate for the broom cupboard must also be halved to 0·85 ml/h per m^2 (this corresponds to a maximum concentration of CO_2 of 0·5% v/v whereas in practice one would expect to set a 'target' of say 0·125–0·25% v/v).

Crowhurst and Beever (ref. 5.37) point out that in the case of landfill gas consisting of 55% v/v methane and 45% v/v carbon dioxide which is diluted by air so that the methane concentration is only 4% v/v in air (i.e. below its LEL value), the concentration of carbon dioxide would be 3·3%; that is, above the short term (10 min TWA value) occupational exposure limit of 1·5% v/v. Even at 1% methane, the concentration of carbon dioxide would be 0·82% v/v; that is, above the long term exposure limit and the suggested maximum acceptable concentration (0·5% v/v).

Oxygen concentrations of less than 18% are unacceptable; that is, situations in which 3% or more of the oxygen has been replaced by other gases such as methane or has been 'used up' in combustion, or in microbial or oxidation processes. Such conditions can be independent of the presence of other gases considered hazardous, and oxygen concentrations should always be monitored in boreholes. A 'rate' of oxygen depletion can be measured in a way analogous to that described for methane above. If a working limit of 1% deficiency (i.e. an oxygen concentration of at least 20%) is applied then equivalent limiting rates may be derived.

Radon

Radon has been a cause for increasing concern in recent years (see also section below on radioactivity). Initially the potential problem was identified in the UK and other countries as arising from the use of certain materials — wastes from the uranium processing industry (USA), metal-mining wastes (UK) and some naturally occurring materials containing relatively high amounts of certain radioactive elements — as fill and/or hardcore beneath buildings. It is now recognised as a matter of concern in areas with high natural background levels (e.g. granite areas) and where certain other wastes have been used. The potential problem is compounded by lower ventilation rates in modern houses associated with attempts to conserve energy. Some 1500 deaths per annum (ref. 5.38) are said to be attributable to radon (i.e. a number far in excess of that attributed to any other form of soil contamination). The National Radiological Protection Board is expected (refs 5.38, 5.39) to produce guidance on acceptable doses related to radon and, in association with the Building Research Establishment, on control measures for existing and new houses. These limits are likely to be very much more restrictive than those existing at present for occupational exposure — which it can be anticipated will have to be revised downwards.

Combustibility

A fire hazard exists when smouldering can occur in the ground mass following 'self-ignition' or ignition from an external source. The assessor will be faced with deciding in which of three categories or classes a site belongs (there is a strong parallel with the assessment of chemical contamination).

- o Category I. There is no potential for combustion because combustibles are absent or not present in sufficient amount.
- o Category II. There is an uncertain potential for combustion.
- o Category III. Combustibility is not in doubt.

The assessor has two further questions to answer for sites in categories II and III.

- o Is there a potential for self-heating or self-ignition?
- o Is the combustible material in such a condition or position that ignition from an external source is possible?

It should be easy to place some sites into classes I and III (there may, for example, be deposits of coal or of fresh refuse), but there may be considerable difficulties classifying many sites because of the uncertainties regarding the factors governing combustibility in practice (these are not limited to inherent properties such as calorific value but include, for example, access of oxygen, density, moisture content).

An alternative classification has been proposed (refs 5.2, 5.40) based initially on the propensity for spontaneous ignition.

- o Category A. The material is 'spontaneously ignitable'; or, more correctly, the rate of self-heating (by slow oxidation etc.) exceeds the rate of heat loss sufficiently to raise the temperature to a point at which self-sustaining smouldering becomes possible, given a supply of oxygen.
- o Category B. Spontaneous ignition through self-heating is not possible, but the material may otherwise ignite through triggering by an external source of heat (surface fires, electric cables, etc.) or through the migration of an underground fire from another area.
- o Category C. No fire hazard exists because the combustible material is either

    (a) absent
    (b) too diluted to ignite
    (c) rendered incapable of ignition (e.g. compacted to reduce the air supply)
    (d) so protected that its temperature can never rise to ignition point (cover layers, cut-off 'fire fences' etc.).

Conditions (b), (c) and (d) may already exist on the site or may be achieved as part of the remedial works.

Table 5.18. Characteristic calorific values

Material	Calorific value: MJ/kg
Arable soil	0·5
Other soils	Up to 2·2
Refuse feed to incinerator	9·9
Dried peat	17·5
Wood (12–15% moisture)	16·7–18·5
Dried pine-wood	21
Coal	27·8

Sites in category A must receive treatment before development to eliminate the hazard.

Sites in category B must be dealt with to prevent ignition from an external source (thus effectively moving them, for example, into category C(d)).

The two systems of classification are combined in Fig. 5.9. Judgement of where in this matrix a site lies is difficult. For example, at present it is not possible to say whether any given material will be liable to self-ignition in the ground. Volume will be an important factor as this will govern the quantity of heat produced and the rate of heat lost to the surroundings. Experience suggests, however, that spontaneously ignitable materials tend to ignite through self-heating sooner rather than later. Thus, if a combustible, such as colliery spoil, has stood for an appreciable time after deposition without catching fire, it is unlikely to do so in the future unless the external conditions change (ref. 5.41).

In many cases the potential for combustion may be obvious because of the presence of certain materials in large quantities (e.g. fresh refuse, coal, wood) or because of a history of fires on the site. In other cases the combustile content may be so low that no doubts arise. Between these two extremes a broad band of uncertainty exists.

Various properties of materials have been measured in order to assess combustibility. The principal of these, and the most useful, is calorific value. Others include loss on ignition, flammable volatile content and ignition temperature.

Present research suggests that materials with calorific values no higher than 2 MJ/kg may be capable of smouldering (this can be compared with a 0·48 MJ/kg for typical arable soils). Characteristic calorific values of a range of materials are given in Table 5.18.

Loss of ignition (after drying at 105°C) can sometimes provide a useful indirect empirical measure for known materials (e.g. colliery spoil from a particular location).

Assessment of the other factors governing the likelihood of combustion (e.g. accessibility to oxygen) is very difficult. Although it might be contended that combustible material encountered in a dense state should not present a hazard (e.g. colliery spoil placed by engineering techniques), a burning underground fire tends to make its own air access channels once started. It is essential, therefore, to protect even compacted fills that have stood safely for many years from external sources of ignition when development is to be carried out.

Aggressive attack on building materials

The durability of building materials depends on the environment in which they are placed: in the present context, the amount and type of chemicals present, certain other factors such as redox potential, and the 'availability' of the potentially aggressive agents. In general the substances of major concern will be acids, strong alkalis, 'organics', sulphides, sulphates and chlorides. However, the presence of metals in solution or metal fragments may have some implications for corrosion.

Regard must be paid to concrete, metals, fired clay products, calcium silicate products, plastics, rubber, and bituminous and asphaltic materials.

In addition to chemical attack, regard must be paid to possible microbial action, and the presence of such materials as ash and cinders, and other materials containing carbon (which can help to set up electrolytic cells).

Except on certain limited topics, the guidance available on the assessment of conditions potentially damaging to building materials is limited and is generally not comparable, for example, to that regarding sulphate attack on concrete contained in BRE digest 250 (ref. 5.14), to which reference has already been made. The problem is partly that the information on which to base guidance is not available, and partly that the guidance and information that is available is not in a readily accessible form or from authoritative and independent sources: reliance often has to be put on the claims of manufacturers. The overall problem of the use of materials in aggressive ground conditions has been reviewed by Nixon *et al.* (ref. 5.42) and by Barry (ref. 5.43), and is mentioned in the CIRIA report on difficult sites (ref. 5.2).

The BRE formal guidance on naturally occurring sulphates (BRE digest 250) has recently been extended by informal guidance on acidic conditions (ref. 5.30), but no general guidance is yet available in the UK on how to select coatings or protective membranes for particularly aggressive conditions. Nor is there a general appraisal available of what can be achieved by the use of specialist admixtures in concrete to improve durability — for which quite remarkable claims are made.

Decaying matter is aggressive to ferrous metals and possibly to cement-based products. Although plastics may be chemically resistant, they are temperature-sensitive and generally perform less well at elevated temperatures such as may be encountered on an active refuse tip. Some hydrocarbon contaminants can penetrate plastic pipes used for water supply, causing tainting of the water: uPVC, high-density and low-density polythene and polypropylene may be susceptible, and the durability of such pipes subject to continuous hydrostatic pressure could be adversely affected. Some organic substances can promote environmental cracking in polyolefins.

Synthetic organic polymers used in manufacturing plastics for engineering purposes (e.g. geotextiles) show a fairly strong chemical resistance under laboratory conditions, particularly at normal temperatures (ref. 5.44). Compounds like polyethylene, polypropylene and polyvinylchloride (PVC) are reportedly bio-inert, but commercial products can be more susceptible to both chemical and microbiological attack, depending on the additives used and the monomers present. There are usually micro-organisms present in soil that can use buried plastics as a growth medium and in some cases cause deterioration of the product. Under certain severe conditions, marked deterioration may occur. For example, in acid sulphate and related soils, the formation of sulphuric acid (pH as low as 2) and the activity of sulphate bacteria can cause deterioration of products based on PVC and nylon; in 'organic soils', depending on the nature of the decomposing matter and whether conditions are aerobic or anaerobic, micro-organisms can cause deterioration of plastics made of polyamide, polyester, plasticised PVC, polystyrene and others that support microbial growth (there can also be a solvent action); and in salt-affected soils, dominated by alkali and alkaline earth compounds, plastics can be degraded by chemical corrosion or mechanical stress.

The corrosiveness of soil to a wide range of metals and to certain other materials has been reviewed by King (ref. 5.45). Several attempts have been made to relate bulk properties of soils to their aggressiveness to buried metals (Table 5.19). Important independent factors are moisture content, salt content, hydrogen uptake, soluble iron content, pH, presence of organic matter and availability of oxygen.

In general, soils in order of aggressiveness are as follows

- o   gravelly soils (least aggressive)
- o   sandy soils
- o   silt soils (loam)
- o   clays
- o   peat and organic soils
- o   made-ground containing cinder (most aggressive).

Calcium carbonate, if present, will reduce corrosion rates. The least corrosive soils will tend to have high resistivity, alkaline pH, and low sulphate and chloride content, and will tend to contain little organic matter.

Table 5.19. Aggressiveness of soils (from King (ref. 5.45))

Aggressiveness	Resistivity: ohm/cm	Redox potential (corrected to pH 7): mV
Very corrosive	< 700	< 100
Corrosive	700–2000	100–200
Moderately corrosive	2000–5000	> 400
Mildly or non-corrosive	> 5000	> 430 if clay soil

Radioactivity

Radioactivity requires specialist assessment. Advice and guidance is available from Her Majesty's Pollution Inspectorate at the Department of the Environment and from the National Radiological Protection Board (NRPB). Increased worldwide concern for the hazards arising from the presence of radon in homes has led to assessment programmes and to research (e.g. between BRE and NRPB) into ways of mitigating any potential problems (refs 5.38, 5.39).

Although the entry of radioactive gases into buildings appears to be the principal hazard (see section above on radon), regard must also be paid to more specific exposure. For example, one source is the luminous paint on vehicle and aircraft instruments (from, for example, World War II). These, and certain other artefacts, such as minefield markers, are attractive items that may be collected and handled by both children and adults.

Biological contamination

The assessment of biological contamination is a specialist task. However, the non-specialist should appreciate that certain potentially harmful micro-organisms (e.g. tetanus) are ubiquitous. As with other forms of contamination, it is not only the presence that matters, but also the concentration. Assessment of biological hazards must begin during the preliminary investigation (i.e. development of site history etc.). The main potential hazard is infection by micro-organisms. Thus areas that have received medical wastes, sewage or similar liquids, or been used for the processing of animals and by-products (abattoirs, tanneries, rendering plants) should be viewed with caution. Land believed to contain anthrax should not be disturbed.

Geotechnical and other assessment

The geotechnical assessment will generally be made against existing standards or using engineering practices that permit the estimation of effects, as in the case of tolerable settlement of buildings. If there appear to be no difficulties due to contamination, then it will usually be possible to adopt a design solution that in engineering terms (there may be interactions with contamination that limit the design options) will bring settlement, for example, within acceptable limits.

Appraisal of 'made ground'

When a building is to be located on 'made ground', the appraisal is generally concerned with the ability of the fill to support the imposed loads without excessive movement. This requires an assessment of probable future settlement of the fill and its likely effect on structures, services and the like, and the feasibilitiy of combating the effect of settlement by remedial treatment of the ground and by design options.

The potential settlement which the building may undergo during its lifetime is predicted and then assessed against criteria which have been established by observation of actual building performance under distortion. In practice, this requires much judgement and experience. Because the behaviour of fill is not, in general, amenable to quantification of settlement by normal soil mechanics theory, which even in the case of natural soils may only provide figures with an accuracy of $\pm 50\%$, the prediction of settlement of a fill has a high margin of uncertainty and even an experienced geotechnical engineer can only be expected to derive an assessment of settlement potential which at best will indicate the order of overall movement which might be expected.

Overall or total settlement in itself is not a danger to buildings as it does not cause distortion. The problem is really differential movement. Although limiting distortions for various types of damage in buildings have been suggested (ref. 5.2), based on differential movements, this information is not really of practical use because of the inherent heterogeneity of fill and the difficulties of predicting even total settlement.

Recent work has been directed towards a broader approach derived from observations of fill performance. As stated above, the basic criterion is whether the fill is capable of sustaining the superimposed structural load without unacceptable movement. The appraisal must determine whether the fill satisfies this essential requirement and, if not, whether remedial treatment to improve its engineering properties is feasible. In other words, the fill will fall into one of three grades according to the feasibility of remedial treatment

  o   grade I   treatment unneccessary
  o   grade II   treatment advisable
  o   grade III   treatment of limited efficacy and possibly not economic-
                   ally feasible.

Most made ground falls into grades II or III. The only fills generally likely to classify as grade I are probably recent opencast backfills which have been deposited with due compaction of the uppermost 15 m, and other rare cases where materials have been placed and compacted in a controlled manner. Allocation of a fill to grade III is tantamount to abandoning a building project or (if applicable) delaying execution until 'collapse' settlement is complete.

Given their extreme heterogeneity and the fact that their discrete components are frequently large, fills are rarely amenable to analysis from results of small-scale laboratory tests. However, large-scale field trials carried out by various workers over the past three decades have provided sufficient data to establish at least a qualitative relation between the following essential parameters

  o   feasibility of remedial treatment
  o   predicted settlement under building load
  o   identifiable characteristics of fill.

The feasibility, or otherwise, of remedial measures depends largely on the magnitude of the settlement likely to be suffered by the untreated fill under the imposed structural load. The classification of fills can thus be expanded (after Charles and Burland (ref. 5.46)) as follows

o grade I: very small settlements — vertical compression nowhere more than 0·5%
o grade II: significant settlements — vertical compression 0·5–2·0%
o grade III: very large settlements — vertical compression estimated to exceed 2·0%.

Grade I is typical of a granular fill placed under controlled conditions with adequate compaction. Such fill forms good foundation material; treatment is normally unnecessary and there should be few problems.

Grade II is typified by granular fill, placed without compaction, with but little organic content and already in place for some years. Ground improvement treatment is desirable to convert the fill to a grade I material. Failing that, careful attention is required in design of adequate foundations.

Grade III is typical of recently placed domestic refuse with high organic content liable to decay and decomposition, or fine-grained materials transported in suspension and discharged into lagoons to form highly compressible, cohesive fill, liable to liquefaction. This grade also includes all fills (opencast backfills and the like) that are liable to, and have not yet undergone, collapse settlement. Problems with settlement will be very severe, ground improvement techniques will be limited in what they can achieve, and the site may be prohibitively expensive to develop.

The principal advantages of this approach are firstly that appraisal can be carried out based on an assessment of total settlement, and secondly that a preliminary appraisal can be made on the basis of the observed characteristics of the fill material.

It should, however, be noted that the classification is not universally applicable and should be used with caution in certain cases, such as where the fill is very deep or of varying thickness (e.g. at quarry edges), and where structures are founded below the fill mass.

Factors affecting appraisal

Important features of made ground that must be identified before an adequate appraisal can be made include

o age of fill
o depth of fill
o nature and quantity of fill
o particle size distribution
o state of compaction
o extent of fill site
o water table
o nature of underlying ground.

These all affect the rate and extent of settlement. They thus have an influence on the classification of the fill site, and the design of remedial measures and of foundations.

The age of the fill is of major importance because of the potential dominance of self-weight settlement in the total settlement to be expected. If the age of the fill can be determined from the initial assessment and investigation work, then the self-weight element of predicted settlement can be assessed. Self-weight settlement is approximately proportional to the logarithm of time for all types of fill and a considerable proportion of such settlement therefore occurs in the early years of the life of the fill. Consequently the difference between, say, 2 years and 5 years is significant.

Age is also significant in the appraisal of domestic-refuse fills. The gradual increase in the putrescible content of domestic wastes since the early 1950s corresponds to increased gassing and combustibility hazards, and inferior density and engineering properties in the younger domestic fill sites. Settlement of younger fills results from a combination of normal 'creep' settlement and the effects of decay. Furthermore, uncontrolled recent fills with abundant putrescible content are scarcely amenable to densification by compaction techniques.

With older fills there is more probability that biodegradation will have been completed and that the self-weight creep will have diminished to acceptable proportions. However, careful appraisal is necessary before any decision is made to build on domestic-waste landfill less than about 30 years old. Such fills will almost certainly require extensive remedial treatment (assuming such treatment is economically feasible) or special design measures, or both.

Depth of fill is important as it controls the amount of overall settlement to be expected in a given fill. Fills may be approximately designated according to their depth, up to 4 m being considered shallow, 5–15 m being considered medium and over 15 m being considered deep.

Deeper waste fills containing refuse are more likely to be varied in composition, and to take longer to reach a stable density under natural compaction and to cease gas generation. Deeper fills of all types suffer greater overall settlement. This may be acceptable provided that the movement is uniform, but attention must always be paid to the possibility of differential movement.

In shallow fills, superimposed structural loads exert a significant vertical stress throughout the depth of the fill. With increasing depth of fill the influence of superimposed loadings diminishes, and in deep fills the self-weight creep of the fill mass becomes the more important. Both medium and deep fills may be subject to serious effects from collapse upon inundation.

Depth also affects the cost and choice of remedial measures and design. In deep fills the costs of all ground improvement treatments will be closely related to the depth to which the fill is to be treated.

A proper understanding of the nature and type of fill, together with information on particle size distribution, is important for the qualitative assessment of a fill. If it can be established that a fill does not contain organic or potentially biodegradable materials, an important element of uncertainty regarding prediction of settlement is eliminated.

Where there are natural soils in fill they should be classified as either fine or coarse in accordance with BS 5930 (ref. 5.47) as this defines their behaviour. Coarse materials may be densified by compaction whereas fine materials rely upon consolidation. It is important to realise, however, that the behaviour of fill consisting of lumps of fine material in a partially saturated state is similar to that of coarse materials.

The degree of compaction is another important factor in the assessment of fill behaviour. Good compaction can reduce the self-weight settlement potential to 25–50% of that of the same fill in an uncompacted state. The majority of fill materials encountered will have been placed at low density, usually by high tipping, and with no compaction; end-tipped into water; or left to settle out from suspension in a lagoon. Such materials have poor engineering properties and high settlement potential.

A knowledge of the extent of a filled site is vital, as the appraisal of differential settlement potential requires knowledge of the changing depths of the fill, and the location and slopes of the fill site boundaries. Decisions on remedial measures require knowledge of the volume of the fill, especially quantities to be removed.

Detailed knowledge of the position of the water table and its potential fluctuations or permanent rise are critical to the assessment of the 'collapse' potential of a fill.

Prediction of settlement

The vertical compression to be considered for appraisal in the classification of the fill is the total movement to be suffered by the building supported on the fill, comprising normally

- o   residual self-weight compression (creep) of unloaded fill
- o   'primary compression' of fill under structural load
- o   additional 'creep' due to structural loading
- o   settlement of underlying strata.

If applicable, 'collapse' settlement must also be included.

The estimation of settlement of the underlying strata is carried out by conventional techniques. It is very important to know the properties of the strata. The ability of the underlying soils to carry the loads imposed by and through the fill must be demonstrated.

Prediction of self-weight settlement

There are three approaches to the assessment of consolidation settlement due to the self-weight of fill

- o   estimation from monitoring results
- o   estimation from fill characteristics
- o   estimation from pseudo-theoretical.methods.

Given the approximately linear relation of the settlement against log time, the monitoring of ground levels over an extended period (at least 3 months, and preferably 6 months) may be extrapolated to predict the total consolidation of a free unloaded fill settling under its own weight over the potential life of a structure (say 50 years). This method will generally give a slight overestimate as in practice the relation tends to weaken with time.

The second approach is to characterise the fill material to estimate from known experience of similar materials the total expected settlement

Table 5.20. Self-weight settlement potential of fill materials (ref. 5.2)

Material	Potential self-weight settlement: % depth of fill
Well compacted and well graded sand and gravel	0·5
Well compacted shale, chalk and rock fills	0·5
Medium-compacted rockfill	1·0
Well compacted clay	0·5
Lightly compacted clay and chalk	1·5
Lightly compacted clay placed in deep layers	1·0–2·0
Nominally compacted opencast backfill	1·2
Uncompacted sand	3·5
Poorly compacted chalk	1·0
Uncompacted (pumped) clay fill	12·0
Well compacted mixed refuse	30·0
Well controlled domestic refuse placed in layers and well compacted	10·0
Opencast backfill compacted by scrapers	0·6–0·8

(Table 5.20). To estimate the potential self-weight settlement remaining from the time of appraisal requires knowledge of the age of the fill. It is now considered prudent (ref. 5.2) to assume that self-weight settlement occurs in 10 years, and to use curves based on this period to predict self-weight settlement potential for all fills devoid of biodegradable material where adequate compaction is not confirmed. Although figures are quoted for refuse fill, the extreme heterogeneity of such material dictates that they should not be used except in a broad qualitative manner. Refuse fills are known to have taken 30 years or more to stabilise.

A theoretical approach has been suggested following work carried out at BRE (ref. 5.48). Considerable judgement, however, is required in the application of theoretical methods and in the selection of suitable values for the parameters. The results can only be regarded as indicative, but they can be used in the classification of a given fill (refs 5.2, 5.48).

For unsaturated inert fill, prediction of the long term self-weight creep settlement involves the use of a parameter α, defined as the percentage vertical creep in a thickness H of fill ($100\Delta H/H$) occurring during one log cycle of time (e.g. between one year and ten years after the placing of the

Table 5.21. *Creep settlement rate parameter* α *(from BRE digest 274 (ref. 5.48))*

Fill type	Typical value of α
Well compacted sandstone rockfill	0·2%
Uncompacted opencast-mining backfill	0·5 – 1%
Domestic refuse	2 – 10%

fill). Typical values of α are given in Table 5.21. Any given value of the α parameter is valid only so long as the conditions within the fill (effective stress, moisture content etc.) remain constant. Further, the magnitude of α can depend on the depth of the deposit and the nature and compaction of the fill material. Given α and the age of the fill, the potential self-weight settlement expected during the life of a structure can be estimated. Values are available for only a very limited range of materials, and as can be seen from Table 5.21 they show wide ranges. This method should be used in conjunction with the other methods outlined above.

Prediction of settlement under load

For natural soil and rock fills of sufficient age for the self-weight element of the settlement to be negligible, settlement resulting from imposed loading can be assessed from a knowledge of the material by consolidation theory in the conventional manner.

In other cases two approaches are available

o estimation from load tests
o estimation from pseudo-theoretical methods.

The 'primary compression' under a building and the subsequent loaded 'creep' can be extrapolated from an appropriate loading test. For the correct simulation of soil stressing, however, the test load must be comparable in dimensions and weight to the definitive structural loading. Such a requirement can only be satisfied in practice for shallow fills (up to about 4 m deep) where narrow strip footings exert a significant vertical stress down to about 2·5–3·5 m. A simple load test has been described (ref. 5.46) for shallow fills using a building waste skip, of bearing and loading similar to that of a strip footing. Such footings, with independent floor slabs, are suitable for light industrial buildings or warehouses of large extent.

For deep fills with massive raft foundations it would obviously be impracticable to monitor a test load of comparable size. Generally, however, the settlements of deep fills are more influenced by the residual self-weight creep of the fill mass than by imposed loads. Projected monitoring of self-weight movements should, therefore, be sufficient for the classification of a deep fill, in cases of light-development loading.

A theoretical method for computing likely settlement of fills under loading has resulted again from work carried out at BRE (ref. 5.48). As in the case of self-weight settlement, the selection of parameters requires considerable judgement and the results must be considered as indicative rather than definitive.

The long term creep is generally the more serious problem affecting the structure. BRE suggests (ref. 5.48) that its prediction can be made using the parameter α, as in Table 5.21, with the proviso that day 0 now corresponds to the application of the load.

In the special case of domestic refuse the parameter in Table 5.21 is not applicable. BRE suggests that a value of 1% is appropriate to the loaded case.

Collapse settlement

The possibility of a future collapse settlement would be a sufficient deterrent to rule out a fill site for any type of building construction which depended directly on the supporting capacity of the fill itself. As its name implies, collapse movement upon inundation is sudden and large. It may amount to 2–6% of the total inundated depth (i.e. sufficient to classify it as an untreatable grade III fill). Even piling down to good ground may be at risk from overstressing due to downdrag in the event of subsequent collapse.

In general, the quantification of collapse settlement is neither possible nor warranted, as its mere possibility would preclude development. It is, however, not a problem with adequately compacted materials, particularly if they are granular in nature. The poorer the fill and state of compaction the greater the collapse movement to be expected under inundation.

A rising water table is the normal cause of collapse, and particularly affects opencast workings and pits, which are usually dewatered during excavation and filling. Once operations cease, the water-table should return to its earlier level within a year.

On larger sites, however, with deep pumping maintained locally, isolated areas of the backfill may remain sensitive for several years. Collapse due to inundation from the surface is less common, but must always be considered.

The economic solution for a fill liable to collapse is to delay construction until the collapse can be verified as having taken place. If there is any tendency for the water-table to rise, it should be allowed to reach its highest predictable level well in advance of any building work. The suitability of the fill can then be judged exclusively on the residual creep and primary compression likely to be produced by the proposed building. These are likely to be small in comparison with the potential collapse movement.

Reliable techniques to forestall the eventuality of collapse do not exist. Attempts to accelerate collapse by artificial inundation of opencast fills from the surface have proved singularly unsuccessful (ref. 5.49). Ideally, long term monitoring of ground and water-table levels is required before a reliable estimate of the likelihood of future collapse can be made. Failing this, it is at least essential to be sure that the water-table is currently standing at the highest probable level before any building work is contemplated. Such assessment demands a detailed study of the local hydrology and hydrogeology by appropriate specialists.

Differential settlement

As stated above, it is not possible to predict settlement to such an accuracy as to permit direct evaluation of differential settlement. Recourse should therefore be made to the generally accepted rule based on observation of structural behaviour that differential movement will not exceed 75% of average total settlement. Thus, once predictions of potential settlement have been made, the likely order of differential movement can be assessed.

The foregoing covers the effects of local variations in fill quality and condition but there are particular situations where the dangers of differential movement are permanent and preclude development. These are

o   abrupt changes of fill depth
o   steeply sloping surface of natural ground in contact with fill.

The dangers effectively preclude the siting of structures above such features. Thus the edges of old pits, quarries and mines, and the high walls of open pit mines should be avoided in the siting of buildings.

Expansive fills

It is important to recognise that some fills, rather than settling, may expand. These may be of natural origin (refs 5.50, 5.51) or man-made. By far the greatest problems have been encountered with steelmaking slags and old 'banked' slags. There can be a considerable time delay between placement of the slags and occurrence of expansion. Slags should never be used as fill or hardcore without proper characterisation and specialist assessment of their expansive properties (ref. 5.52). Attempts to overcome the expansion problems by re-implacing the slag in a controlled manner have been unsuccessful.

Options available

Potential settlement of grade I fill of shallow and medium depth will, by definition, permit development using 'normal foundations' as for green field sites. On the deeper fills, however, foundations must be specially designed to secure the building against settlement damage.

If the fill is classified as grade II, the potential settlements will be such as to require some measures to be taken. It will be necessary to adopt remedial measures (i.e. to remove the problem), to treat the ground to achieve compatibility between the state of the fill and the end use, or to adopt a design solution (e.g. special foundations, piling).

Physical removal is usually not technically or economically attractive for fills more than about 3 m in depth. The choice of improvement of the fill by ground treatment to upgrade it to, or near to, a grade I condition, or of piles, will be governed by site-specific factors. If ground improvement is chosen it is likely that it will also be necessary to plan for dealing with any latent problems remaining after treatment.

For shallow fills, remedial measures involving earthmoving are probably the most economic; piling and/or compaction methods are not usually competitive owing to the relatively high mobilisation costs. For medium depth fills, piling may generally be a competitive solution for all types of building. In deep fills, piling is only likely to be competitive for high-rise structures, owing to the high cost of long piles compared with the value of a simple low-rise structure.

For high-rise structures (over six storeys), large-span portals, cranes, heavy machines, silos and process plants, the improvement potential of a fill is unlikely to be sufficient to permit direct founding on the fill. Logical solutions are piling or, in medium depth or shallow fills, removal and replacement with gravel, broken stone etc. In contrast, ground improvement should be advantageous for low-rise buildings on rafts, lightly loaded framed warehouses and the like in medium or deep fills.

If the fill is classified as grade III, then the technical difficulties will be large and may render development uneconomic.

References

5.1. Interdepartmental Committee on the Redevelopment of Contaminated Land. *Guidance on the assessment and redevelopment of contaminated land.* Department of the Environment, Central Directorate on Environmental Protection, London, 1987, 2nd edn, ICRCL 59/83.
5.2. Goodger H.K. and Leach B.A. *Building on derelict land.* Construction Industry Research and Information Association, London 1990.
5.3. Roscoe G.H. and Driscoll R. *A review of routine foundation design practice.* Building Research Establishment, Garston, 1987.
5.4. Uff J.F. and Clayton C.R.I. *Recommendations for the procurement of ground investigation.* Construction Industry Research and Information Association, London, 1987, CIRIA special publication 45.
5.5 British Standards Institution. *Draft for development: code of practice for the identification of potentially contaminated land and its investigation.* BSI, London, 1988, DD 175.
5.6. Lord D. Appropriate site investigations. *Reclaiming contaminated land* (ed. Cairney T.C.). Blackie, Glasgow, 1987, 62–113.
5.7. Davies B.E. *Science of the Total Environment,* 1978, **9**, 243–262.
5.8. Interdepartmental Committee on the Redevelopment of Contaminated Land. *Notes on the redevelopment of landfill sites.* Department of the Environment, Central Directorate on Environmental Protection, London, 1988, 7th edn, ICRCL 17/78.
5.9. Interdepartmental Committee on the Redevelopment of Contaminated Land. *Notes on the redevelopment of gasworks sites.* Department of the Environment, Central Directorate on Environmental Protection, London, 1986, 5th edn, ICRCL 18/79.
5.10. Interdepartmental Committee on the Redevelopment of Contaminated Land. *Notes on the redevelopment of sewage works and farms.* Department of the Environment, Central Directorate on Environmental Protection, London, 1983, 2nd edn, ICRCL 23/79.
5.11. Interdepartmental Committee on the Redevelopment of Contaminated Land. *Notes on the redevelopment of scrapyards and similar sites.* Department of the Environment, Central Directorate on Environmental Protection, London, 1983, 2nd edn, ICRCL 42/80.
5.12. Bridges E.M. *Surveying derelict land.* Clarendon Press, Oxford, 1987.
5.13. Montgomery R.E. *et al.* Rapid on-site methods of analysis. *Contaminated*

land: reclamation and treatment (ed. Smith M.A.). Plenum, London and New York, 1985.

5.14. Building Research Establishment. *Concrete in sulphate-bearing soils and groundwaters*. HMSO, London, 1981, BRE digest 250.

5.15. Smith M.A. and Ellis A.C. An investigation into methods used to assess gas works sites for reclamation. *Reclamation and Revegetation Research*, 1986, **4**, 183–209.

5.16. Thornton I. Background levels of heavy metals in soils. *Proc. Conf. Reclamation of Contaminated Land, Eastbourne, 1979*. Society of Chemical Industry, London, 1980, C5/1–12.

5.17. Berrow M.L. and Burridge J.C. In: *Inorganic pollution and agriculture*. HMSO, London, 1980, Ministry of Agriculture Fisheries and Food reference book 326, 159–183.

5.18. Archer F.C. In: *Inorganic pollution and agriculture*. HMSO, London, 1980, Ministry of Agriculture Fisheries and Food reference book 326, 184–190.

5.19. Thornton I. and Webb J.S. Regional distribution of trace element problems in Great Britain. *Applied soil trace elements* (ed. Davies B.E.). Wiley, Chichester, 1980, 381–440.

5.20. Davies B.E. and White H.M. Cadmium and lead contamination in soils and vegetables in relation to historic base metal mining. *Proc. Conf. Reclamation of Contaminated Land, Eastbourne, 1979*. Society of Chemical Industry, London, 1980, C8/1–8.

5.21. Parry G.D.R. *et al. Environmental Pollution* (B), 1981, **2**, No. 1, 97–107.

5.22. Joint Unit for Research on the Urban Environment. *State of the West Midlands environment*. JURUE, University of Aston, Birmingham, 1981.

5.23. Fleming G. *et al. Feasibility study on the use of dredged material from the Clyde estuary for land renewal*. University of Strathclyde, Glasgow, 1988.

5.24. Alford-Stevens A.L. Analysing PCBs. *Environmental Science and Technology*, 1986, **20**, No. 12, 1194–1199.

5.25. Creaser C. (School of Chemical Sciences, University of East Anglia). Personal communication.

5.26. Shimell P. PCBs are everywhere — and dioxins may be too. *Surveyor*, 1987, 12 Mar., 10–11.

5.27. Badsha K. and Eduljee G. PCB in the UK environment — a preliminary survey. *Chemosphere*, 1986, **15**, No. 2, 211–215.

5.28. Jones K.C. Polynuclear aromatic hydrocarbons in the soil system: long-term changes, behaviour and current levels in the UK. *Contaminated soil '88* (eds Wolf K. *et al.*). Kluwer Academic Publishers, Dordrecht, 1988, 351–358.

5.29. Heeps K.D. Reclamation of a disused sewage works. *Public Health Engineer*, 1982, **10**, No. 4, 213–214 and 218.

5.30. Harrison W.H. Durability of concrete in acidic soils and waters. *Concrete*, 1987, Feb., 18–24.

5.31. Moen J.E.T. *et al.* Soil protection and remedial actions: criteria for decision making and standardisation of requirements. *Contaminated soil* (ed. Assink J.W. and van den Brink W.J.). Martinus Nijhoff, Dordrecht, 1986, 441–448.

5.32. Lewis W.K. *et al.* Contamination of groundwater resources and impact on potable supplies. *1987–88 handbook of the Institution of Water and Environmental Management*. IWEM, London, 1988, 39–47.

5.33. Dai-xing Z. and Ding-nan L. Chronic thallium poisoning in a rural area of Guizhou Province, China. *Journal of Environmental Health*, 1985, **48**, No. 1, 14–18.

5.34. Haines R.C. *Report of soil analysis undertaken on JURUE's state of the environment soils*. Joint Unit for Research on the Urban Environment, University of Aston, Birmingham, 1982, report to the Department of the Environment.

5.35. Deegen J. Looking back at Love Canal. *Environmental Science and Technology*, 1987, **21**, No. 4, 328–331; and 1987, **21**, No. 5, 421–426.

5.36. Building Research Establishment. *Ventilation requirements*. HMSO, London, 1981, BRE digest 206.

5.37. Crowhurst D. and Beever P. *Fire and explosion hazards associated with the redevelopment of contaminated land*. Building Research Establishment, Garston, 1987, IP2/87.

5.38. Ridout G. Radon — the seeping sickness. *Building*, 1988, 22 Apr., 60–61.

5.39. O'Riordan M.C. *et al. Human exposure to radon decay products inside dwellings in the United Kingdom*. National Radiological Protection Board, Didcot, 1983.

5.40. Palmer K.N. Fire and explosion hazards with contaminated land. *Proc. Conf. Reclamation Contaminated Land, Eastbourne, 1979*. Society of Chemical Industry, London, 1980.

5.41. Beever P.F. Assessment of fire hazard in contaminated land. *Contaminated soil* (eds Assink J.W. and van den Brink W.J.). Martinus Nijhoff, Dordrecht, 1986, 515–522.

5.42. Nixon P.J. *et al.* Durability and protection of building materials in contaminated soils. *Proc. Conf. Reclamation Contaminated Land, Eastbourne, 1979*. Society of Chemical Industry, London, 1980, E4/1–10.

5.43. Barry D.L. *Material durability in aggressive ground*. Construction Industry Research and Information Association, London, 1983, report 98.

5.44. Rankilor P.R. *Membranes in ground engineering*. Wiley, Chichester, 1981.

5.45. King R.A. *A review of soil corrosiveness with particular reference to reinforced earth*. Transport and Road Research Laboratory, Crowthorne, 1977, supplementary report 316.

5.46. Charles J.A. and Burland J.B. Geotechnical considerations in the design of foundations for buildings on deep deposits of waste materials. *Structural Engineer*, 1982, **60A**, No. 1, 8–14.

5.47. British Standards Institution. *Code of practice for site investigations*. BSI, London, 1981, BS 5930.

5.48. Building Research Establishment. *Fill: classification and load carrying characteristics*. BRE, Garston, 1983, BRE digest 274.

5.49. Charles J.A. *et al.* Treatment and subsequent performance of cohesive fill left by opencast ironstone mining at Snatchill experimental housing site, Corby. *Clay fills*. Institution of Civil Engineers, London, 1979, 63–72.

5.50. Nixon P.J. Floor heave in buildings due to the use of pyritic shale as fill material. *Chemistry and Industry*, 1978, **4**, Mar., 160–164.

5.51. Wilson E.J. Pyritic shale in the Lower Lias at Barry, Glamorgan. *Quarterly Journal of Engineering Geology*, 1987, **20**, 251–253.

5.52. Smith M.A. Expansive slags. *Building Technical File*, 1987, No. 17, 29–32.

6 Options available for problem-solving

ANDREW LORD, MA(Cantab), PhD, CEng, MICE, AFPWI
Director, Ove Arup & Partners

The success of any development relies on close co-operation between the developer, the architect, the engineer and the quantity surveyor — success being the fulfilment of the developer's requirements at an economical cost. In the case of redevelopment of derelict land the need for close co-operation is paramount, with the engineer assuming an even more important role than normally (including the essential task of co-ordination) if an economical scheme is to be achieved.

Although almost any derelict land could be redeveloped for almost any purpose at a price, the cost of such development would probably be prohibitive in comparison with that for a green field site, for which very few constraints would exist. (However, it is likely that the land cost for a green field site would be greater than that for derelict land.) Consequently it is essential in any redevelopment of derelict land to maximise and harness its strengths as far as is possible (e.g. in docklands to retain water features as part of the scheme), and to minimise and overcome its weaknesses (for example, pollution).

The hazards posed by derelict land take a wide variety of forms. Basically they can be grouped under the headings

o *chemical contamination of soil and groundwater*: noxious chemicals arising from previous industrial use of site (e.g. gasworks) or waste effluent tipping; organic matter derived principally from landfill, whose organic decay can lead to the generation of methane
o *infrastructure of former industries*: massive old foundation or underground structures (e.g. gasholders and retorts); massive old walls (e.g. quay walls in docklands); 'filled' ground which is extensive both vertically and laterally (also applicable to landfill sites); large areas of open water (e.g. docks and former gravel pits)
o *areas of surface or subsurface mining and associated spoil tips*: stability; pollution.

These different hazards require differing techniques to overcome the problems posed; these are discussed subsequently in the chapter.

As mentioned previously, the end use of derelict land has a profound influence on the cost of redevelopment. Nevertheless, on any such site, the question that must first be asked is, 'Is the site contaminated?' If the answer is no, then the site and the ground conditions can be assessed on a strict geotechnical basis; that is, in terms of the provision of adequate foundations if structures are envisaged, and ensuring the stability of civil engineering works, for example against subsidence of fill or mine workings. Various techniques for dealing with these problems of 'ground improvement' are discussed later in this chapter.

If the site is found to be contaminated to an extent that gives cause for concern (as identified in previous chapters), taking appropriate action to reduce or overcome the problem becomes the principal engineering task. Nevertheless, in undertaking this task it is essential to bear in mind the possible foundation options that are available; this is necessary to ensure compatibility between the ground treatment — both chemically (i.e. rendering innocuous) and from a geotechnical standpoint (e.g. ground improvement) — and the proposed structure or end use of the site.

Guidance available and case histories

Available reclamation methods are discussed by Smith (ref. 6.1, chapter 5), but only for problems of chemical contamination, and that largely on a theoretical basis — only one or two case histories are quoted. The proceedings of both the first and second international conference on contaminated soil (refs 6.2 and 6.3) present a few case histories, but many of these concern laboratory or small-scale field trials of different methods of soil decontamination. The most abundant source of case histories is the proceedings of the conference on building on marginal and derelict land (ref. 6.4).

Knowledge of contaminants

For any chemically contaminated site it is important to know what the principal contaminants are and how they might affect the proposed development; also, whether the contaminants are present in solid, liquid or gaseous phases, or in combination, for each requires different methods of treatment. Even if leachates are not present, it should be remembered that they can be generated by the ingress of rainwater or the passage of groundwater through the contaminated solids, as this can result in contamination with soluble chemicals.

Gaseous contaminants pose similar problems to leachates insofar as they can migrate freely both vertically and laterally; however, the generation of gases on contaminated sites, in particular methane generated from landfill sites and the increased public awareness of its explosive properties, warrants separate consideration being given to means of dealing with gases.

Methods of treating contaminated sites

Smith (ref. 6.1) has identified various options for the treatment of contaminated land. Basically these are

A: excavate the material
B: leave in situ.

Excavated material can be

A.1:   deposited elsewhere on site in a controlled environment (e.g. as at Stockley Park (ref. 6.5))

A.2:   deposited off-site, generally at licensed tips

A.3:   cleaned up on site or off site, or the contamination stabilised.

If the material is left in situ, the following options are possible

B.1:   to do nothing other than prevent access to the site and deal with any immediate environmental problems (e.g. remove any deposits of asbestos, control surface run-off)

B.2:   to contain or isolate the site by superimposing cover and providing underground barriers as necessary to prevent contamination migration

B.3:   to clean up the soil or stabilise the contaminants in situ; this could include biological treatment.

The most common reaction to the discovery of contamination on a site is that the contaminated material should be removed from site to a licensed tip (case A.2). However, Tables 6.1 and 6.2, taken from a summary by Lord (ref. 6.6) of papers relating to landfill and sites of former industries, show the actual ground treatment and end use of various landfill and chemical waste sites, and sites of former industries. It is evident from Table 6.1 that where it was originally intended the chemical waste should be excavated and removed from site (e.g. refs 6.10, 6.13, 6.14), subsequent reassessment led to its being left in place, as the cost and risks of removing the waste were found to be prohibitively high. Even at Stockley Park (ref. 6.5), where landfill was excavated to permit construction on clean fill, the landfill was reused on site for landscaping and for golf-course construction (case A.1).

Thus, in the UK, option A is not pursued as vigorously as might be expected, and instead there is a marked tendency to leave contamination in situ. Many environmentalists argue that this is simply burying the problem and leaving it for future generations. Certainly, if this approach is adopted, additional measures may be necessary to control groundwater movement, and to contain or treat leachate and contaminated groundwater. The following arguments support the case for leaving the contaminated material in situ.

o   The transport of hazardous wastes to a licensed tip increases the risk to communities through which vehicles pass.

o   Deposition on licensed tips is merely moving the problem elsewhere.

o   Knowledge is constantly growing as to how hazardous certain contaminants really are.

o   Advances in 'cleaning up' contaminants are likely to continue, and it is probably simpler to clean up a known contaminant than a lethal cocktail of contaminants at a licensed tip.

The pros and cons of excavation (cases A.1 and A.2), soil treatment (cases A.3 and B.3), and containment (case B.2) are discussed below, but no specific recommendations are given, since each site must be treated on its own merits.

Table 6.1. Landfill and chemical wastes (after Lord (ref. 6.6))

Type of fill or waste	Thickness: m	Ground treatment	End use
Municipal waste (ref. 6.7)	25	Dynamic compaction; 1·5 m cover	Bus station
Domestic and industrial waste (ref. 6.8)	8	Removal of 3½ m; dynamic compaction	M25 on 3 m embankment
Chemical works waste — alkaline (ref. 6.9)	11–15*	Footings on granular fill	Church
Industrial and chemical waste: liquors/leachate (ref. 6.10)	10	Leaving in place; raising road alignment; 1 m rock blanket	Trunk road
Household refuse (ref. 6.11)	–	Piles	Housing
Industrial and domestic waste (ref. 6.12)	12–17	Dynamic compaction	Road embankment

Domestic and industrial refuse and leachate (ref. 6.5)	12½	Removal from beneath buildings and reuse	Business park and golf course
Tar and chemical works (ref. 6.13)	6½	Up to 2·4 m removed; replaced by granular fill	Industrial units
Old gasworks (ref. 6.14)	5*	Minimum removed	Crown and county courts
Old gasworks (ref. 6.15)	4½	Some excavation; 1 m thick seal; piles	Solid waste transfer station
Industrial and domestic refuse (ref. 6.16)	9	Stone columns	Warehouse
Landfill (3 cases) (ref. 6.17)	4	Sealing layer	Housing
Industrial waste (ref. 6.18)	1½–4†	Excavation up to 1·4 m and replacement with capping	Site preparation only

* Plus underlying contaminated ground.
† Underlain by peat up to 5 m thick.

Table 6.2. Sites of former industries (after Lord (ref. 6.6))

Site	Ground treatment	End use
Queen's Dock, Glasgow — infilling (ref. 6.19)	Arisings; dynamic compaction	Scottish Exhibition Centre
London Docks — infilling (ref. 6.20)	Crushed arisings; dynamic compaction	Housing
Industrial basements — backfilling (ref. 6.21)	Dredged aggregate and crushed arisings (footings)	Housing
4 infilled docks; 3 former industrial sites; 1 colliery-discard site (ref. 6.17)	Dynamic compaction	Housing and light industrial use; car park
Dock, Barrow-in-Furness (ref. 6.22)	Vibro-compaction	Dockyard
2 docks; 3 steel/iron works; quarry (ref. 6.23)	Dynamic compaction	Refinery; factory; housing
Methil Docks (ref. 6.24)	Colliery discard; dynamic compaction and rolled fill	Industrial yard
Demolished housing (ref. 6.25)	Vibro-replacement	Housing
Iron works, brickworks and infilled brick quarry (ref. 6.26)	Vibro-replacement	Bus garage and workshops

Excavation

Despite the comments made above, excavation of contaminated material for deposition elsewhere and replacement with clean imported fill (Fig. 6.1) remains a viable option for dealing with contaminated sites. However, the cost of long-distance haulage can form a significant proportion of the cost. For example, in the rehabilitation of the Old Palace Gasworks site for the Norwich Crown and County Courts, Collins *et al.* (ref. 6.14) found that, as there were no hydrogeologically secure tips in Norfolk, solid contaminated materials would have had to be transported to a pit at Cambridge and contaminated slurries and liquids to Pitsea in Essex (a round trip of 350 km); hence other means were sought for dealing with the contaminated liquids, such as controlled discharge to sewers through treatment tanks.

At Stockley Park (ref. 6.5) it was necessary for commercial reasons to remove some $2.7 \times 10^6\,\mathrm{m}^3$ of landfill from beneath the proposed business park. As the removal of such large volumes of material by road to licensed tips would have been prohibitively expensive and would have caused unacceptable congestion on an already crowded road network, it was decided that all landfill except special waste should, if possible, be accommodated on the site. The material was used to construct the golf course.

To minimise the environmental impact of the M42 motorway to the south of Birmingham, the preferred route had to pass through a number of old landfill sites formed from both industrial and domestic waste. The vertical alignment of the motorway required the removal of considerable volumes of waste material. It was possible to re-deposit the domestic refuse on the area of the tip lying outside the motorway, but all the excavated industrial waste had to be disposed in licensed tips off site. The contractor obtained a licence for his own tip adjacent to the motorway some 3 km from the site. This greatly reduced disposal costs and as the tip was reached by travelling along the motorway route, the nuisance of carting wastes on public roads was avoided. Gabryliszyn (ref. 6.27) has described how the motorway was 'floated' across the tip material on a 2.5 m thick layer of natural material to minimise the volume of waste to be moved.

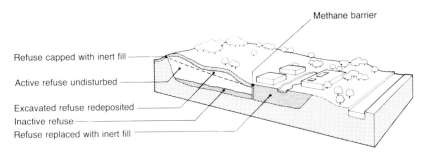

Refuse capped with inert fill

Active refuse undisturbed

Excavated refuse redeposited

Inactive refuse

Refuse replaced with inert fill

Methane barrier

Fig. 6.1. Excavation of contaminated material and replacement with clean imported fill

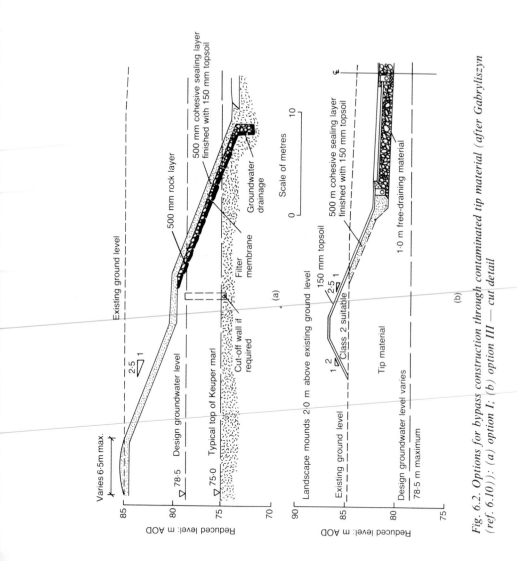

Fig. 6.2. Options for bypass construction through contaminated tip material (after Gabryliszyn (ref. 6.10)): (a) option I; (b) option III — cut detail

Gabryliszyn (ref. 6.10) has also compared and costed three options for the construction of a bypass through a landfill site composed of industrial and chemical wastes, liquors and leachate. Option I was to construct the cutting on the originally proposed vertical alignment and to accept the problems associated with both the tip material and the groundwater. Option II was to maintain the original proposed vertical alignment but to replace the cutting side slopes over their lower section with a retaining wall. Option III was to raise the vertical alignment of the road through the tip, in order both to minimise the volume of material to be excavated and to avoid the problems associated with the groundwater. Options I and III are illustrated in Fig. 6.2. The latter was eventually adopted since it was considered that the financial savings of £2·2 million outweighed the environmental disbenefits.

Despite the thoroughness of any chemical site invesigation, it is still highly likely that significant contamination 'hot-spots' will be encountered during excavation of landfill. (At the M42 motorway site described above, this took the form of 147 drums of cyanide compounds.) In such circumstances it is essential that a resident chemist be present on site to inspect the waste as it is excavated and to identify any materials requiring neutralisation and special disposal.

In addition to the foregoing problems of cost, Smith (ref. 6.1) has identified other complications

o   an indistinct edge to the area of contamination
o   previous movement of contamination to areas outside the site, including beneath neighbouring buildings
o   possible hydrogeological problems caused by excavation
o   difficulty finding suitable clean fill material
o   environmental problems: traffic movement, noise, atmospheric and surface water pollution, odour problems.

Also, it may be necessary to

o   underpin adjacent buildings
o   temporarily lower groundwater levels
o   collect, treat and dispose of contaminated water
o   monitor working environment and neighbourhood
o   take extensive health and safety measures to protect workers and neighbours.

Soil treatment by cleaning or by stabilising contaminants

The treatment of contaminated soil by cleaning or stabilising it in situ or after excavation has not been pursued in the UK to any great extent. However, considerable research is currently being undertaken in both the Netherlands and Germany to identify and improve such techniques. Enthusiasm for this form of treatment stems from a desire to remove the problem of contamination once and for all. In the case of a relatively small and low-lying country such as the Netherlands, there is an awareness of the absence of alternative disposal sites, and the need to prevent sterilisation of large tracts of contaminated land and pollution of the ground-water. In such circumstances it is perhaps fortunate that the principal soil type in the Netherlands is a fine sand, as opposed to the silty clays that predominate in the UK. The former lend themselves much more to the techniques of cleaning or stabilisation, since their considerably higher permeability permits the cleaning medium easier access to the contaminant.

In the first international conference on contaminated soil, held in 1985 (ref. 6.2), various remedial techniques were discussed. A comprehensive review of the treatment methods which are theoretically available has been provided by Rulkens *et al.* (ref. 6.28)

- o *physical*: solvent leaching, gravity separation, particle sizing, settling velocity, magnetic, flotation
- o *thermal*: direct heating, indirect heating, incineration, steam strip-ping
- o *chemical*: neutralisation, chemical reduction, hydrolysis, electrolysis, ozonation, photolysis
- o *microbial*
- o *stabilisation/solidification*: cement-based systems, polymer-based systems.

By the time of the second international conference on contaminated soil, in 1988 (ref. 6.3), small-scale pilot plants capable of operating on contaminated sites had been developed from laboratory research techniques for many of these treatment methods. Furthermore, Ebel and Weingran (ref. 6.29) discuss soil decontamination centres that have been set up to deal with contaminated industrial sites, principally by excavating the contaminated soil and then treating it. However, Haines (ref. 6.30) and Mischgofsky and Kabos (ref. 6.31) conclude that greater savings can be achieved if the contaminated soil can be treated with in situ methods as a result of large-scale research and development programmes. There are reviews of physico-chemical treatment methods (ref. 6.32), thermal and extraction soil treatment techniques (ref. 6.33), and biological soil treat-ment techniques (ref. 6.34), all in the Netherlands, and solidification/stabilisation in the USA (ref. 6.35). It would appear that although thermal treatment is often very successful at laboratory or pilot plant scale, the energy resources required for full-scale treatment are often prohibitive.

Biological soil treatment, which relies on microbial activity and which has occurred naturally for years in the decomposition of refuse and sewage, has been used successfully to clean clayey sands contaminated with a variety of oils, kerosene and aromatics (ref. 6.34). In addition the technique can be used to deal with other organic contaminants, including phenols, polychlorinated hydrocarbons, chlorinated hydrocarbons and dioxins. In predominantly clayey soils such as are found in the UK it is difficult to aerate the soil to permit degradation of the contaminants, but in fills which are essentially granular in nature, in situ biological treatment has been used successfully; for example, in the cleaning-up of disused gasworks sites at Blackburn and Doncaster.

Successful treatment of contaminated land by cleaning soil of its contaminant by a variety of techniques has still largely only been implemented in laboratory experiments or at pilot-plant scale.

Nevertheless, extensive research is continuing in various countries, notably the Netherlands, Germany and the USA, which may identify appropriate, cost-effective techniques in the future. Clearly more work is required before such techniques can be accepted as routine methods for treating contaminated land. It is recommended that reference is made to the technical press, particularly in the Netherlands and Germany, to assess the state of the art current at any time. The applicability of the techniques to soil conditions in the UK will also have to be assessed.

Containment

Treatment of contamination by containing or isolating the site by superimposing cover and/or providing underground barriers to prevent migration of contamination would appear to be one of the most commonly adopted techniques in the UK. In fact, the provision of a 'clean soil' cover to a contaminated site is often adopted as a 'minimum action' alternative to the 'do nothing' option of case B.1. On other occasions, the contaminant may surround the whole site — top, bottom and sides — but frequently only partial containment is carried out.

Childs (ref. 6.36) has reviewed the techniques available to construct horizontal and vertical barriers in situ. However, many of these techniques require the introduction of cement or chemical grouts into the ground, and the efficacy of their penetration, setting (or solidification) and durability in the presence of chemical contaminants is all too frequently inadequately known. Consequently the containment barrier is likely to leak slightly and there is a high risk of deterioration with time. Even a relatively inert material such as clay can react with contaminants so that its permeability to water is increased (refs 6.37–6.39). Furthermore, chemical grouts themselves can be toxic or degrade with time (ref. 6.40).

As with soil treatment by cleaning (preceding section), considerable research is being undertaken on encapsulation techniques. These are discussed in the proceedings of the second international conference on contaminated soil (ref. 6.3); contributions mainly relate to surface coverings and seal wall barriers, although Alyanak and Bihlmaier (ref. 6.41) consider the long-term behaviour of encapsulation materials. It is anticipated that continuing studies over the next few years will provide better information on the performance of different types of seal.

Horizontal subsurface barriers

Very frequently in the UK, contaminated sites are underlain by naturally occurring clayey strata of relatively low permeability. Even sites which are underlain by relatively weak jointed rock, such as Keuper marl or chalk (e.g. that described in ref. 6.14) possess a relatively impermeable layer beneath the contaminant, since the upper surface of the natural stratum has frequently weathered to a structureless mélange, thereby destroying the natural drainage path along the joints. For contaminated

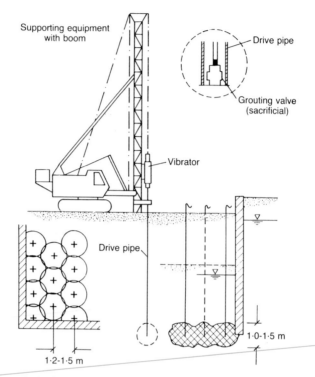

Fig. 6.3. Method of construction of horizontal membranes (after Tausch (ref. 6.42))

sites underlain by deposits such as sands and gravels or sandstone, naturally occurring barriers do not exist.

Childs (ref. 6.36) has identified three possible methods of forming horizontal barriers

- o   jet grouting
- o   chemical grouting
- o   claquage grouting.

Although jet grouting has been used to construct horizontal cement-grout layers, it can only be used effectively in fine-grained soils and cannot be guaranteed to give 100 % coverage, thus running the risk of leakage. Alternatively, a hollow-stem flight auger or drive pipe with sacrificial grouting valve (Fig. 6.3) can be used in coarser material. The auger or pipe is inserted to the required depth and, as it is withdrawn, grout is injected down the hollow stem emerging at the tip, thereby filling the hole created. Grout injection is stopped when the tip reaches the top of the proposed horizontal barrier. Thereafter insertions are repeated at centres about 70 % of the auger or drive pipe diameter. Although the method is relatively effective in creating a barrier, it is considered that frequent passages of the auger through overlying contaminants would tend to contaminate the grout and may interfere with its setting.

In claquage grouting and to a certain extent chemical grouting, it is very difficult to control placement of the grout, particularly in non-homogeneous soil; grout under pressure will always tend to flow into areas of weaker ground (ref. 6.43). Hence claquage grouting is unlikely to form a sufficiently uniform barrier capable of being impermeable. A wide range of chemical grouts exist which are appropriate for different soil conditions and different end uses (ref. 6.43). However, as noted previously, chemical grouts can themselves be toxic or degrade with time.

Vertical barriers

Childs (ref. 6.36) has identified and described various vertical barrier systems. Basically these can be divided into those involving little or no disturbance of the ground (e.g. driven steel sheet piles), and those in which material, possibly contaminated, is excavated or otherwise removed from the ground and replaced by an impermeable barrier.

The latter type of barrier can be

o   a trench dug by an excavator and backfilled with compacted clay, cement–bentonite slurry or a membrane (which may take the form of precast elements)
o   a diaphragm wall
o   a secant bored pile wall.

Alternatively, jet grouting or chemical grouting can be adopted, as in the case of horizontal subsurface barriers (preceding section), but may suffer from the problems mentioned.

The trench system is generally limited to a maximum practical depth of dig of 6–7 m if conventional bucket-type tracked excavators are used. Tracked excavators with clamshell buckets can be used to construct cut-off walls to about 13–14 m depth. Diaphragm wall rigs have satisfactorily excavated dam cut-off walls to more than 100 m depth. However, this form of construction requires particular care to ensure that adjacent elements do not deviate from each other sufficiently to cause leakage between the elements. Even at relatively shallow depths, deficiences in the integrity of the concrete forming the wall can lead to loss of watertightness. A recent notable example of this was leakage through the bored pile cofferdam around part of the new nuclear power station at Sizewell in Essex; difficulties were subsequently encountered in trying to form a seal by alternative techniques such as grouting (ref. 6.44).

Gordon et al. (ref. 6.5) give examples of a clay bund acting as a vertical barrier, and a cement–bentonite cut-off wall of 600 mm minimum width. The clay bund, which was formed around the perimeter of the business park at Stockley Park, was provided with a drain from which leachate could be pumped in order to prevent it entering the nearby canal (Fig. 6.8). Interestingly the cement–bentonite cut-off wall was constructed around the northern perimeter of the site to prevent southerly-flowing ground-water from entering the site and becoming contaminated. The cut-off wall

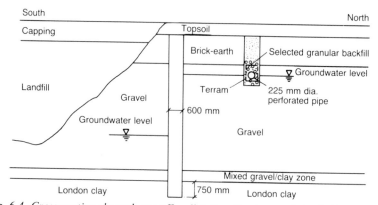

Fig. 6.4. Cross-section through cut-off wall (after Gordon et al. (ref. 6.5))

was 5–6 m deep and penetrated 750 mm into London clay (Fig. 6.4.). Trial panels, of the dimensions shown in Fig. 6.5, were constructed through landfill and gravel. Water was pumped from wells within the panel boxes, and drawdown on the inside and outside of the cement–bentonite walls was measured. These tests indicated that the cut-off wall had a permeability of about 10^{-8} m/s. A similar cut-off wall has been satisfactorily constructed between the southern edge of the tip described by Gabryliszyn (ref. 6.10) and the top of the adjacent A427 northern cutting slope, to prevent long term leachate flow into the cutting from the tip.

Nevertheless, knowledge of the long term behaviour and durability of cement–bentonite walls is very limited: practice is leading theory and understanding. Alyanak and Bihlmaier (ref. 6.41) have considered long term behaviour, and Muller-Kirchenbauer et al. (ref. 6.45) have tested a cement–bentonite wall on a hazardous waste dump. Smith (ref. 6.1) considers that with cement–bentonite mixtures seepage will occur primarily due to convection. Systems based on Portland cement will be vulnerable to attack by sulphates and acids, and the hydration reactions may be detrimentally affected by various organic substances (e.g. sugars, phenols) and alkali-soluble metals (e.g. zinc, lead, arsenic).

In selecting a barrier system the following factors require consideration

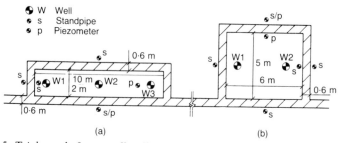

Fig. 6.5. Trial panels for cut-off wall tests (after Gordon et al. (ref. 6.5)): (a) gravel trial panel; (b) landfill trial panel

o   knowledge of the geology and hydrogeology of the site, including permeability of the various strata and depth to 'impermeable' stratum

o   degree of integrity required

o   proposed seal into low-permeability stratum or inserted horizontal barrier

o   resistance to corrosion and other forms of interaction with contaminants

o   costs.

Surface barriers

Since, as discussed earlier in this chapter (under 'Methods of treating contaminated sites'), excavation of all contaminated material present on a site is seldom pursued vigorously in the UK, the provision of a surface barrier is a frequent occurrence. In many instances this may only take the form of a 'clean soil' cover. Smith (ref. 6.1) has noted that a covering system must be designed and carefully installed if it is to fulfil the demanding functions (which are often conflicting in their solutions) of

o   sustaining vegetation

o   fulfilling an engineering role.

Clean soil cover. The principal objective of using clean soil cover is to improve the appearance of the contaminated site by an ability to support vegetation. At the same time, the soil cover will prevent erosion, dust blow and odours, and reduce fire hazards and vermin. The selection of an appropriate soil cover is complex. If methane is being generated, a good thickness of silty sand, rich in organic matter capable of oxidising the methane, is ideal, but seldom available in the UK (although common in the Netherlands); whereas control of water ingress into a contaminated site (and the ensuing risk of generating more leachate) requires a clay capping. Further details are given in refs 6.46 and 6.47, but the advice of an agronomist or topsoil consultant should be sought.

In most instances the inhibiting factors are cost and the shortage of topsoil. Various ways have been sought to overcome this problem: the Dutch have reduced the topsoil cover necessary on landfill sites by creating an 'intermediate zone', about 600 mm thick, between topsoil and landfill by rotovating organic silty sand into the top of the landfill; while at Stockley Park (ref. 6.5), sewage sludge cake was mixed with weathered London clay to provide a topsoil, checks having shown that the sludge cake was not contaminated with phytotoxic metals (copper, nickel and zinc) which would inhibit plant growth.

Cover for engineering purposes. The cover required for engineering purposes is such as to provide protection for any development constructed above the contaminants. In this role, it is required to control gas movement if appropriate (but see also the section below on 'Controls for preventing or regulating gas emissions from landfill'), and to prevent water ingress and upward moisture movement including leachate. There are no hard and fast rules for the cover, since the form and degree of contamina-

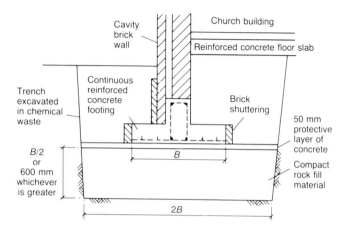

Fig. 6.6. Protection of footing against sulphate attack (after Thorburn and Buchanan (ref. 6.9))

tion, the presence of leachate, the degree of integrity required and the proposed after-use of the site are all controlling factors. However, an essential prerequisite is a resistance to corrosion and any form of interaction with the contaminants. This would appear to be most frequently achieved by the use of chemically inert stone or rockfill.

Thorburn and Buchanan (ref. 6.9) report excavations in alkaline chemical waste to depths of at least 600 mm below the underside of the foundation, the latter being 5 m or more above the highest recorded position of the groundwater table. Crushed dolerite rock, graded 50 mm down, was vibration-compacted in layers into the wide trench excavations to form dense, chemically inert and durable formations for the continuous reinforced concrete foundations, constructed using sulphate-resisting cement. The formations were covered by 50 mm protective layers of sulphate-resisting concrete, and sulphate-resisting cement mortar was used in the construction of the brick shuttering for the foundations (Fig. 6.6).

Gabryliszyn (ref. 6.10) describes how a road was constructed through a tip, in which the leachate level could rise to the underside of the formation, by building the carriageways on a 1 m thick rock blanket of free-draining material (Fig. 6.2).

Buchanan and Thorburn (ref. 6.13) describe how, at an old tar and chemical works, made ground up to 2·4 m below the finished platform level was removed and replaced by granular material compacted in layers, with an upper 225 mm of compact crushed rock. The granular fill provided a dense layer suitable for shallow foundations and roads, together with ground conditions free from contamination within the depths anticipated for excavations for services.

Similarly, at the former Norwich gasworks site described in ref. 6.14, the existing ground was excavated to a minimum depth of 500 mm below the invert level of services etc., and beneath the foundations of the building it was excavated to the top of the natural sandy gravel. The resulting excavations were filled with well compacted granular material. To avoid a complex geometry for excavation and filling, the proposed underground services were clustered together and, where possible, benched into the sides of the main foundation excavation.

At another former gasworks site (ref. 6.15), which was being redeveloped as a solid-waste transfer station, the entire site was sealed by a 1 m thick barrier, the bottom 450 mm comprising a well compacted impermeable clay-bound granular material having the advantages of suitable plasticity and relatively low compressibility. Beneath underground services the barrier layer was locally thickened, with a 100 mm thick mass concrete slab cast on top to prevent puncturing of the barrier layer during revisions or repair of services at a later date.

At the site of a residential development in the Isle of Dogs which was locally heavily contaminated, particularly with oils and with significant combustible matter, Nutt and Britnell (ref. 6.18) adopted a 0·7 m thick capping layer using clean inert granular material to prevent contaminants dissolved in the groundwater migrating upwards by capillary action. In heavily oil-contaminated areas a 1·5 m thick sealing layer of clean cohesive material was placed below the capping layer. Where significant combustible matter existed, the capping material was thickened to 1·0 m to insulate the lower fill material from the effects of a surface fire.

It should be noted that in the design of capillary breaks, the design principles set out by Lambe and Whitman (ref. 6.48) should be followed, since the capillary head in silty gravel can be greater than 1 m and in medium sand greater than 2 m.

Methane-generating sites

The hazards posed by methane and other gases have been described in Chapter 3. Barry (ref. 6.49) has listed typical or possible occurrences of hazardous gases on contaminated and other sites. Of these gases, the most emotive is methane (CH_4), on account of its explosive properties. In redevelopment of derelict land, the most frequent sources of methane are refuse disposal sites. However, coal-miners have always been aware of the hazard of methane in coal seams. The disaster at the Abbeystead water pumping station (ref. 6.50) has drawn attention to the risk that methane derived from such seams and from peaty ground can migrate considerable distances both laterally and vertically along joints and fissures in the rock. Similarly, the presence of peaty or marshy ground in low-lying riverside or coastal areas, and organic silt trapped in docks, has prompted an awareness of the methane risks in the redevelopment of docklands.

Although Pecksen (ref. 6.51) in 1985 noted that 'the lack of a universally accepted procedure for dealing with generation of methane gas on sites which are to be developed for housing and other buildings has led to the adoption of fail safe solutions which are expensive and in some cases totally unwarranted', he added that 'it cannot be assumed that sites which have a potential for gas generation need only cursory examination because the number of accidents attributed to this cause is relatively small'. The occurrence of recent accidents as a result of lateral migration of methane gas from landfill sites into domestic dwellings and the increased incidence of new housing developments being built close to landfill sites have prompted the Inspectorate of Pollution in the UK to issue much stricter guidelines in such circumstances (ref. 6.52). These recommend that until the wastes are biologically stabilised, the after-uses of landfill sites should be restricted to agricultural or similar uses. Furthermore, no housing with gardens should be built on any landfill site with flammable gas concentrations greater than 1 % by volume and carbon dioxide concentrations greater than 0·5 % by volume. Nevertheless, it is accepted that the presence of methane in the ground should not necessarily preclude development, provided that the risks are recognised and appropriate precautionary measures are taken. Both the need for and the design of remedial measures will depend on the proposed type of development; land which is left open, such as playing fields or golf courses, as exemplified by Stockley Park (ref. 6.5), usually presents little or no problem other than the preservation of trees and plants, which may be affected by oxygen starvation.

As mentioned above, there are two principal types of redevelopment area likely to be affected by methane gas: on or adjacent to landfill sites; and in riverside or dockland areas where either peaty ground exists (possibly at depth as a result of filling) or organic silt has accumulated within the docks. In general, the latter areas tend to be the less hazardous, since the biodegradable material tends to form a smaller proportion and be of greater age, resulting in a lower methane-generating potential. In this respect old landfill sites are similar: the proportion of organic matter tipped was smaller than in present-day landfills and substantial biodegradation will have taken place. Nevertheless, on both old and new sites containing biodegradable material, a change in the water regime can reactivate methane generation; for example, following the cessation of pumping, or by water being impounded as a result of changes in drainage. In addition, water can obstruct gas migration routes, but when the water table rises, a pumping effect is achieved and the gas can be forced out in greater concentrations (Fig. 6.7).

Controls for preventing or regulating gas emissions from landfill

Waste management paper 26 (ref. 6.53) has presented information on the steps to be taken during construction of landfills, but the absence of controls on such procedures in the past inevitably produces problems for the future. Many such operations have taken place in the backfilling of old sand and gravel workings, and rock or chalk quarries. Seldom have the sides of the excavation been sealed before backfilling commences, and so methane can migrate laterally through permeable strata or through joints and fissures in the rock. This lateral migration frequently occurs as a result of the surface of the completed landfill having been capped with a cohesive or low-permeability layer in order to reduce ingress of surface water (which would increase the volume of leachate) and to provide a medium in which vegetation can grow, albeit often sparsely. It has been found that the lateral migration of methane gas poses perhaps the greatest problem

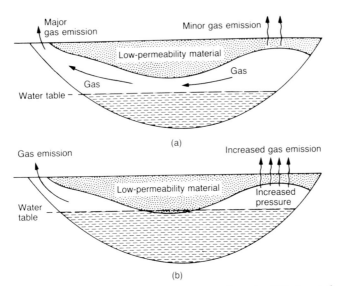

Fig. 6.7. Effect of water-table level on gas emissions from landfill sites (after Barry (ref. 6.49)): (a) normal water table; (b) elevated water table

in any redevelopment. Consequently the greatest need on any methane-generating site is the provision of an adequate cut-off system.

Cut-off system and venting trench. Vertical barriers, such as those described in an earlier section, can be very effective if keyed into a suitable low-permeability layer. The normal minimum practical construction thickness should generally be adequate to prevent critical gas transmission.

Such barriers can be supplemented by (Fig. 6.8), or on occasions

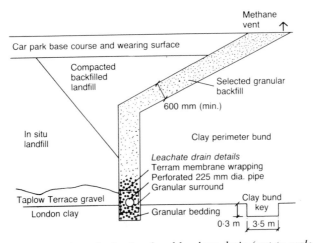

Fig. 6.8. Cross-section through clay bund and leachate drain (not to scale) (after Gordon et al. (ref. 6.5))

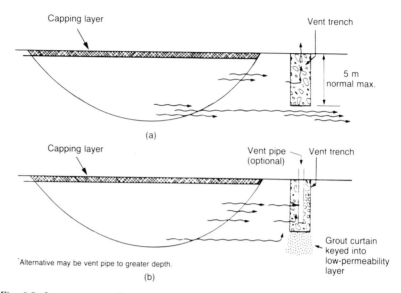

Fig. 6.9. Improvement of vent trench function (after Barry (ref. 6.49)): (a) limitation of vent trench; (b) improvement of effectiveness of vent trench

replaced by, trenches filled with gravel, crushed stone or broken brick; these have been found to be very effective as a means of protecting property adjacent to landfill sites. Pecksen (ref. 6.51) reports such use (in conjunction with naturally venting boreholes) in controlling gas at a landfill site near Dartford, Kent. Barry (ref. 6.49) has drawn attention to the need to ensure that trenches are deep enough (i.e. keyed directly, or with the aid of a grout curtain, into a low-permeability layer (Fig. 6.9)) and properly maintained (e.g. with soil and vegetation cover prevented by periodic maintenance (Fig. 6.10)). Barry also suggests that if gas migration is likely to occur at depths greater than the vent trench, a piling rig can be used to form a 'wall' of stone columns constructed at close centres. It should be noted that venting trenches produce odour problems in their immediate vicinity.

Pumped systems. The commercial exploitation of methane generated from landfill as an energy source at Aveley, Essex, has prompted the developers of old landfill sites to explore similar exploitation of their sites. Unfortunately, the cost of the pumping equipment and infrastructure for cleaning the gas frequently far outweighs the financial gain from old and therefore depleted energy resources; this is often further hampered by the identification of a suitable energy user close to the landfill site.

Opinions differ as to the effectiveness of pumping gas as a means of control. A uniform ground permeability is essential for efficient removal — a condition virtually absent within a landfill. Pecksen (ref. 6.51) notes that for redevelopment of landfill sites, it would be essential to extract at a rate probably equal to or higher than the gas generation rate. This would

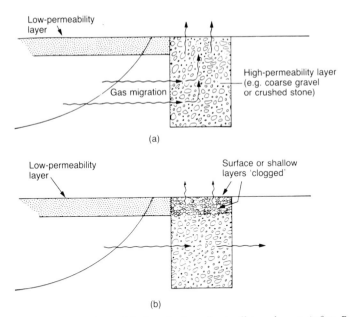

Fig. 6.10. Theoretical and possible functioning of cut-off trench vent (after Barry (ref. 6.49)): (a) theoretical functioning; (b) possible functioning (longer term)

encourage air to move into the ground, with the probable loss of anaerobic conditions within the fill, so that methane concentration would consequently decline to a point where flaring would become impossible.

Cover system. The provision of surface barriers for contaminated sites has been discussed in a previous section. Very often a low-permeability cover composed of either clay, hoggin or concrete has been provided to prevent gas emission. However, such an approach fails to take account of the fact that gas generation relies on decomposition, and decomposition results in a reduction in mass, so that the surface of the ground will inevitably subside, irrespective of the degree of initial ground compaction. Unfortunately such subsidence is non-uniform, so that tension cracks will develop in the covering layer (Fig. 6.11), through which gas will escape. As a result of escaping at one point instead of diffusing uniformly through a wider area, the gas will be more concentrated and have less opportunity for dilution prior to exit.

Furthermore, when a clay seal dries it also shrinks, so that fissures are created through which gas can similarly escape. Thus on a landscaped site, a clay capping will not prevent methane emission. The Dutch have sought to overcome this problem by encouraging a uniform diffusion of methane through organic soil which can oxidise the gas. As stated in the section above on 'Surface barriers', provision of topsoil cover for landscaping of contaminated sites requires specialist knowledge.

The inherent risks of subsidence leading to cracking of concrete slabs requires that floor slabs in buildings should not be constructed directly on

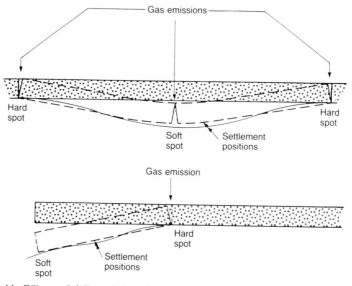

Fig. 6.11. Effects of differential settlements on rigid slabs (after Barry (ref. 6.49))

ground in which methane is being generated. Possible schemes are discussed below.

Controls for preventing gas ingress to critical confined spaces within buildings

Underfloor venting. The breakdown of organic material in river silt trapped by the infilling of Surrey Docks prior to its redevelopment led to problems of gas generation. This prompted the Greater London Council, in conjunction with the developer's consultant, to undertake extensive on-site testing and the construction of full-scale test rigs to investigate underfloor ventilation systems for the prevention of gas accumulation in and beneath dwellings. The provision of a void between the floor slab and the ground prevented methane entering the building by allowing any gas entering the void to mix with air, dilute to a safe level, and discharge to the atmosphere. Removal of gas from the void could be achieved through either natural or forced ventilation. Pecksen (ref. 6.51) describes the experimental and theoretical studies of the required ventilation rates, and how the natural ventilation was influenced by the pattern of wind speeds and direction, the grille area and the void space. It was concluded that the form of ventilation should be determined not only by the level of ground contamination, but by building design, building density and height. Such systems were adopted for habitable buildings throughout the Surrey Docks development.

The development of buildings on landfill sites is becoming more common, prompting the challenge of designing buildings with a sufficient overlap of protective measures to ensure safety of the buildings and their occupants. Whereas passive underfloor ventilation is generally adequate to prevent dangerous gas accumulation from organic clay and peat, where generation rates are low, active underfloor ventilation is frequently essential for landfill areas, where methane generation rates are high. This requires close co-operation between the architect, structural engineer, mechanical and ventilation engineer, geotechnical engineer and environmental engineer.

A variation on the basic underfloor ventilation is the use of vertical vents through the centre of a large industrial building; the heat generated in the building turns these vents into 'chimneys' to naturally vent the void beneath the floor slab. However, there is a risk that in certain climatic conditions methane might be generated but the 'chimney' not function adequately.

Another variation is the provision of gas sensors within the void beneath the floor slab; on detecting methane the sensors activate fans to provide forced ventilation. Such systems require regular maintenance and standby pumps.

On a large scale, it is considered that the provision of well ventilated (i.e. open) ground level car parking under buildings will provide adequate protection to the building.

Although suggested by Pecksen (ref. 6.51) as a cheaper alternative to a ventilated void, the construction of a floor slab directly on a semi-permeable foundation (e.g. ballast rejects) which provides a relatively easy path for gas to move outside and escape alongside the building, should be treated with considerable caution. Gas does not escape so freely and air is prevented from diffusing back into the ground, so that gas concentration directly below the floor slab may become very high.

Sealing of buildings. In areas of high gas emission it is good practice to incorporate a polythene membrane in floor structures in addition to an intervening ventilated space. Pecksen (ref. 6.51) suggests that where contamination is low, a gas membrane alone will provide a sufficient precautionary measure; however, if this method is adopted, even greater attention should be paid to internal ventilation (as discussed below) since no polymeric membrane can be regarded as totally impervious to gas. The principal criteria in selecting a membrane are cheapness, easy handling and ability to withstand damage. Pecksen suggests that 1000 gauge polythene is generally satisfactory for most building applications.

A common weakness in sealing a floor slab is where service pipes and ducts pass through it. Any drainage penetrating the slab would be provided with puddle flanges; services should be brought in above the slab via an external ventilated box.

Ventilation of buildings. Despite the above precautions there is still a risk that gas will enter buildings through cracks or discontinuities in the concrete floor (or even the walls), through the gas membrane around service pipes or in service ducts. Barry (ref. 6.49) notes that it is not possible to be explicit about the areas within a building that are most at risk, but relatively small rooms or compartments that are poorly ventilated (through, for example, infrequent use) are particularly vulnerable. Careful design and provision of appropriate ventilation is necessary, for example, in electrical switch rooms, where the risks of explosion are not solely related to human interference.

Infrastructure of former industries

Apart from industrial and domestic waste tip sites, most of the problems of chemical contamination discussed previously have derived from the sites of former industries, notably tar and chemical works and gas works. Although the chemical contamination associated with these produces the principal hazards, the infrastructure on which they relied, such as massive old foundations and underground structures, can pose equally challenging problems for redevelopment. In addition, there are sites such as derelict docklands and old iron and steel works where the relict infrastructure poses the greatest problem and the chemical contamination is relatively insignificant or non-existent. The principal problems can be categorised as follows

- o   massive old foundations and underground structures
- o   extensive 'filled' ground
- o   in the case of docklands, large areas of open water with associated quay walls.

Backfilled basements and cellars from former tenement properties bridge the first two categories.

Massive old foundations and underground structures

When any site is to be developed it is essential to examine old maps and records to ascertain the previous history of the site. This is particularly valuable in the case of former industries, because maps such as the old Ordnance Survey maps (available for study in the British Museum Map Room), 18th century maps (such as undertaken by Rocque in London) and insurance plans (such as those prepared by Goade in London) are frequently the first indication of former structures, long since demolished, whose foundations still remain buried. For more recent structures, such as Lots Road Power Station, Battersea, and Eland House, Stag Place, London, the original foundation drawings still exist or, in the case of the former, have been published. Nevertheless, care needs to be taken to ascertain whether the foundations were built in accordance with the drawings: a representative number should be exposed by means of trial excavations to determine their extent and depth.

It is natural to seek to reuse existing foundations, particularly if massive, to support the new structure, but all too frequently the new column grid fails to coincide exactly with the old foundations. In such a situation the old foundations will either interfere with new foundation construction or create a 'hard spot' (e.g. beneath a raft foundation), thereby causing differential settlement and inducing cracking of the new structure. In these cases it will probably be necessary to break out the old foundations, at some expense if these are massive. Gaba and Hyde (ref. 6.21) adopted a slightly different technique when faced with the old foundations and basements of the Morgan Crucible Works at a riverside site in London. There they backfilled the basement in a carefuly controlled manner with crushed arisings and sea-dredged gravel imported into the site, thereby creating a thick granular raft on which a housing estate was built.

Lee House Development in the City of London will replace a 1960s structure with an air rights building spanning Wood Street. The original small-diameter bored piles supporting the orginal structure were inadequate to support the new loads, so large-diameter underreamed bored piles were carefully threaded between existing piles and services.

Both Fenchurch Street and Charing Cross British Rail stations are supported by arches and strip footings founded in the underlying gravel. Although by no means derelict sites, further redevelopment has taken place in the form of structures built over the stations. The existing foundations could not sustain additional loads, and these were supported on caissons sunk between the arches into the London clay (refs 6.54, 6.55).

If reuse of existing foundations is contemplated, an accurate assessment must be made of loads sustained during previous use: application of higher loads in reuse is seldom permitted unless a proof load test to at least $1.5 \times$ new design load is applied. In addition, samples of the material of which the foundations are constructed (e.g. concrete, steel or timber) should be tested for possible loss of strength or decay with time. Such a programme of investigation was instigated in the redevelopment of Tobacco Dock, where the reuse of timber piles was permitted after load testing and sampling of the timber (ref. 6.56). If the new loads to be applied to the old foundations are greater than the former loads, it may be necessary to adopt underpinning or strengthening techniques; for example, by installing micro-piles through a pad footing or by enlarging the footing. Even so, some column loads may still require to be carried on new foundations: it is then important to check the different load–settlement characteristics of the old and new foundations in order to assess whether the structure can accommodate possible differential settlements.

Extensive 'filled' ground

Frequently during excavations for the original structure and subsequent demolition and rebuilding, the spoil and debris were not removed from the site, but were allowed to accumulate in situ, as were by-products and waste from industrial processes. Consequently considerable thicknesses of uncontrolled, uncompacted fill have accumulated on industrial sites (Table 6.1).

Very often during demolition, basements (e.g. of tenement houses (ref. 6.25)) up to 3 m deep, are allowed to fill up with loose demolition debris, generally including timber.

Treatment of such thicknesses of fill can be an expensive item in any redevelopment. Ground improvement techniques are discussed in a later section.

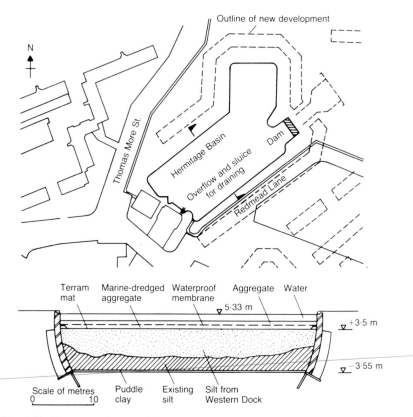

Fig. 6.12. Hermitage Basin infilling, London Docks: plan and section (after Lord et al. (ref. 6.20))

Docklands

The demise of cargo ships allied to increased containerisation and larger vessels has rendered many of our docks derelict, particularly those situated up-river in the heart of our cities — London, Liverpool, Salford, Cardiff and Glasgow, for example.

Such dereliction poses three main problems

- large expanses of open water beneath which substantial quantities of silt, often contaminated with heavy metals and with methane-producing organic content, has accumulated following cessation of dredging schedules
- quay walls with low factors of safety against sliding and hence vulnerable to any permanent reduction in water level and/or dredging
- existing buildings and vaults in various states of disrepair.

In addition, redevelopment highlights other deficiencies

o existing infrastructure — notably surface water drainage —
   inadequate for any large-scale development, particularly if the
   population is to be increased substantially
o inadequate transport, with road networks in need of upgrading.

Consequently, in the redevelopment of docklands, the need to maximise
the site's assets and thus its potential income while minimising its liabilities
with imaginative and innovative engineering is most severely tested. The
water pollution and old foundations are the main liabilities. An important
aspect is the recognition that the water-rich landscape can be a principal
asset.

Dock basins. Contributions to the conference on building on marginal
and derelict land (ref. 6.4) included six papers relating to docks, as listed
in Table 6.2. These would appear to mirror the treatment of old docks
prevalent in the late 1970s and early 1980s, namely infilling the docks with
crushed arisings or colliery discard which was compacted by one of the
ground improvement techniques discussed at the end of this chapter. Silt
trapped in the dock basin was pumped into an adjacent dock, or allowed
to decant and turned into an ornamental lake (Fig. 6.12; ref. 6.20) or
allowed to escape into the open sea (ref. 6.24). The infilling scheme
described in ref. 6.20 related only to the Western Dock of the London
Docks (Fig. 6.13) and the silt was deposited in Hermitage Basin. The value
of a water-rich landscape was recognised by the provision of a 1 m deep
freshwater 'canal' along the South Quay; this canal also collected surface-
water drainage, which was discharged into the River Thames via a flap
valve.

Elsewhere in the London Docks, Shadwell Basin was used as a balancing reservoir for surface-water drainage from the North Quay area. The
massive dock wall construction in Shadwell Basin presented formidable

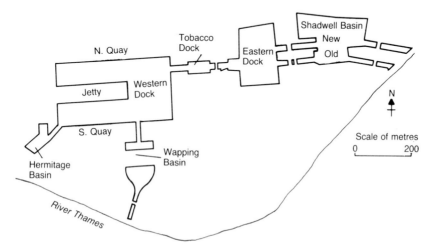

Fig. 6.13. Plan of London Docks (after Lord et al. (ref. 6.20))

obstructions to the future development of the basin, and hence its potential as a water recreation area (which could be combined with use as a balancing reservoir) was pursued.

The Salford Quays Project (ref. 6.57) lies 3 km from the centre of Manchester and represents a further step in the strategy for redevelopment of docklands. The development plan maximised the site's principal asset, the water, by the construction of bunds across the three major basins, which at once united the land and allowed the impounded polluted water to be treated. A single lock connects the internal water to the Manchester Ship Canal, and the three enclosed dock basins are interconnected by two canals (Fig. 6.14). These canals not only allow boat movement between the basins but also extend the valuable water frontage. Considerable attention was paid to preventing anoxic conditions developing within the water in the basins by circulating oxygenated water (Fig. 6.15).

Quay walls. Quay walls were originally constructed 'in the dry'. When the docks were flooded, the water level also rose behind the walls; if the water level in the dock were subsequently lowered, the pressure from the water trapped behind the walls would render them unstable. Lord *et al.* (ref. 6.20) describe how, prior to lowering of the water level in Western Dock, the walls were stabilised against overturning by end-tipping rockfill against the water face of the wall, starting from one corner.

Existing buildings and vaults. Many docks were constructed with vaults underneath the quays. At Tobacco Dock in the London Docks, the vaults were in sufficiently good condition to permit reuse (ref. 6.56). However, those in Western Dock were generally in a poor state of repair and

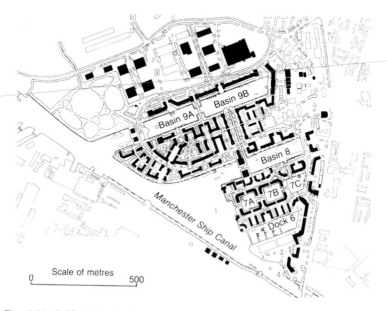

Fig. 6.14. Salford Docks development plan (after Radway et al. (ref. 6.90)).

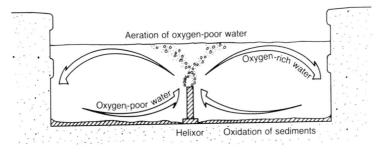

Fig. 6.15. Water quality improvement at Salford Quays: principle of aeration (after Hindle et al. (ref. 6.57))

incapable of supporting all but the lightest loads (ref. 6.20). Accordingly they were either backfilled using pumped pfa or more often demolished, the masonry being crushed and replaced on the old vault floors.

At the Salford Docks (ref. 6.57), old concrete and brick arch service ducts, 1·5 m high and up to 3 m wide, ran behind the entire length of some dock walls. The ducts were structually unsound and constituted a health

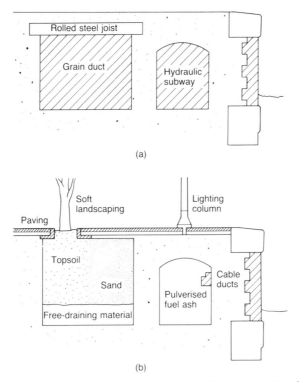

Fig. 6.16. Treatment of derelict service ducts at Salford Quays: (a) derelict service duct; (b) proposed treatment

hazard, but their location rendered them of limited value as ducts for new services. Consequently the ducts were used for quayside tree planting, with a public walkway on top; they also carry electrical feeds to the footpath and dock wall lighting (Fig. 6.16).

Land affected by old mine workings and opencast mining

The problem of ground subsidence following the mining of coal seams has long been recognised. With the adoption of long-wall mining techniques the magnitude of the subsidence and the induced ground strains were more readily predictable, and followed on closely behind the extraction. The incidence of subsidence resulting from the earlier pillar-and-stall mining technique was far less predictable: the practice of pillar-robbing prior to abandoning a seam frequently led to sudden local collapses; and subsequent oxidation and weakening of the pillars allied to roof and floor creep has produced further collapses decades after the seam was abandoned (refs 6.58, 6.59).

Similar problems have been encountered with abandoned limestone mines in the West Midlands of England (ref. 6.60). Such mines have been found to have a more protracted period of deterioration than coal mines before they collapse. An old rule of thumb that limestone mines lying at a depth greater than 60 m could be regarded as 'safe', and unlikely to give rise to surface subsidence, was disproved in 1978 by the collapse of Cow Pasture Mine at 150 m depth, which produced an elliptical surface subsidence, 300 m × 200 m in plan and up to 1½ m deep (Fig. 6.17). As a result it was recognised that all limestone mines would continue to deteriorate with the passage of time, and that this posed a serious threat to the

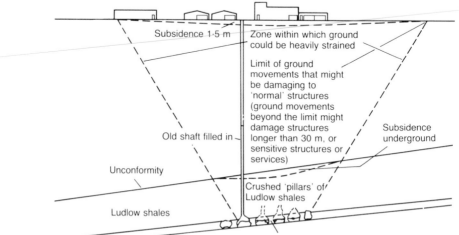

Fig. 6.17. Subsidence at Cow Pasture Mine (after Cole et al. (ref. 6.60))

properties and services over them. In effect, the presence of the mines caused both actual and apprehended dereliction.

Some mining, such as that listed above together with the mining of chalk, ironstone and fireclay, tends to result in mass extraction: it is this that principally causes surface subsidence. Into this category would also fall salt extraction by the former technique of wild-brine pumping. Other mining for mineraliferous ores, such as lead and tin, tends to be less extensive in extraction as a result of following the lodes; this, together with the presence of strong, competent rock surrounding the workings, inhibits the risk of collapse. However, care needs to be exercised when developing adjacent to or over sites where the worked mineral lodes are near vertical but may not be evident at the surface.

Ground subsidence is not the only dereliction associated with mining. Shafts which provided access to the mines are frequently unmapped and/or inadequately backfilled and capped, with the inherent risk of future collapse. Furthermore, such shafts and the workings which they served were often used as a dumping ground for the uncontrolled disposal of highly toxic contaminants such as cyanides. Mining, especially coal-mining, produced large quantities of spoil or waste in the form of mine-stone or colliery shale. These spoil tips have rendered derelict large tracts of countryside; not only does their sheer size pose a problem but the risks of possible combustion of any finely divided coal content and of oil shale also need to be recognised. In addition, coal-mine spoil tips can be a source of water contamination (refs 6.61, 6.62). Colliery discard lagoons and china-clay washings are considered in a later section with other hydraulic fills. Also, later sections on loose tipped spoil and ground improvement techniques deal further with spoil tips and the end result of open-cast mining, and possible solutions for their treatment.

There have been two conferences on the reclamation, treatment and utilisation of coal-mining wastes (refs 6.63, 6.64), at which the need for reclamation has been discussed and the commercial benefits acknowledged. The special interest in coal-mining probably stems from the fact that the responsibility for coal mines is vested in the National Coal Board, whereas there is no single authority responsible for other mines. A conference held by the Engineering Group of the Geological Society on engineering geology of underground movements (ref. 6.65) devoted two sessions to abandoned mine workings.

Identification of mine workings

Towns and cities originally grew up around places where an industry had flourished. The industry itself frequently started on account of local availability of the requisite raw material. Extraction took place, the source became exhausted and the area was frequently refilled with waste products, thereby hiding evidence of the former mining. Consequently, in treating the sites of former industries, it is essential to be aware of the possibility of mining extraction, whether for the raw material used in the industry or for coal, the universal source of power.

Examination of first the 1 : 63 360 and then the 1 : 10 560 geological maps published by the British Geological Survey will provide evidence of natural resources beneath the site. If coal is indicated, the National Coal Board should be consulted for evidence from old plans of former mining, although this should by no means be considered as definitive since it was not compulsory to maintain mining plans until 1873. For other minerals, much information can be gained by studying records in the Public Records Office and local libraries relating to ownership of land and the granting of mining rights. Even the names of fields can provide clues. In the UK, the problems associated with mining have been recognised by the Department of the Environment, who have commissioned a study of all mining activities in England and Wales. The findings will be published as a series of maps covering the entire area, on which known and conjectured mining and mineral extraction will be indicated. Such maps will provide primary guidance to planners and all involved in site redevelopment.

Aerial photographs can also provide evidence of mining. By careful study of the geomorphology, mining subsidence, spoil tips and old shafts can frequently be identified, despite possible covering with fill. Old Ordnance Survey maps may give an indication of past mining activities.

After the desk-study stage, a site investigation consisiting of rotary cored boreholes and probeholes should be instigated to assess whether or not seams have been worked, and if they have, whether the workings are still open or collapsed, either partially or totally. It is then important to determine whether the workings extend only beneath part of the site or cover a larger area.

Stabilisation of mine workings by grouting

The need for and form of remedial treatment of underground workings is dependent on a number of factors

o   whether the workings are still open or have collapsed
o   the depth of the workings
o   the thickness of extraction
o   the competence of the overlying strata.

The principal question that must be addressed is whether collapse is likely in the future and, if so, how it will affect the proposed redevelopment. Even if total collapse appears to have occurred, there are still risks either of uncollapsed areas or of a continuing upward migration of the collapse to the ground surface. Consequently, it is likely that some form of ground treatment will be necessary.

Since direct access into the main workings is unlikely, infilling as a form of stabilisation will have to be carried out from ground level, and hence the infilling medium must be pumpable. Cement or cement–pfa grouts are frequently used, but are expensive if large volumes are to be filled. Minimising the number of injection points can reduce costs, particularly if the workings are at depth. The need to achieve near-complete infilling requires pressurisation of the grout, but if the workings are extensive this can lead to grout travelling well beyond the area to be treated, with consequent wastage and loss.

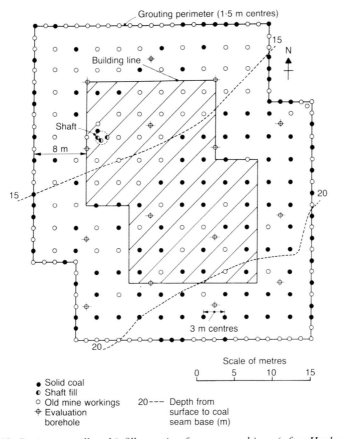

Fig. 6.18. Perimeter-wall and infill grouting for open workings (after Healy and Head (ref. 6.59))

The normal treatment of old coal-mine workings has been described by Healy and Head (ref. 6.59). Initially, inclined holes are drilled in a ring around the perimeter of the site (Fig. 6.18). (These holes are raked away from the site to ensure that any voids immediately outside the site boundary do not collapse and migrate upwards, so forming a cone of depression which could affect the site.) These primary holes are filled with a thixotropic grout, which does not flow laterally outwards and hence forms a perimeter barrier around the site. This is followed by filling inside the barrier with holes on a regular grid, often referred to as secondary grouting. Frequently, pea gravel is first pumped down each hole, to provide bulk, and this is followed by injection of cement–pfa grout under pressure to fill in the interstices. If grout takes are large, tertiary holes midway between the secondary holes may be drilled and grouted.

If contaminated water is displaced by the grouting and emerges at ground level, it must not be allowed to drain away with the risk of polluting watercourses, but should be discharged under the directions of the Pollution Control Officer.

Infilling mine workings with colliery spoil

The large volumes of the limestone mines described by Cole *et al.* (ref. 6.60) and the extensive areas of apprehended dereliction arising from their lateral extent has prompted an investigation into the infilling of these workings with colliery spoil, which exists in abundance in nearby tips, thereby removing a second source of dereliction. Full-scale mixing, pumping and surface-spreading trials of rock paste were first described by Ward (ref. 6.66). Improvement of the rock paste by the addition of pulverised fuel ash and lime to the colliery spoil to produce a slow-hardening bulk fill have been described by Cole and Figg (ref. 6.67). The use of such material to infill limestone mines has been presented by Braithwaite and Sklucki (ref. 6.68). The objectives of the infilling are to provide additional support to existing mine pillars and roof, although the latter is difficult to achieve as a result of the paste tending to 'settle out'. In the event of an incipient roof collapse, the rock paste should be of sufficient strength to support the falling roof and prevent the collapse migrating to the ground surface. Hence it has been found necessary to add small quantities of lime to assist the setting of the rock paste.

As a result of the experience gained in using waste material for bulk infilling, the techniques are continually being developed and improved. It is anticipated that the twofold removal of dereliction, arising from both the mining and the spoil tips, will encourage local authorities to pursue such techniques more vigorously in the future.

Old mine shafts

The existence of mines almost inevitably means the presence of shafts for access or ventilation, or both. These can range from shallow shafts, such as those servicing bell-pits, to the larger lined ones for working deep seams. Both pose their own peculiar problems.

The former, although shallow, were often very widespread and, on account of being among the earliest mines, were seldom recorded, backfilled or capped off. As a result there exists, for example, in the Peak District hundreds of open shallow shafts from which lead was extracted. Those that have been identified have been fenced off or capped, but many more unidentified shafts are thought to exist. Similarly, when redevelopment of a former allotment site was proposed in the county of Durham, it was discovered that each of the tool sheds on the site hid the access to a bell-pit in a coal seam at shallow depth.

Old shafts to deep seams have generally been either loosely infilled or capped off in some way or other (refs 6.58, 6.59). If infilled, the infilling often contained degradable material such as timber, and so decomposition together with consolidation of the loose material frequently caused subsidence of the ground surface. When capped, the capping was often of timber, which rotted with time. A combination of the two techniques, namely blocking off the shaft with timber at about 5–10 m depth and then infilling above with loose material, could be guaranteed to produce the most spectacular collapses when the timber rotted.

Before old shafts can be treated they must be identified; techniques such as those described in the section on identification of old mine workings (see above) should be followed, but there is still an element of 'looking for a needle in a haystack'. Stripping the upper layers of a site and looking for signs of disturbance has sometimes been successful in identifying shafts, as have geophysical techniques, it is claimed (ref. 6.58). Otherwise consideration should be given to designing structures to span up to, say, 5 m should ground support be lost as a result of a collapse.

When shafts are discovered, treatment should be based on their condition, the likelihood of loss of ground, the risks to the proposed development and, in some instances, local authority requirements. If a shaft is loosely infilled, it can sometimes be usefully grouted up to provide a solid plug, although account should be taken of any timber in the infill whose decay could destroy the plugging action. Local authorities frequently require open shafts to be backfilled with bulk fill, such as described in the preceding section. In all instances it is recommended that a permanent reinforced concrete cap be provided; this is often a local authority requirement. Rockhead, or a secure base, should be exposed and the cap should be founded on benches cut into it (refs 6.58, 6.59).

Loose tipped spoil

On old tips, as the name implies, the spoil was loosely tipped, whereas in present-day operations it is spread in layers and compacted, in order to maximise the capacity of the tip. The loose nature of old tipped material renders it prone to subsidence and, in the case of colliery spoil, to spontaneous combustion. The oxidation of iron pyrites in the spoil is an exothermic reaction which can heat fine coal in the spoil (in old tips up to 30 % could be coal dust) to combustion point. Combustion could then take place if there were sufficient air voids arising from the loose nature of the tip.

Opencast mining, which involved stripping and tipping superficial deposits with a dragline excavator in order to expose the seam to be won, also produces considerable thicknesses of loosely tipped deposits. Cole (ref. 6.69) has noted that restoration of such land poses the following problems.

o   How extensive were the pits?
o   How deep were they?
o   How were they filled, and with what?
o   How long does it take before surface subsidence reduces below a given rate?
o   Is it likely that all or part of the fill is in unstable equilibrium?
o   Could a future gradual or sudden change in the environment induce unexpected and unwelcome subsidence?
o   What loads can be safely carried?

In the UK, opencast mining has been carried out principally for the extraction of coal and iron ore. Charles *et al.* (ref. 6.70) measured settlements at various depths in a 70 m deep dumped-spoil opencast mine at Horsley in Northumberland. The results of their measurements showed considerable variations, but it was found that a rise in groundwater level of 34 m caused collapse and consolidation of the fill it encroached upon, with settlements up to 0·7 m measured. The same team (ref. 6.71) studied the restoration for housing of a 30 m deep opencast ironstone mine at Snatchill, Corby, in the Midlands. Here the surface was given various types of treatment, such as dynamic compaction and surcharge (see section below on ground improvement techniques) and inundation. One area was not treated. The inundation produced large settlements, including differential settlements. The authors concluded that collapse settlement caused by inundation could be avoided by precompressing the ground to reduce the air voids below a critical level. This was best achieved by surcharge which, because of the inevitable large scale at which it had to be undertaken, penetrated deeply and largely eliminated the effects of underground collapses caused by rising groundwater.

Schulz *et al.* (ref. 6.72) have also considered the effect of changes in the environment (notably surface flooding) on foundations. They found that after five years the settlement induced by self-weight and groundwater was essentially complete, but infiltration of surface water caused large abrupt differential settlement, generally in the top 1½ m of the spoil. A prototype of foundation, 8 m × 10 m in plan and 2 m deep, was therefore placed on a compacted mat of soil and flyash: this was to obviate water ingress and to provide a dense, settlement-resistant zone beneath the foundation footings.

Lange (ref. 6.73) describes building on uncompacted dumps, up to 150 m deep, in the Rhenish brown coal area of the Federal Republic of Germany. Four zones were identified in the fill.

o   Zone 1 was the seasonally affected crust about 1·5 m thick.
o   Zone 2 was uncompacted mixed material, about 7·5 m thick, with insufficient self-weight to cause self-compaction, and hence changes in density occurred only by external influence.
o   Zone 3, from about 9 m depth to the mine floor, was the same material as zone 2, but partially consolidated by overburden pressure.
o   Zone 4 was the mine floor, which may have risen due to overburden pressure relief and dewatering.

If structures were founded below the seasonally affected crust, subsidence in zone 2 was expected to cause greater differential settlements than subsidence in zones 3 and 4. Accordingly, Lange studied the effects of different ground improvement techniques, as discussed in a later section.

Hydraulic fills and colliery-discard lagoons

Insofar as derelict land is concerned, hydraulic fills are the deposits formed by pumping and discharging a suspension of waste materials mixed with a sufficient quantity of water. This has principally been used for the disposal of materials such as dredgings and various mining and industrial wastes, notably from the coal-mining and china-clay industries. In these the common method of disposal has been to pump the waste product, usually termed 'tailings', in the form of a slurry through a pipeline which discharges into a lagoon. After sedimentation has occurred, the water is decanted and may be reused.

Hydraulic filling is also used for the reclamation of derelict land, by filling worked-out pits and quarries. An example of this is the filling of worked-out brick pits at Peterborough with pulverised fuel ash (pfa), which began in 1965, with the object of returning the land to agricultural or building use.

The use of hydraulic fills has been reviewed by Charles (ref. 6.74). In considering the engineering properties of hydraulic fills, he distinguishes between coarse fills, whose behaviour is essentially that of a granular material, and fine fills, that are cohesive in character. Most of the fills associated with derelict land fall into the latter category. This includes lagoon pfa, which is composed of non-plastic silt-size particles, and has properties somewhat intermediate in character between coarse granular fills and plastic clay fills. The submerged density of lagoon pfa may be as small as 4 kN/m³, since its particle density is very low (2·0–2·3). Consequently, with a high water table, effective stresses will be particularly low.

Charles states that many of the problems associated with hydraulic fills are related to the level of the water table, which is frequently close to or at ground level. This causes practical problems not only for construction on the site but also for subsequent use, since the low effective stresses create poor load-carrying characteristics. The problem may be dealt with by raising the ground level by leaving surcharge material permanently in position, or by lowering the water table. The latter method depends on the permeability of the fill.

Charles identifies various methods for improvement of hydraulic fills, such as preloading, vacuum well points, natural desiccation, dynamic compaction, vibro methods, blasting, electro-osmosis and chemical methods. Many of these techniques are described in more detail in the following section. In the case of fine hydraulic fills, preloading, probably combined with some drainage measures to speed up the rate of consolidation, is considered by Charles to be the most appropriate method.

Charles et al. (ref. 6.75) describe the results of a trial carried out to assess the effectiveness of temporary preloading as a means of improving the load-carrying characteristics of lagoon-placed pfa in the worked-out brick pits at Peterborough. In this an 8 m high surcharge of brickbats was used to load an 11 m depth of lagoon pfa. As a result of further recent (1988) trials in which full-size raft foundations for houses have been loaded, the decision has been taken to construct 900 dwellings on the infilled former brick pits. Difficulties were anticipated with the installation of deep services such as sewers. A trial indicated that these could be overcome by temporary vacuum dewatering adjacent to the proposed sewer trench during the installation stages.

Ground improvement techniques

The frequent decision to leave in situ the products of former land use, and with it the cause of dereliction, prevents the redevelopment enjoying the benefits of a green field site as far as foundations are concerned. The reasons for leaving fill material in situ, whether on account of contamination, high transport costs, planned disposal of hydraulic fills, or, in the case of opencast mining, part of the planning constraints, has been discussed in the preceding sections. The end result is one in which either piled foundations are required or some form of ground treatment; following the latter, conventional foundations such as pad footings or rafts may be adopted. If the depth of fill is great, piling may not be an economic solution; and if contamination exists which might attack the concrete, piling may not be feasible unless permanent protection can be provided, such as that described by Bartholomew (ref. 6.76). In such circumstances ground improvement may be an appropriate solution, provided that the performance criteria for the building are satisfied.

The Construction Industry Research and Information Association (CIRIA) has recently commissioned Mitchell (ref. 6.40) to undertake a detailed study of ground improvement techniques. Those techniques which are considered appropriate for derelict land are discussed below. It is recommended that source documents where indicated, and the CIRIA report when available, are consulted for further information. The processes have been grouped together by related method and in order of popularity of use in the UK. It is not unusual to use several methods in combination (e.g. precompression and deep drains, or vibro-replacement and dynamic compaction).

- o *Group 1. Improvement by vibration*: vibro-replacement (stone columns), vibro-compaction, dynamic compaction
- o *Group 2. Improvement by adding load and increasing effective stresses*: precompression, deep drains (sand, band or wick), inundation, dewatering (vacuum preloading)
- o *Group 3. Reinforcement or replacement*: reinforced soil (reinforced earth, geotextiles); remove and replace (structural fill—see earlier section), displace, or reduce loading; compaction or jet grouting (see earlier sections).

Vibro-replacement (stone columns) currently forms about 90 % of all ground improvement by vibration carried out by specialist geotechnical contractors in the UK, with dynamic compaction making up the remaining 10 %. Much of this work is undertaken on derelict sites where uncompacted fill of varying thickness exists. The techniques in group 2 are principally applicable to derelict land arising from loose tipped spoil (see earlier section), hydraulic fills (see earlier section) and soft clay fills; precompression is sometimes applied to housing and industrial sites, occasionally in conjuction with deep drains to speed up consolidation. Dewatering has been used to assist the excavation of trenches in hydraulic fills. The use of geotextiles, reinforced earth, and jet grouting is developing rapidly.

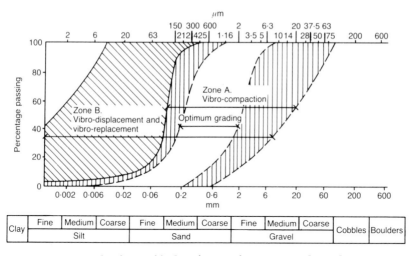

Fig. 6.19. Range of soils suitable for vibrational processes (after ref. 6.78)

The most common ground improvement processes have been used for more than 30 years, except dynamic compaction. However, Greenwood's opinion (ref. 6.77) that the 'art of compaction' is still largely empirical in nature should be heeded. Although there have been some advances recently in theories, difficulties in accurately determining soil properties, or fabric, still inhibits progress. It is therefore prudent not to try to apply processes to soil conditions in which they are only marginally applicable.

Table 6.3. Situations unsuitable for the use of stone columns

1.	In soft clay with cohesion $c_u < 15\,\mathrm{kN/m^2}$
2.	Through a layer of peat thicker than about 0·6 m or stone column diameter, or through several layers of peat
3.	In voided filled ground, e.g. old water tanks, pottery, concrete rubble, shallow mine workings, brick fill
4.	In chalk and clay fill subject to collapse settlement due to inundation, or rising or fluctuating groundwater levels
5.	In filled ground still settling under self-weight, e.g. with high organic content and decay continuing
6.	In contaminated ground or toxic waste, or where methane generated
7.	Across edges of pits or quarries
8.	Where site level to be raised after treatment — surcharge can cause additional settlement
9.	Where site to be reduced in level
10.	Adjacent to crest of slope or cutting
11.	Near soakaway or drainage run
12.	On sites with obstructions or hard ground
13.	Near trees
14.	Where only small structural settlements permitted
15.	Where the structure is intolerant to stone columns out of position

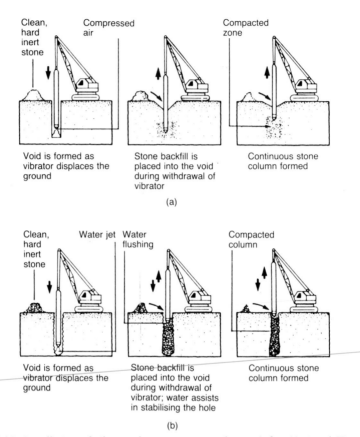

Fig. 6.20. Installation of vibro-replacement stone columns (after National House Building Council (ref. 6.80)): (a) dry process; (b) wet process

Vibro-replacement (stone columns)

Stone columns were developed independently in Germany and the UK in the late 1950s for use in variable ground conditions, usually soft clays and silts, but later filled ground. The range of application of vibro-replacement and vibro-compaction in relation to the grain size of the soil to be treated is shown in Fig. 6.19. Details of the technique are given by St John *et al.* (ref. 6.79). A large volume of low-pressure water, or compressed air, assists penetration of the vibrating poker and removes soil debris during the construction process (Fig. 6.20). The wet process is used in soft to very soft ground and fills, while compressed air is applicable where the ground is soft to firm, producing a stone column of slightly smaller diameter than the wet process. Columns are typically 0·6–0·8 m in diameter and can be up to 30 m deep. Typical spacings, on a triangular or square grid, are 1–2 m for isolated loads, and 2–3 m for spread loads such as ground slabs.

In very weak soils an alternative to the use of water is the bottom-feed vibrator, in which compressed air feeds stone to the tip of the vibrator as

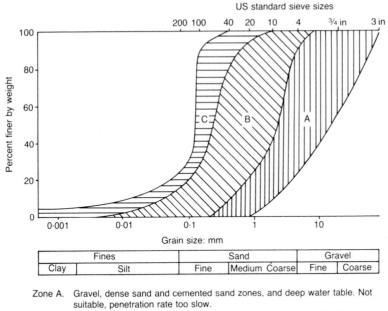

Zone A. Gravel, dense sand and cemented sand zones, and deep water table. Not suitable, penetration rate too slow.

Zone B. Very loose sands below the water table that have grain size distributions falling entirely in zone B. Most suitable.

Zone C. Clay layers, excessive fines, cementation, and organic ground affect vibro-compaction. If soils fall entirely within zone C, most difficult to compact. Portions of grain size can be in zone C, but densities achieved decrease with increasing silt and clay content.

Fig. 6.21. Suitability of soils for vibro-flotation and vibro-compaction (after Brown (ref. 6.81))

the column is formed. The method is applicable to weak fills and very soft clays below the water table. Constraints on the use of the vibro-replacement (stone column) process are given in Table 6.3.

Vibro-compaction

The vibro-compaction technique was developed to penetrate loose saturated fine sands or deep hydraulic fills. Compaction was achieved through the application of horizontal vibration. The process is similar to that of vibro-replacement (Fig. 6.20). The range of application related to grain size is given in Fig. 6.21. Treatment points are typically at 1·8–3·0 m spacings. Vibro-compaction cannot be employed if the fines content (silt and clay) exceeds 20 %. Deep deposits of saturated fine sand are unusual in the UK, although Bell *et al.* (ref. 6.22) report treatment of 28½ m of hydraulic sand fill in conjunction with surcharging.

Dynamic compaction

Dynamic compaction consists of a large weight being dropped from a great height on to the ground to form an imprint or crater. Typically weights of 5–20 t are used, with drops of up to 20 m, to treat ground to about 15 m depth. Weights are often of mass concrete, or steel plates welded together, and are usually about 2 m square. Typically a 1 m layer of granular fill is placed first, then the weight is dropped on a square grid of about 5–10 m. In each pass of the weight 5–10 blows are applied to each imprint. The ultimate aim is to form a crater about 0·5–2·0 m deep. Groundwater may have to be lowered to ensure that it does not enter the imprints. Craters are backfilled and the process is repeated until the required induced settlement of the site is achieved. This can vary between 0·5 m and 2 m. The process can be applied economically to sites of 5000 m² or greater, and has been used mainly to compact sands, silty sands, hydraulic fills, and silty clay fills. More recently dynamic compaction has been applied to refuse and colliery waste fills. Welsh (ref. 6.82) reports that the treatment can cause up to 25 % compression of 10 m of recent refuse. However, Gabryliszyn (ref. 6.27) and Buchanan and Thorburn (ref. 6.13) report rejection of dynamic compaction because of the presence of con-tamination: in the former case, past experience of dynamic compaction at Surrey Docks had shown that, after treatment, methane was generated in large quantities; in the latter case, tar inpregnation was considered to have an unpredictable effect on the efficacy of the treatment. Further limitations are listed in Table 6.4; ground-borne vibrations and the sensitivity of local buildings to vibration was one reason for the rejection of such compaction by Collins *et al.* (ref. 6.14).

Precompression

Precompression is the deliberate act of compressing the ground prior to the application of structural load. It is economical on moderate to large sites (ref. 6.83), and for full economy the fill should be reused, but an area larger than the proposed site needs to be loaded. Precompression takes two forms

- *preloading*: the placement and removal of filling similar in weight to the structural load
- *surcharging*: the placement and removal of filling greater than the structural load.

Table 6.4. Constraints on the use of dynamic compaction

1.	Soft clays with cohesion $c_u < 30 \, kN/m^2$
2.	Karstic rock, or voided ground below treated ground, e.g. old mine workings
3.	Vibration effects: minimum distance 30 m to closest structure; effects worst where groundwater is high; also ejection of missiles to more than 100 m distance
4.	Clay working surface: a granular surface is essential for operating equipment
5.	Groundwater: water table should be at least 4 m below ground level, otherwise dewatering is required; after treatment of dewatered site, rising groundwater could cause clay to swell or could cause collapse settlement
6.	Regeneration of biological action

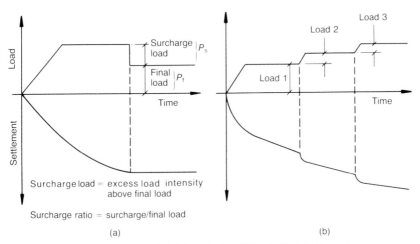

Fig. 6.22. Precompression — definitions (after Pilot (ref. 6.84)): (a) surcharging; (b) step-by-step construction

The concept is shown in Fig. 6.22(a). Stage construction is used where the ground is so weak that it has to gain sufficient strength before the next lift of preloading or surcharge can be added (Fig. 6.22(b)).

The main constraint is the time available for drainage, and thus deep drains are often used in conjunction with precompression to accelerate the rate of settlement. The surcharge ratio, defined in Fig. 6.22, is typically between 0·5 and 1·0 for buildings, with loading maintained for 1–5 months. For embankments, surcharge ratios are 0·3 or less, with the preload or surcharge maintained for a few months to several years. A maximum height of about 10 m is practical.

Charles *et al.* (ref. 6.75) describe nine preloading case histories applied to uncompacted fills on derelict sites. They suggest that preloading is very effective because the fills are unsaturated and highly permeable, and will consolidate rapidly. Most settlement occurs during the placing of the surcharge itself, but this may not apply to the silt at the base of infilled docks. Charles *et al.* also advise that all forms of settlement have to be considered, as well as the possibility of gas generation.

In a further recent case history, Jones *et al.* (ref. 6.85) describe how a 2 m surcharge was applied to deep deposits of soft clays and peats to allow the construction of up to 4 km of roads, drainage and services.

Inundation
Inundation as a form of ground improvement has been applied worldwide, principally to unsaturated collapsible soils. The loose honeycomb type structure and various types of bond which holds the grains in place are shown in Fig. 6.23. Inundation causes collapse by breaking or destroying these cementing bonds. Water can be added by ponding or through trenches.

Charles *et al.* (ref. 6.71) describe a site at Corby involving unsaturated cohesive backfill, in which treatment by inundation was compared with dynamic compaction and preloading. Five trenches 1 m deep were dug at 10 m centres across a 50 m square area, and kept filled with water for four months. Inundation proved to be the least successful form of improvement. Charles *et al.* suggest that inundation is best applied to ground that is dry of its optimum moisture content. Deeper, more closely spaced drains would also have been more effective. However, the results demonstrate the hazards to ground caused by unintentional inundation of drainage or foundation excavations. Inundation can occur in two other ways: by groundwater rising after deep pumping ceases, and through recharging of dewatered excavations to control settlement of surrounding ground.

Charles *et al.* (ref. 6.87) give data for a number of opencast mines backfilled with colliery waste consisting of fragments of mudstone and sandstone. Dewatering had been discontinued, and at Horsley the groundwater rose 34 m in three years. Vertical compressions of 1–2 % were caused, mainly in the upper 10 m of unsaturated backfill. However, vertical compressions of 4–6 % have been reported by Charles *et al.* (ref. 6.71).

Comparison of ground improvement techniques

It is considered that a comparison of the different techniques is difficult, since such techniques are often site-specific.

Charles *et al.* (ref. 6.71) have compared the average settlements produced by dynamic compaction, inundation and precompression, together with the costs of the respective treatments, for a backfilled site at Corby: their findings are reproduced in Table 6.5. As noted above, inundation proved to be the least successful form of treatment, although considerably cheaper.

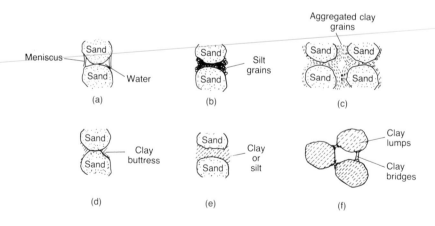

Fig. 6.23. *Typical collapsible soil mechanisms which hold loose, bulky grains in place (after Barden et al. (ref. 6.86)): (a) capillary tension; (b) silt bond; (c) aggregated clay bond; (d) flocculated clay bond; (e) mud flow type of separation; (f) clay bridge structure*

Table 6.5. Average settlements produced by ground treatment, and cost of treatment (after Charles et al. (ref. 6.71))

	Dynamic compaction	Inundation	Surcharge 9 m high
Average settlement: mm			
At surface	240	100	410
At depth 4 m	90	40	230
At depth 10 m	< 10	< 10	40
Cost:* £	£15 000†	£2 500	£12 000‡

* Cost of treatment of 50 m × 50 m square at late 1974 prices.
† Dynamic consolidation could have been considerably cheaper if a large area had been treated.
‡ Average haul distance was 100 m for placement of surcharge.

The 'instantaneous' improvement afforded by dynamic compaction in comparison with the longer term precompression could have obvious cost benefits, but these must offset against the costs of designing for additional long term settlements of up to 30 mm following dynamic compaction (ref. 6.71).

St John *et al.* (ref. 6.79) have undertaken a survey on the use and application of deep vibratory ('vibro') ground treatment techniques, and found that

o   they can be a cost-effective way of reducing settlement and creating more uniform foundation conditions
o   treatment can be localised under footings and slabs; it is unnecessary to treat large areas as with dynamic compaction or preloading
o   the methods can be used closer to existing structures than, for example, dynamic compaction
o   the supply and disposal of water can be difficult for the wet process
o   extensive buried obstructions can seriously impair treatment unless identified and removed ahead of the works
o   vibrations may cause settlement of adjacent existing structures and buried services.

The increased use of vibro-replacement and vibro-compaction has prompted the NHBC to issue practice note 16 (ref. 6.80), which advises on the precautions to be taken for vibratory ground improvement techniques for low-rise housing, including garages. Furthermore, Mitchell (ref. 6.88) has given clear guidance on the responsibilities of the Engineer (or designer) and the specialist contractor for ground improvement schemes.

For all ground improvement techniques, treatment should reduce ground movements, but is unlikely to eliminate them. If the building function demands very small movements then ground improvement may not be appropriate and another solution, such as piles, may have to be adopted. Each project must be treated strictly on its merits.

Concluding remarks

Cragg and Walker (ref. 6.89) have stated that, in addition to the commercial risks inherent in any development project, building on derelict land includes technical risks, such as subsidence and contamination. Technical risks can be reduced by increasing either the cost or commercial risk of the project. Thus there is always a need to strike an equitable balance between technical and commercial risks.

This chapter has indicated the various considerations and constraints on the options available for solving the problems associated with derelict land. Case histories have been represented illustrating the successful implementation of various schemes. However, these are by no means exhaustive. In 1986 CIRIA initiated a research project entitled 'Building on derelict land' which will doubtless identify further case histories. Furthermore, it is anticipated that over the next decade new techniques and solutions to overcome contamination problems will be identified. To anyone faced with the problems of engineering derelict land, it is recommended that they study the literature for details of recent case histories. However, the scheme adopted should always seek to be efficacious and cost-effective, by maximising the site's assets and by minimising its liabilities by imaginative and innovative engineering.

References

6.1. Smith M.A. Available reclamation methods. *Reclaiming contaminated land* (ed. Cairney T.). Blackie, Glasgow, 1987, ch. 5, 114-143.

6.2. Assink J.W. and Van den Brink W.J. (eds). *Proc. 1st Int. TNO Conf. Contaminated Soil, Utrecht, 1985*. Martinus Nijhoff, Dordrecht, 1986.

6.3. Wolf K. *et al*. (eds). *Contaminated soil '88: Proc. 2nd Int. TNO/BMFT Conf. Contaminated Soil, Hamburg, 1988*. Kluwer, Dordrecht, 1988.

6.4. Institution of Civil Engineers. *Building on marginal and derelict land*. Thomas Telford, London, 1987.

6.5. Gordon D.L. *et al*. The Stockley Park project. *Building on marginal and derelict land*. Thomas Telford, London, 1987, 359-379.

6.6. Lord J.A. Discussion contribution: Derelict sites of former industries. *Building on marginal and derelict land*. Thomas Telford, London, 1987, 594-598.

6.7. Frydman S. and Baker R. Construction of a bus parking station on a waste deposit site. *Building on marginal and derelict land*. Thomas Telford, London, 1987, 255-266.

6.8. Perelberg S. *et al*. M25 Bell Lane pit: ground improvement by dynamic compaction. *Building on marginal and derelict land*. Thomas Telford, London, 1987, 267-280.

6.9. Thorburn S. and Buchanan N.W. Building on chemical waste. *Building on marginal and derelict land*. Thomas Telford, London, 1987, 281-296.

6.10. Gabryliszyn J. The design of a road cutting through a contaminated waste tip. *Building on marginal and derelict land*. Thomas Telford, London, 1987, 297-314.

6.11. Sargunan A. and Rajamani K. Foundation problems of waste disposal fills in Madras. *Building on marginal and derelict land*. Thomas Telford, London, 1987, 315-322.

6.12. Swain A. and Holt D.N. Dynamic compaction of a refuse site for a road interchange. *Building on marginal and derelict land*. Thomas Telford, London, 1987, 339-357.

6.13. Buchanan N.W. and Thorburn S. Development of land occupied formerly by tar and chemical works. *Building on marginal and derelict land.* Thomas Telford, London, 1987, 423-433.

6.14. Collins S.P. *et al.* Rehabilitation of the Old Palace Gasworks site for the Norwich Crown and County Courts. *Building on marginal and derelict land.* Thomas Telford, London, 1987, 449-496.

6.15. Mills G. and Clark J.C. The redevelopment of Wandsworth Gasworks site. *Building on marginal and derelict land.* Thomas Telford, London, 1987, 497-520.

6.16. Skilton E.J. Vibro-flotation and jackable foundations combined to cut costs. *Building on marginal and derelict land.* Thomas Telford, London, 1987, 759-764.

6.17. Crossley A.D. and Thomson G.H. Land redevelopment involving ground treatment by dynamic compaction. *Building on marginal and derelict land.* Thomson Telford, London, 1987, 785-790.

6.18. Nutt R.D. and Britnell M.F. Site preparation for residential redevelopment on the Isle of Dogs, London. *Building on marginal and derelict land.* Thomas Telford, London, 1987, 807-813.

6.19. Reid W.M. and Buchanan N.W. The Scottish Exhibition Centre. *Building on marginal and derelict land.* Thomas Telford, London, 1987, 435-448.

6.20. Lord J.A. *et al.* Western Dock and Hermitage Basin reclamation, London Docks. *Building on marginal and derelict land.* Thomas Telford, London, 1987, 521-537.

6.21. Gaba A.R. and Hyde R.B. The redevelopment of a former industrial site at Morgan's Walk, Battersea, London. *Building on marginal and derelict land.* Thomas Telford, London, 1987, 539-558.

6.22. Bell A.L. *et al.* Vibro-compaction densification of a deep hydraulic fill. *Building on marginal and derelict land.* Thomas Telford, London, 1987, 791-797.

6.23. Slocombe B.C. and Moseley M.P. Experience with dynamic compaction on derelict sites. *Building on marginal and derelict land.* Thomas Telford, London, 1987, 799-806.

6.24. Somerville M.A. Infilling a dock with colliery discard. *Building on marginal and derelict land.* Thomas Telford, London, 1987, 821-826.

6.25. Wrigley W. Load settlement characteristics of demolition debris treated by the dry process of vibro-replacement. *Building on marginal and derelict land.* Thomas Telford, London, 1987, 827-835.

6.26. Mitchell J.M. Discussion contribution: Derelict sites of former industries. *Building on marginal and derelict land.* Thomas Telford, London, 1987, 581-594.

6.27. Gabryliszyn J. M42 motorway: landfill sites. *Arup Journal*, 1988, **23**, No. 2, 18. (Ove Arup Partnership, London.)

6.28. Rulkens W.H. *et al.* On-site processing of contaminated soil. *Contaminated land: reclamation and treatment* (ed. Smith M.A.). Plenum, New York and London, 1985, 37-90.

6.29. Ebel W. and Weingran, Chr. Experiences, problems and possible solutions for a redevelopment of contaminated industrial sites. *Contaminated soil '88* (eds Wolf K. *et al.*). Kluwer, Dordrecht, 1988, 495-503.

6.30. Haines R.C. Contaminated land: the scale of the problem in Europe — costs of clean up and application of novel techniques to reduce clean up costs. *Contaminated soil '88* (eds Wolf K. *et al.*). Kluwer, Dordrecht, 1988, 481-485.

6.31. Mischgofsky F.H. and Kabos R. General survey of site clearance techniques:

trend towards in situ treatment. *Contaminated soil '88* (eds Wolf K. *et al.*). Kluwer, Dordrecht, 1988, 523-533.

6.32. Assink J.W. Physico-chemical treatment methods for soil remediation. *Contaminated soil '88* (eds Wolf K. *et al.*). Kluwer, Dordrecht, 1988, 861-870.

6.33. Verhagen E.J.H. Review of thermal and extraction soil treatment plants in the Netherlands. *Contaminated soil '88* (eds Wolf K. *et al.*). Kluwer, Dordrecht, 1988, 797-808.

6.34. Soczo E.R. and Staps J.J.M. Review of biological soil treatment techniques in the Netherlands. *Contaminated soil '88* (eds Wolf K. *et al.*). Kluwer, Dordrecht, 1988, 663-670.

6.35. Wiles C.C. *et al.* Status of solidification/stabilisation in the United States and factors affecting its use. *Contaminated soil '88* (eds Wolf K. *et al.*). Kluwer, Dordrecht, 1988, 947-956.

6.36. Childs K. Contributions to chapters on groundwater and treatment. *Contaminated land: reclamation and treatment* (ed. Smith M.A.). Plenum, New York and London, 1985, 141-205.

6.37. Brown K.W. *et al.* Permeability of compacted soils to solvent mixtures and petroleum products. *Proc. 10th Annual Research Symp. Land Disposal of Hazardous Wastes.* US Environmental Protection Agency, Washington DC, 1984, report EPA 600/9-84-007, 124-137.

6.38. Anderson D.C. *et al.* Barrier–leachate compatibility: permeability of cement/ asphalt emulsions and contaminant resistant bentonite/soil mixtures to organic solvents. *Proc. Conf. Management of Uncontrolled Hazardous Waste Sites, Washington DC, 1983.* Hazardous Materials Control Research Institute, Silver Spring, Maryland, 1984.

6.39. Beine P.R.A. and Geil M. Physical properties of lining system under percolation of waste liquids and their investigation. *Proc. 1st Int. TNO Conf. Contaminated Soil, Utrecht, 1985* (eds Assink J.W. and Van den Brink, W.J.). Martinus Nijhoff, Dordrecht, 1986, 863-886.

6.40. Mitchell J.M. *Guide to ground improvement.* Construction Industry Research and Information Association, London, in preparation.

6.41. Alyanak I. and Bihlmaier B. Long term behaviour of encapsulation materials — especially for cleaning up hazardous waste landfills. *Contaminated soil '88* (eds Wolf K. *et al.*). Kluwer, Dordrecht, 1988, 621-623.

6.42. Tausch N. A special grouting method to construct horizontal membranes. *Proc. Symp. Recent Developments in Ground Improvement Techniques, Bangkok.* Balkema, Rotterdam, 1985, 351-361.

6.43. Greenwood D.A. Underpinning by grouting. *Proc. Symp. Building Appraisal, Maintenance and Preservation, Bath, 1985.* Echo Press, Loughborough and London, 97-112.

6.44. Stent struggles to stop Sizewell leak. *New Civil Engineer*, 1988, 21 Jan., No. 773, 6-7.

6.45. Muller-Kirchenbauer H. *et al.* Test seal wall for Gerolsheim hazardous waste dump. *Contaminated soil '88* (eds Wolf K. *et al.*). Kluwer, Dordrecht, 1988, 635-637.

6.46. Cairney T. Soil cover reclamations. *Reclaiming contaminated land* (ed. Cairney T.). Blackie, Glasgow, 1987, ch. 6, 144-169.

6.47. Parry G.D.R. and Bell R.M. Landscaping and vegetating reclaimed sites. *Reclaiming contaminated land* (ed. Cairney T.). Blackie, Glasgow, 1987, ch. 10, 213-222.

6.48. Lambe T.W. and Whitman R.V. *Soil mechanics.* Wiley, New York, 1969, 245-247.

6.49. Barry D.L. Hazards from methane on contaminated sites. *Building on marginal and derelict land.* Thomas Telford, London, 1987, 323-338.

6.50. Health and Safety Executive and Her Majesty's Factory Inspectorate. *The Abbeystead explosion: a report of the investigation by the Health and Safety Executive into the explosion on 23 May 1984 at the valve house of the Lune/Wyre Water Transfer Scheme at Abbeystead.* HMSO, London, 1985.

6.51. Pecksen G.N. Methane and the development of derelict land. *London Environmental Supplement*, No. 13, Summer 1985, 1-18.

6.52. Her Majesty's Inspectorate of Pollution. *The control of landfill gas.* HMSO, London, 1989, HMIP waste management paper 27.

6.53. Her Majesty's Inspectorate of Pollution. *Landfilling wastes: a technical memorandum for the disposal of wastes on landfill sites.* HMSO, London, 1986, HMIP waste management paper 26.

6.54. Jacobs A.F. *et al.* Fenchurch Street Station development. *Structural Engineer*, 1984, **62A**, Dec., No. 12, 365-372.

6.55. Grose W.J. Hand-dug under-reamed piles at Embankment Place, London. *Proc. Int. Conf. Piling and Deep Foundations, London, 1989.* Balkema, Rotterdam, 1989, 51-62.

6.56. Courtney M.A. and Matthew R.J. Tobacco Dock. *Structural Engineer*, 1989, **67**, No. 18, 19 Sept., 325-331.

6.57. Hindle B.R. *et al.* Salford docks urban renewal: design, construction and management of civil engineering works. *Proceedings of the Institution of Civil Engineers*, Part 1, 1989, **86**, 1067–1087.

6.58. Littlejohn G.S. Surface stability in areas underlain by old coal workings. *Ground Engineering*, 1979, **12**, No. 2, 22-30.

6.59. Healy P.R. and Head J.M. *Construction over abandoned mineworkings.* Construction Industry Research and Information Association, London, 1984, special publication 32.

6.60. Cole K.W. *et al.* Removal of actual and apprehended dereliction caused by abandoned limestone mines in the West Midlands of England. *Building on marginal and derelict land.* Thomas Telford, London, 1987, 177-196.

6.61. Nutting M. Minestone and pollution control. *Proc. 2nd Int. Conf. Reclamation, Treatment and Utilisation of Coal Mining Wastes, Nottingham, 1987* (ed. Rainbow A.K.M.). Elsevier, Amsterdam, 1987, 281-293.

6.62. Szczepanska J. and Twardowska I. Coal mine spoil tips as a large area source of water contamination. *Proc. 2nd Int. Conf. Reclamation, Treatment and Utilisation of Coal Mining Wastes, Nottingham, 1987* (ed. Rainbow A.K.M.). Elsevier, Amsterdam, 1987, 267-280.

6.63. Rainbow A.K.M. (ed.). *Proc. Symp. Reclamation, Treatment and Utilisation of Coal Mining Wastes, Durham, 1984.* NCB Minestone Executive, Houghton le Spring, 1984.

6.64. Rainbow A.K.M. (ed.). *Proc. 2nd Int. Conf. Reclamation, Treatment and Utilisation of Coal Mining Wastes, Nottingham, 1987.* Elsevier, Amsterdam, 1987.

6.65. Bell F.G. *et al.* (eds). Engineering geology of underground movements. *Proc. 23rd Annual Conf. Engineering Group of Geological Society, Nottingham, 1987.* Geological Society, London, 1988.

6.66. Ward W.H. Full scale mixing, pumping and surface spreading trials of rock paste for filling mines. *Proc. 2nd Int. Conf. Reclamation, Treatment and Utilisation of Coal Mining Wastes, Nottingham, 1987.* Elsevier, Amsterdam, 1987, 307-318.

6.67. Cole K.W. and Figg J. Improved rock paste: a slow hardening bulk fill based on colliery spoil, pulverised fuel ash and lime. *Proc. 2nd Int. Conf. Reclamation, Treatment and Utilisation of Coal Mining Wastes, Nottingham, 1987.* Elsevier, Amsterdam, 1987, 415-430.

6.68. Braithwaite P.A. and Sklucki T. The infilling of limestone mines with rock paste. *Proc. 2nd Int. Conf. Reclamation, Treatment and Utilisation of Coal Mining Wastes, Nottingham, 1987.* Elsevier, Amsterdam, 1987, 615-638.

6.69. Cole K.W. Review paper of land affected by old mine workings. *Building on marginal and derelict land.* Thomas Telford, London, 1987, 213-227.

6.70. Charles J.A. *et al.* Settlement of backfill at Horsley restored open cast coal mining site. *Proc. Conf. Large Ground Movements and Structures, UWIST, Cardiff.* Pentech Press, London, 1977, 229-251.

6.71. Charles J.A. *et al.* Treatment and subsequent performance of cohesive fill left by opencast ironstone mining at Snatchill experimental housing site, Corby. *Clay fills.* Institution of Civil Engineers, London, 1979, 63-72.

6.72. Schulz T.M. *et al.* A study of urban restoration of surface mine land in Western Canada. *Building on marginal and derelict land.* Thomas Telford, London, 1987, 125-136.

6.73. Lange S. Building on uncompacted dumps in the Rhenish brown coal area of the Federal Republic of Germany. *Building on marginal and derelict land.* Thomas Telford, London, 1987, 137-153.

6.74. Charles J.A. Review paper on hydraulic fills and colliery discard lagoons. *Building on marginal and derelict land.* Thomas Telford, London, 1987, 95-109.

6.75. Charles J.A. *et al.* Improving the load carrying characteristics of uncompacted fills by preloading. *Municipal Engineer,* 1986, **3**, Feb., 1-19.

6.76. Bartholomew R.F. The protection of concrete piles in aggressive ground conditions: an international appreciation. *Recent developments in the design and construction of piles,* Institution of Civil Engineers, London, 1980, 131-141.

6.77. Greenwood D.A. Summary of discussion, speciality session 3. *Proc. 8th Eur. Conf. Soil Mechanics Foundation Engineering, Helsinki, 1983.* Balkema, Rotterdam, 1984, **3**, 1131-1132.

6.78. Vibro flotation: treating weak ground. *Civil Engineering* (London), 1984, Apr., 39 and 41.

6.79. St John H.D. *et al. The use of 'vibro' ground improvement techniques in the United Kingdom.* HMSO, London, 1989, BRE information paper IP5/89.

6.80. National House Building Council. *Precautions to take for vibratory ground improvement techniques for low-rise housing, including garages.* NHBC, Amersham, 1988, practice note 16.

6.81. Brown R.E. Vibroflotation compaction of cohensionless soils. *Proc. Geotechnical Engineering Division American Society of Civil Engineers,* 1977, **103**, Dec., GT12, 1437-1451.

6.82. Welsh J.P. Dynamic deep compaction of sanitary landfill to support superhighway. *Proc. 8th Eur. Conf. Soil Mechanics Foundation Engineering, Helsinki, 1983.* Balkema, Rotterdam, 1984, **1**, 319-321.

6.83. Broms B. Problems and solutions of construction in soft clay. *Proc. 6th Asian Regional Conf. Soil Mechanics Foundation Engineering, Singapore, 1979,* **2**, 3-38.

6.84. Pilot G. State of the art — Methods of improving the engineering properties of soft clays. *Selected papers/abstracts of papers presented at an int. symp. in Bangkok in July 1977 by the Laboratoires des Ponts et Chaussées, Paris.* Special edition, UNESCO Institute of Education, 1978, 140-178.

6.85. Jones D.B. *et al.* Ground treatment by surcharging on deposits of soft clay and peat: a case history. *Building on marginal and derelict land.* Thomas Telford, London, 1987, 679-695.

6.86. Barden L. *et al.* The collapse mechanism in partly saturated soil. *Engineering Geology,* 1973, **7**, 49-60.

6.87. Charles J.A. *et al.* The effect of a rise in water table on the settlement of backfill at Horsley restored opencast coal mining site, 1973-1983. *Proc. 3rd Int. Conf. Ground Movements and Structures, UWIST, Cardiff, 1984.* Pentech Press, London, 1984, 423-442.

6.88. Mitchell J.M. Discussion contribution: Hydraulic fills and colliery discard lagoons. *Building on marginal and derelict land.* Thomas Telford, London, 1987, 115-116.

6.89. Cragg C.B.H. and Walker B.P. To accept or avoid settlement when developing marginal land. *Building on marginal and derelict land.* Thomas Telford, London, 1987, 59-67.

6.90. Radway A. *et al.* Water quality improvement at Salford Quays. *Journal of the Institution of Water and Environmental Management,* 1988, **2**, Oct., 523-531.

Logistics for selecting the final solution

ALISTAIRE GILCHRIST, FICE, FIHT
Head of Environmental Unit, Scottish Development
Agency

The final decision on how derelict land will be treated can only be taken after all technical investigation has been carried out. This work can be regarded as the provision of all the basic facts about the condition of the site and its constraints, together with cost options for the various solutions.

This information has to be set against general planning criteria and land use requirements. Only after consideration of all these aspects can a final solution be adopted.

Land uses

The responsibility for land use policies rests with central and local authorities. These policies are developed through the authorities' planning function. It is a statutory requirement for each region to produce Structure Plans, which are reviewed at predetermined intervals. These plans identify land uses in general terms and state overall land use policies in a regional context. Local Plans are also produced, setting out in greater detail the requirements of the Structure Plans. It is from these documents that ultimate land uses are determined.

The land in question will already be categorised by its previous use but it may not be desirable to reclaim the site for a similar after-use. In these cases, local authority permission has to be obtained for change of use, and the various options would have been agreed when the proposals to carry out reclamation were being examined.

In many cases planners have been proposing new uses for derelict sites principally because of supply and demand. For instance, industry now occupies much less space than before, and as a result most areas have a large overprovision of zoned industrial land. Reclamation provides the opportunity for changes to be introduced.

The reclamation process can in itself also provide a temporary change of use, as in the case of, say, an open casting operation to remove the problem of shallow unconsolidated mineral workings.

It is therefore essential that reclamation options are fully discussed and developed with the local planning authority before final decisions are made.

The foregoing has tended to suggest that derelict land occurs within the urban areas, and while this tends generally to be the case there are also many examples of rural dereliction, mainly as a result of the extraction industries such as coal, sand, gravel and stone. In these cases the reclamation options are unlikely to be other than agricultural, forestry or public open space.

There is also in this category sometimes an intermediate development — prior to completion of the final restoration — which can involve a temporary change of use and which in certain cases can be controversial. For example, holes in the ground have been valuable assets to the waste-disposal industries and satisfactory solutions have generally been attained. There have, however, been examples of poorly planned facilities creating major problems to the surrounding landowners from such things as wind-borne litter, water pollution, methane gas generation, vermin, spontaneous combustion or simply noxious odours.

Reclamation proposals using landfill are usually self-financing but can take a few years to complete, depending on their extent and the availability of fill material — a factor which has to be considered and which is not always appreciated by those who are affected by the project. Much of the same problem arises with the washing of colliery spoil in the reclamation of tips: the process can last a number of years, depending on the size of the tip.

In recent times a special problem of reclamation schemes on the urban fringe has emerged. Schemes in this zone need careful consideration because of the limited options available to the developer. Studies have been carried out by the Countryside Commission for Scotland under the heading of *Countryside around towns* (ref. 7.1) and are worthy of consideration.

There is a widely held view that the urban fringe should act as a buffer zone or a no-man's-land between housing and farming. This proposal, while commendable, often creates the problem that the reclamation seeks to resolve. Poor maintenance and subsequent vandalism, fire and general rubbish-dumping are the usual characteristics of these areas.

Attempts at creating fringe forestry have been reasonably successful but again success depends on the general outlook of the local residents. High levels of unemployment coupled with poor-quality housing stock are the characteristics of many peripheral housing estates, and schemes in such areas run a high risk of whole or partial failure. A recent proposal which has had some success has been the development of a linear park, with opportunity for informal recreation along a few miles of a peripheral housing estate.

In areas where the quality of development is higher, few of the foregoing problems exist. Agricultural solutions in such locations usually provide effective reclamation.

Land value

A key issue in the selection of the reclamation solution is consideration of land value. Two aspects need to be taken into account: first, the considered value of the land in its existing condition, and secondly, the perceived value of the treated site.

If the acquisition or existing-use land value plus the cost of reclamation per unit of area is equal to or less than the perceived after-value, the project is viable without public assistance. In this case all values are positive.

However, for most derelict sites the initial land value plus reclamation cost will be considerably more than the realisable land value. Reclamation is then not a viable proposition unless this 'negative land value' is subsidised. In the UK, central government funding is provided to bring this negative value back to a positive commercial proposition.

This approach is reasonable where the derelict land is valued at nil consideration or where the site is gifted to the developing authority. The situation does exist, however, when a developer pays more for the land than what it is worth. This excess valuation would normally be deducted from any assistance being provided from central government funds.

Another scenario exists where the proposed cost of treatment becomes excessive. In this situation, limits have to be set and an alternative cheaper solution found.

Due to the considerable variation in land values between different parts of the country, it is not possible to set national specific targets for assistance on a unit-cost basis. These have to be established on a regional basis.

Unit-cost targets are discussed in a later section of this chapter. For guidance, however, treatment costs of up to £20/m^2 may be considered reasonable where the current market value of the land after treatment might be in the order of £15/m^2.

In England, where Derelict Land Grant is administered by the Department of the Environment, variations in the level of grant payable will vary with the status of the area, whereas in Scotland and Wales, where the grant is administered by the respective development agencies, it can be at the discretion of these agencies. Such assistance is available to developers in both the public and the private sector. Conditions are usually built into any agreement to ensure that if treated land is disposed of at a higher value than that used in the calculation of assistance, the grant-giving agency is entitled to be reimbursed that excess.

Land use criteria

The criteria used for the selection of potential after-use will vary with the different uses proposed. Most uses are covered by the general categories considered below.

A general methodology for assessing projects is shown in Fig. 7.1.

Industrial/commercial

In the industrial/commercial category, the planning zoning will follow that of the existing use, which will generally be compatible with the proposed after-use. However, consideration will have to be given to the existing land supply in this category in the area: if it is in excess of the Local Plan provision, thought needs to be given to possible alternative uses.

Where the likely development is known, treatment of the dereliction can be purpose-designed to suit the development, by far the best method of dealing with the problem.

Where treatment is proposed for an unknown after-use, it is advisable to carry out only such works as are necessary to bring the site to an

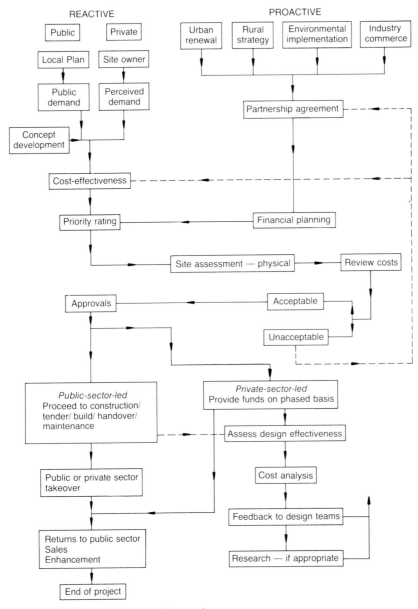

Fig. 7.1. *Project assessment and procedures*

acceptable visual condition. For example, excessive ground consolidation of fill material might be unnecessary if some form of piling solution was preferred for the ultimate new development. Ground profiling also has to be carefully considered, particularly if large relatively flat areas are to result. In an interim situation land drainage would not be provided, and as a consequence these areas could be difficult to drain by natural means.

Sites with a contamination problem need careful investigation, but in many cases removal of this material may not be necessary since it can normally be capped with an inert material. Care will be necessary in making such decisions to take account of the effects of the contaminants on foundation materials and on services. On old gasworks sites, for example, phenols can present a particular hazard.

The presence of methane in infilled sites should be thoroughly investigated and the problem fully dealt with before any building on the site is contemplated.

If the superficial materials have a carbonaceous content, proper precautions will be necessary to preclude the risk of spontaneous combustion.

Housing

Where it is proposed to designate the restored site for housing, many of the criteria laid down for industrial sites will still apply. There are, however, some notable exceptions.

Ground profiling will not normally require large flat areas, and thus drainage of the site can be easier.

The use of unburnt colliery shale is generally not acceptable as fill because of its combustion possibilities. However, a site has been prepared in Bathgate in Scotland using this material: the methods were such that the criteria set down by the National House Building Council were satisfied. This was an experimental site and was treated to a very high standard.

Sites with contaminated materials require a very high standard of treatment. The acceptable solution will either be complete removal of the offending material or capping with a minimum of 2 metres thickness of inert clay material. This level of treatment would apply where it was proposed that the houses would have gardens. Vegetables are known to take up contaminants from the soil and if the uptake exceeded the levels laid down in guidelines there could be a risk to health. Where the development was for flats without gardens, the same conditions as for industrial uses would be appropriate.

The pressure of methane gas in the fill is totally unacceptable for a housing after-use. The methane would have to be eradicated if that use was to continue.

Agriculture

An agricultural after-use can fall into one of two principal categories

o   a return to full agricultural use
o   a minimal agricultural use.

In the case of the former it is necessary to provide a sufficient depth of subsoil, together with an appropriate topsoil thickness to match that of the surrounding good quality agricultural land. This will involve fairly extensive drainage and the establishment of proper gradients. A scheme designed to this standard would normally cost considerably more than a lower-grade option. It is also necessary in a case like this to carefully select the subsoil and topsoil and have these properly analysed and treated, as appropriate, with lime, fertilisers or organic materials to ensure that good quality soil will result.

It is probably also necessary to continue a period of aftercare. It would be necessary to rip-plough the land for more than the first year and it is unlikely that quality crops could be anticipated before the third year.

In the case of the minimum standard of agricultural use, the land would be intended purely for grazing and would need to have only a minimum subsoil/topsoil cover to ensure the establishment of grass. This, obviously, is the cheapest option.

Sometimes it is possible to use soil substitutes such as sewage sludges or other types of material to enable a grass sward to be established. The problems with schemes of this nature are that, because of the minimum depth of soils and the extremely limited amount of surface-water drainage, the land in question will be very easily damaged if overgrazing is permitted, particularly in the early years before a reasonable soil structure has been re-established. Again, because of the very poor quality of material involved, extensive testing of the soils is necessary to ensure adequate fertilisation. Grass mixes need to be carefully considered in these cases since only the most robust species are likely to succeed.

Forestry

The development of forestry after-uses on reclaimed sites has become more prevalent in recent times. This option is usually chosen where neither of the agricultural options previously mentioned are necessary. Changing agricultural land use policies can dictate in many cases that this is probably the most effective after-use for many reclaimed sites. In recent years there has been a downturn in the need for production of good quality agricultural land as a process of restoration.

In this case it is usually necessary to make an accurate survey of the appropriate adjoining landscapes to ensure that indigenous species of trees are used in the regeneration process. Trees can be seeded or transplanted from forests, the latter option giving the quicker response.

Extensive research work has been undertaken in the processes of tree seeding. Although some successes have been achieved, these have been of a limited nature, and until greater success can be guaranteed it is more appropriate to consider the forestry-transplant method. Schemes of this nature still require extensive analysis of the soils into which the transplants will be planted, and extensive aftercare is also necessary to ensure the continued success of the work. This option provides a relatively low-cost treatment and one which has a relatively low cost of maintenance. In the early years after planting, growth will be slow, but from about the fifth year onwards the full effect will begin to show.

Public open space

In towns a more positive use has to be sought for reclamation sites. Where commercial or industrial uses are not appropriate, playing fields and informal recreation in the form of urban parks are the most likely after-uses.

Where the site is big enough to be used for an urban park, it is possible to have a variety of standards of reclamation throughout the park. For instance, the areas required for playing fields require to have reasonably good quality subsoil and topsoil to ensure the continued growth of the grass cover. Lower standards can be accepted in the informal grass areas. Shrub areas need adequate soils to sustain growth and ensure success.

Schemes of this nature do require fairly careful planning to ensure that the best uses are selected for the particular areas. Adequate drainage has to be provided, particularly for playing fields. The design process on these schemes has to be carefully considered and all who are likely to be involved, including the managers of the scheme in the long term, have to be brought into the design team to ensure that all aspects are properly catered for.

Schemes of this nature are usually considerably more expensive than the equivalent agricultural and forestry schemes.

Urban, rural and urban-fringe schemes

Different criteria have to be established for urban, rural and urban-fringe schemes. Urban schemes are generally schemes with a productive end use, but they are more expensive in view of the likely after-uses. The opportunity presents itself to reclaim the sites for productive uses such as commerce, industry and housing, or in the case of public open space for small parks and recreation areas. These schemes are highly visible and usually affect many people. Therefore, if budgets are a consideration, they have higher priority than some of the more remote rural schemes.

Rural schemes are by far the cheapest option for reclamation. Since many are associated with the extraction industries or disused railway lines, they generally can be of a much lower standard than the urban schemes. The exception is where it is intended to carry out the reclamation in such a way as to provide good-quality agricultural land. However, this is now less likely due to changing agricultural policies, as discussed earlier in this chapter.

Urban-fringe schemes are probably the most difficult to deal with since they form the interface between the town and the countryside. Schemes of this nature should aim to encourage positive links between the key sites on the urban fringe and the countryside beyond in order to achieve a harmonious transition between town and country which reflects the different values and lifestyles inherent in each way of life.

Within this category it is possible to provide access via footpaths, picnic sites and other countryside features in close proximity to the urban conurbations. It allows the countryside to come within towns in many cases and acts as a major buffer to the better quality agricultural land beyond.

There are problems, of course, associated with schemes of this nature

— particularly where extensive planting works have been carried out — due to the high risk of vandalism and the possibility in dry weather of grass fires. However, by careful ranger servicing it is possible to provide some degree of management and generally to educate the population at large as to the benefits of schemes of this nature. There are considerable educational benefits in these schemes in developing the flora and fauna and general wildlife.

Aftercare and cost-effectiveness

Land reclamation is the cost of taking the negative value out of the land development process. The reason that derelict land is not cleared as a result of the normal economic process is that the cost of reclamation greatly exceeds the likely return from the sale of the land for its designated purpose.

Schemes should not be designed without due care being given to the effectiveness of the proposals. It is important to consider carefully whether a scheme with low initial cost and a high cost of aftercare is more effective than one with higher initial cost and a lower cost in use. Modern philosophy of land use is tending to move towards the latter: the costs of reclamation are rising as more positive uses for the land are found.

Whatever the intended after-use, it is essential that the design of any scheme is carefully considered, along with the potential long term maintenance aspects. It is not sufficient that designers design and managers manage: it is necessary for both to be involved in the design process, and feedback from earlier schemes is essential. Attempts have been made over the years to ensure that costs are kept within reasonable bounds. In view of the scale of the problem countrywide it is not possible to allow unlimited resources to be spent in clearing these problems. Various publications have been written on the cost-effectiveness of land renewal and these generally tend towards the thinking that judicious consideration of after-use and appropriateness of the design solution have managed to keep the initial design cost reasonable without unduly prejudicing the aftercare costs.

It is recommended that existing schemes be closely monitored, and checked at regular intervals against the intentions of their original design. This enables the success of some of the design techniques to be monitored and thus the techniques can be either improved upon or discarded for future schemes.

More work should be done to improve designers' awareness of the problems and to allow proper research to be carried out.

Land reclamation schemes provide an excellent opportunity for experimental works since the sites in question generally are not required immediately for a specific purpose. In fact, the use of reclamation sites for experiments can be a very effective method of reclamation and provides excellent background information.

In design, careful consideration must be given to the interaction between the scheme itself and its users, whether they be the users of public open space or, in fact, the maintaining authority.

Project selection criteria

Various authorities have tried to establish how best to apply criteria to enable judgements to be made as to which schemes should be carried out in which order. Normally with limited budgets it is necessary to apply certain criteria to ensure that money is spent wisely on the most appropriate schemes.

It has proved difficult to compare and reconcile the economic benefits of reclamation with the environmental benefits. Techniques have been established, but to date there is no known simple method of forming an evaluation, and judgement is still necessary. It is possible, however, by using a number of criteria to establish certain parameters which can be used in this respect.

Initially, the after-use of the site is a key factor in this process. That is closely followed by the degree of dereliction, and the location of the site either in relation to people's dwellings or, in the case of main communication routes, in relation to the number of people who will see the site as they pass through the area. The following headings give some idea of some of the aspects that can be considered in these processes.

Economic impact criteria

Activities are appraised in terms of their cost-effectiveness in increasing the aggregate income of the population and aggregate employment.

Activities are appraised primarily in terms of their cost-effectiveness in generating additional labour earnings within the economy. Such earnings are additional to the extent that they would not have been generated without the initiative and are net of displacement. There are three levels at which these additional earnings can be generated

o   directly within the initiative
o   indirectly in the economy by purchase of goods or services from other firms within the initiative
o   externally.

A system based on this concept of additional labour earnings plays an important role by highlighting the aspects of a scheme which are most likely to generate net additional output and employment.

Other economic factors which have to be considered are leverage (additionality) and employment generation (cost per job).

The system, therefore, has four specific components

o   economic impact (direct)
o   external economic impact
o   leverage/additionality
o   net cost per job.

Each of these elements can be ranked on a scale of 1 to 10: the scores are then averaged and an overall economic score between 1 and 10 is arrived at.

No attempt is made here to detail the elements which make up each of these headings since weightings will vary throughout the country. The user can assess these as they may apply to a particular area of the country. If a national scheme were to be developed, different weightings would be necessary for separate areas of the country.

Environmental score
An environmental score can be based on the theory that the 'best' projects (from a purely environmental viewpoint) are those which secure the maximum visual impact for the greatest number of people at the net lowest cost. The score can be calculated as

$$\frac{\text{degree of visual improvement} \times \text{number of beneficiaries}}{\text{net cost}}$$

In the assessment of visual improvement, two elements are taken into account: how bad the site or building is initially in visual and safety terms relative to the local environment, and how well, relative to the local average, it would exploit its environmental potential if the project were undertaken.

The site is assessed on a 'before' and 'after' basis on a scale of -5 to $+5$, with twice as much weight being given to the 'before' score. This latter point indicates the primary emphasis on improving below-average environments.

The assessment of visual impact is necessarily subjective.

The number of people assessed as benefitting from any environmental improvement is based on the location of the project and the size of the site. Full weighting is given to local residents, and a weighting of 20% is given to tourists (daily average), 10% to passers-by and 2% to travellers.

Net cost is taken as a unit cost, that is as a cost per square metre.

The environmental score can then be calculated using appropriate values for the variables, to give a score which will lie between 0 and 100.

Final selection
By using combinations of the economic score and the environmental score, schemes can be selected to suit the corporate priorities of the appropriate authority.

Recommendations for good landscaping practice

The process of land renewal can be regarded as a process with three phases: feasibility; use and implementation; and management.

During the feasibility phase the potential users and managers of the site should be identified. The characteristics and context of the site should be thoroughly understood and alternative approaches to renewal evaluated before a budget for the proposed development is finally formulated.

In the use and implementation stage, user and management requirements are taken into account and site modification is carried out to achieve cost-effective establishment of vegetation or land use. The site should not be brought into use until vegetation has been properly established.

During the management stage the site is inspected on a regular basis, its performance in use is reviewed, and adjustments to management and/or design are made to reflect demand to achieve optimum growth performance towards achieving a diverse system of vegetation.

As the majority of sites treated will have some form of landscaping they should be treated within a Landscape Structure Plan or strategy which is subject to regular review in accordance with changing land use demands.

In predominantly industrial or inner city locations there is generally far more land zoned for industrial use than will ever be required for the less space-demanding modern industries. In situations such as these it is necessary for the local planning authorities to reassess their land use policy and to identify new land usage for the sites. Only when this exercise has been completed is it possible to apply the appropriate landscape treatment, following the Landscape Structure Plan framework, to the particular sites.

Sufficient resources should be allocated at feasibility stages of site investigations. Maximum effort should be directed to identifying potential user groups within the community and to making realistic assessments of management resources.

At the feasibility stage the physical and biological characteristics of the sites should be thoroughly investigated and evaluated, especially insofar as they will affect the rate of establishment of vegetation. Approaches which involve the importation of topsoil should only be considered as a last resort.

The cost of a project is an important criterion but should not be pre-eminent. Widespread use can be made of yardstick costings to provide a general cost plan, but this should not be rigidly adhered to since specific sites may require specific levels of commitment.

Designs should require the preparation of a landscape context study to ensure the proposals are fully integrated into their surroundings.

The basic objective of planting design should be to improve soil structure and fertility and increase the amount of woody vegetation to generally increase diversity of plant species. There is a need to re-treat over a longer period the area laid down for grass, and this may involve the occasional ploughing and resowing of these areas. This is something which is not done at present, the general perception being that once the grass seed is sown that is all that needs be done.

In both site planning and design and during construction priority should be given to protecting existing plant and soil systems since these form the effective basis of regeneration. Unnecessary disturbance should be avoided at all costs.

Where vegetation is proposed, more attention should be given to the need to create root-permeable substrates as the key to successful plant establishment and stability. Techniques of ground preparation are equal in importance to good plant handling. More attention should be paid to ensuring that the natural processes of weathering are developed as an aid to establishment, even where this may lead to a series of phased contracts instead of an attempt to carry out all the work at one particular time.

Where it is intended to give a fairly instant impact the use of pioneer plant species is a normal design method. However, management plans should allow for the planting of more mature species, and the subsequent removal of the pioneer species to allow the new mature planting to develop.

The use and amount of grass included in schemes should be carefully considered. If grassland is intended for recreational use it should be designed to a high standard in order to achieve a high wear performance. Where it is otherwise included its primary function should be to improve soil fertility and structure, and therefore adequate provision should be made for ploughing and reseeding during the management phases of the contract.

Where community users or client groups can be identified, their full participation in all stages of a scheme should be encouraged, especially where public use is intended in either the short or long term.

The design and management of public open space on the urban fringe and significant spaces within towns should create more diverse habitats and a more natural appearance relevant to future community needs.

Planting designs should be subject to a performance evaluation to ensure that they will achieve growth corresponding to the management objectives of the scheme.

A 20 year management plan should be prepared for each site. This plan should be subject to regular review by the managers or client users groups.

Conclusion

As can be seen from the foregoing the process of selecting a solution for land renewal works is not simple and has to be constantly kept under review. This chapter has attempted to set out some of the main criteria to be considered.

Reference
7.1. Fladmark J.M. *The countryside around towns*. Countryside Commission for Scotland, Battleby, 1988.

Index